May You Live in Interesting Times

Books by Conor O'Clery

The Billionaire Who Wasn't: How Chuck Feeney
Secretly Made and Gave Away a Fortune
(PUBLICAFFAIRS, 2007)

Panic at the Bank: How John Rusnak Lost AIB $700 Million
(co-author with Siobhan Creaton)
(GILL & MACMILLAN, 2002)

Ireland in Quotes: A History of the Twentieth Century
(O'BRIEN PRESS, 1999)

The Greening of the White House: The Inside Story of how
America Tried to Bring Peace to Ireland
(GILL & MACMILLAN, 1996)

America: A Place Called Hope?
(O'BRIEN PRESS, 1993)

Melting Snow: An Irishman in Moscow
(APPLETREE PRESS, 1991)

Phrases Make History Here: A Century of Irish
Political Quotations, 1886–1986
(O'BRIEN PRESS, 1986)

May You Live in Interesting Times

CONOR O'CLERY

POOLBEG

Published 2008
by Poolbeg Press Ltd
123 Grange Hill, Baldoyle
Dublin 13, Ireland
E-mail: poolbeg@poolbeg.com
www.poolbeg.com

1 3 5 7 9 10 8 6 4 2

A catalogue record for this book is available from the British Library.

ISBN 978-1-84223-325-2

Typeset by Patricia Hope in Berling 11.5/16
Printed by Litographia Rosés, S.A., Spain

ABOUT THE AUTHOR

Born in Belfast and educated at Queen's University Belfast, Conor O'Clery worked for *The Irish Times*, Ireland's leading national newspaper, for over thirty years in various positions, including news editor and foreign correspondent based in London, Moscow, Washington, Beijing and New York. He wrote for *The New Republic* from Moscow, contributed columns to *Newsweek International*, and has been a frequent commentator on RTÉ, BBC, NPR and CNN. He has won several awards, including twice Journalist of the Year in Ireland: in 1987 for his reporting of the Soviet Union, and in 2002 for his reporting of the 9/11 attack on the World Trade Center, which he witnessed from his office three blocks away.

To my grandchildren,
Ben, Conor, Joseph, Sam, Maeve and Annie

He comes, the herald of a noisy world,

With spatter'd boots, strapp'd waist, and frozen locks;

News from all nations lumb'ring at his back.

WILLIAM COWPER
"The Task". Book IV,
The Winter Evening

CONTENTS

INTRODUCTION

The Second Rough Draft of History

A newspaper flourished briefly in Downpatrick in the 1950s. It was called the *Hilltop Herald*. It had editorial comment, news, features, sports, music and film reviews, cartoons, short stories and poetry. The first edition, dated 16 December 1957, had six pages and cost sixpence. It promised that subsequent issues would be larger, and announced that the proprietor/owner hoped to raise substantial capital to buy improved printing equipment. And indeed by June 1958 the *Hilltop Herald* had expanded to twelve pages. That month's issue contained an editorial extolling the pleasure of learning a foreign language, a news story about accidents on snow-covered roads (we had snow in those days), a review of the film *The Rising of the Moon* (verdict: "It didn't rise too high."), a piece on the "phenomenal success" of Elvis Presley's "Jailhouse Rock", a review of a local pageant of Irish history, and a page and a quarter of ads for shops such as Fox's of Market Street, "specialists in sportswear and religious goods".

Alas, it was to be the last edition, despite the fact that it was a profitable venture that had accumulated a surplus of £43. The person who published the *Hilltop Herald*, who edited it, wrote the leaders and news stories, commissioned the arts, literary and sports coverage, tramped the streets to get advertisements from local shopkeepers, spent hours typing up the stories and rolling the ink drum by hand to duplicate each page for each individual copy, had to abandon the venture and study for his A Levels.

Thus ended my first spell in the newspaper business. I had founded the *Hilltop Herald* as the student organ of St Patrick's High School, Downpatrick, which was run by the De La Salle Brothers. The school was perched on top of one of County Down's steep drumlins; hence the title of the newspaper. There were in fact only three editions over seven months. It was an obsessive venture for me, and time-consuming. At seventeen years of age I now had to knuckle down and study for my exams. I abandoned my media creation to swot up on Latin, English, geography, history, physics, science and mathematics. I stood down the publicity agent, my best pal, Dan McNeill; the assistant editor, Albert Sage; the business manager, Raymond Jennings; the pop music and film reviewer, Conor Bradley; the short story writer, Cyril Jamison; and drama critic, Tom King. It was a mass downsizing, but they were quite happy. They all had exams too.

However, one thing was surely clear. I was cut out for the newspaper business. I was passionately interested in news. My most exciting childhood memory is as a three-year-old watching American soldiers rehearsing for the 1944 Normandy landings on the beach in Newcastle, County Down. I followed foreign affairs on the radio from an early age. In my mid-teens I had a fist fight with my friend Frank Lacey on the beach in Newcastle, because he wanted to kick a ball around while I wanted to go home and listen to radio bulletins about the uprising against communist rule in Hungary. I wrote to foreign radio stations asking for their English-language schedules so I could listen to their broadcasts on my father's big Pye radio. Radio Moscow and Radio Prague sent me picture postcards along with their programme listings. My mother eventually asked me to write and tell these two stations to end the correspondence, because a clerk in the post office was telling people I was "a bit of a communist". I certainly had early leanings in that direction. I used my pocket money every Saturday to buy the British Labour Party newspaper *Reynolds News*, now defunct, at McNaughton's tiny newsagents on Newcastle's main street.

But the thought of a career in journalism never occurred to me, nor to my teachers or my parents, Ben and Ita O'Clery-Clarke (in later life I dropped the "Clarke" from my surname). I can't, for the life of me, explain this. Founding and editing the *Hilltop Herald* was seen by me I suppose and by everyone else as just an extra-curricular activity, a hobby and a passing phase. My passion for news and for all things foreign was considered a mere quirk of character. The De La Salle High School in those days mostly prepared us for careers as teachers or civil servants. My father and mother were teachers, as were many of my aunts and uncles. My younger brother Brendan became a science teacher in Belfast and my sister Marie a nurse in Washington DC, where she sometimes teaches other nurses. I myself did not have the patience to be a teacher. I liked the idea of teaching in principle but not in practice. However, there was no great tradition of writing that I knew of in my family – other than that my great-grandfather, Thomas McConville from Portadown, wrote a semi-autobiographical novel about emigrating to Australia in the Gold Rush of the 1850s, called *The Artist of Collingwood*, and published by Gill (now Gill & Macmillan) in Dublin, after he returned to Ireland to make a living in the linen business.

So I drifted. My parents wanted me to aspire to a profession, and I articled myself to an accountant in Belfast, Peter O'Hara. "Articled" in those days meant working for next to nothing. His clients were mostly Catholic publicans in West Belfast. Every week I was sent out to different public houses on the Crumlin Road, Falls Road and in Ligoniel to do the books. I would write down in a huge ledger, item by item, how much stock there was in the bar in terms of beers, wines and spirits, down to half-measures in opened bottles, compare it with the stock a week earlier, and factor in the cash receipts and bills paid. If it didn't balance out, it meant the barman was on the take. The friendly curate at the Clock Bar in Ligoniel was fired after I couldn't get the numbers to add up. It transpired he liked giving free drinks to his mates. Peter O'Hara also did the books for the Ulster Group Theatre, and local celebrities like Harold Goldblatt, Elizabeth Begley and James Young, later of *Z Cars*, would occasionally come trooping through the office in Ann Street.

During this time our family suffered a great tragedy. On 15 November 1959 my older brother Michael, who was training for the priesthood at St Malachy's College, Belfast, died from leukaemia. I was at his bedside in the Mater Hospital when he simply stopped breathing. My father was never the same afterwards, and he passed away five years later from "hardening of the arteries", a condition aggravated, I suspect, by a broken heart. I always wondered if there was a connection between Michael's death and the nuclear accident at the Sellafield power plant (then called Windscale) on the Irish Sea coast in Cumbria two years earlier, on 10 October 1957. There were reports of clusters of leukaemia in County Down afterwards. It gave a personal edge to my reporting of the Chernobyl nuclear disaster some thirty years later.

It took me two years of penury to realise that I was not destined to be an accountant, and I joined the Northern Ireland Civil Service at the age of nineteen to earn some real money. I was assigned to the National Assistance Board, a creation of the welfare state designed to ensure that people with no income had something to live on. On presenting myself on the first day to Mr McMaster, the manager of the Ballymena office, I was told to bring in my bible to take an oath to the Queen. This was a problem for someone who was not just a "bit of a communist" but a bit a nationalist as well. I got around it by following the example of Eamon de Valera, who swore an oath to the King on entering the Dáil in 1927, while declaring that it didn't really count. I brought in my Catholic missal, which looked like a bible, and took the oath on that, and so convinced myself it didn't count either. In truth it didn't bother me very much. There is a degree of ambiguity in most Irish families on the constitutional question. My Great Uncle Peter Clarke fought in the Old IRA and my Aunt

Eileen McConville served in the Women's Royal Naval Service in Malta and I was immensely proud of both of them. I was moved around a bit by the National Assistance Board, to Downpatrick, Kilkeel, Newcastle and Belfast, seeing at first hand the shocking poverty and squalor that existed in those times.

In my mid-twenties I had something of a personal renaissance. I resurrected the defunct Newcastle Amateur Dramatic Society, which flourished for a couple of years as a cross-community project before collapsing in a welter of arguments about the merits of English plays, favoured by the director, a formidable unionist lady, and Irish plays by the likes of J.B. Keane, favoured by me.

I also thought I might improve my financial prospects by further education, and at age twenty-eight I applied to enter Queen's University as a mature student to study computer science – then the coming thing. By this time I was married, to Della McAnulty from Kilkeel, and I was father of four children, soon to be five, so it was a bit of a gamble for me and my family. But there were generous grants available from Down County Council for married students. The university agreed to admit me if I would sit one A Level examination over again to prove my worth. I chose English and took lessons at my old school from Brother Damien, a brilliant teacher who opened my eyes to the joys of poetry and prose and helped me get the desired result. I was accepted for a full-time computer science course in the arts faculty, and resigned from the civil service, despite a stern lecture from a senior official at Stormont about my irresponsibility in giving up a pensioned job, and presented myself at Queen's University admissions office on the first day of the 1968/69 academic year. The admissions officer informed me, in a rather offhand way, that the computer science course had been scrapped at the last minute because of a lack of lecturers. "Pick something else," he suggested.

So I selected English, and thereby got to know other undergraduates on the same course, like Bernard Loughlin and

Tony Dumphy, who recruited me to help run *Gown*, the student newspaper, of which both were to become editors. The moment I walked into the *Gown* office in the Student Union I knew that the media world was where I was meant to be all along. I began writing regularly for *Gown* and eventually inherited a monthly column in *The Irish Times* called "QUB Notes". My by-line unaccountably appeared once on "QUB Notes" as Bishop O'Clery. I won the UK newspaper award for student feature of the year in 1970, and edited the *Student Handbook* for 1971, which allowed me to strike a small blow for Irish freedom. The entry submitted by the university hockey club referred to planned trips to the "mainland", meaning England. I changed "mainland" to "foreign parts".

In my last year at Queen's I wrote to the editor of *The Irish Times*, Douglas Gageby, asking for a job. As luck would have it, Gageby and his news editor, Donal Foley, had come to the conclusion that there was a deficit of Northern Catholics with student journalism experience on the staff of the traditionally Protestant paper. I was accepted. Only my Aunt Edith, our formidable family matriarch who lived on the Falls Road in Belfast, expressed disapproval, asking me, "Could you not get a job on a Catholic paper?" Gageby told me to start work in Dublin in the week immediately after my final examination. I had been hoping to take a holiday but knew better than to mention that.

Former civil servant that I was, I presented myself at precisely nine o'clock on the following Monday morning at *The Irish Times* office in D'Olier Street in Dublin, only to find no one there. I kept coming back until people began appearing around eleven o'clock and let me in. I loved it immediately, the noise, the smell of the ink, the sense of being where I belonged. Within a week I was writing headlines on stories. I am very proud of my first effort, "Library Seeks to Balance Books", over an article about Waterford Library's financial woes. Having been admitted to the staff, no one seemed to care about my academic qualifications and, to this day, no one in *The Irish Times* has ever asked me whether I graduated or not. (I did.)

After a year writing headlines and a few news features, I was appointed Northern editor in Belfast, mainly because hardly anyone in the senior editorial staff in Dublin wanted to live full-time north of the border. Donal Foley often complained that many high-profile performers in the newsroom had joined *The Irish Times* only as an extension of their social life in Dublin. I spent three years in Belfast covering the Troubles and was then transferred to London. After two years there I returned to Dublin, where I spent the next few years as assistant editor, news editor and roving foreign correspondent. I went on assignments to Afghanistan, the Soviet Union, Iraq, Iran and the United States.

Della supported me in making the transition from salaried life to one of student grants and then moving house from Newcastle to Dublin, Belfast, London and back to Dublin. However, in the mid-1980s I left home, and later moved back to the UK alone for a second spell as London editor and got divorced. When Conor Brady was appointed editor to succeed Douglas Gageby in December 1986, and aspired to further Gageby's efforts to make *The Irish Times* a proper European newspaper, he offered me the job of opening the first staff bureau in Moscow where big things were beginning to happen. In Russia I met and married an Armenian, Zhanna Naumova, who was widowed. After almost five years in Moscow reporting on the collapse of the Soviet Union, we moved to Washington where I opened the paper's first staff bureau and after five years there, we were transferred to the other side of the world to Beijing, where I opened the paper's first Asia office. Finally, after another five years, we returned to the United States where I set up the newspaper's first Wall Street bureau.

In New York I wrote a column called "On Wall Street". It was, I believed, a first in Irish journalism. But then my California-based cousin Ted McConville, delving into old family papers, found long-forgotten cuttings of articles my great-grandfather Thomas McConville had written for the *Ulster Observer* during a tour he made of the United States. One of his columns, dated 12 December 1862, was written from Wall Street. The discovery confirmed that the urge to communicate was in my genes, handed down over the generations and passed on to my five children, Cathy, Michael, Joan, Patrick and Emer, who are all involved in the media and the arts.

This then is a political travelogue, a retrospective on events I have witnessed beyond Irish shores on every continent (except Antarctica) in thirty-three years with *The Irish Times*, many of which have shaped modern history.

News stories were described memorably by former *Washington Post* publisher Philip Graham, as "the first rough draft of history". This book is something of a second rough draft of history, as I have updated and brought stories to a conclusion that was not evident or foreseeable in the heat of reporting. There is a Chinese saying, "May you live in interesting times". It is of course a curse. The word "interesting" is a synonym for "dangerous" or "troubled". It is the first of a trilogy of curses, the other two being "May you come to the attention of the authorities" and "May you get what you wish for". I lived through some dangerous and troubled times, managed to avoid attracting too much attention from the authorities, and professionally got much more than I ever could have wished for. This book will, I hope, provide some insights, entertainment and historical information for the reader who shares with me a fascination for the news from abroad.

I cannot hope to thank by name all those who have helped me in my career and my reporting around the world, including diplomats, translators, drivers, government officials, the editors and staff of *The Irish Times*, readers (especially those who sent me letters), the friends and colleagues I made here and abroad, and above all, the members of my family, who at all stages of my career put up with more, and gave me more support, than I ever deserved. I would also like to give special thanks to fellow-journalists Robert Fisk and Mary Kay Magistad, and my agent Jonathan Williams for making invaluable suggestions on the manuscript; Brian Langan at Poolbeg Press, whose idea the book was; and Zhanna, for her superb editing skills. I alone bear responsibility for any errors.

Conor O'Clery
Dublin, 2008

1

Paradise Lost

Everyone remembers where they were and how they first heard of the planes crashing into the twin towers of the World Trade Center in New York on 11 September 2001. It was a catastrophe that killed over 2,600 people, some of them my neighbours and acquaintances, transformed Wall Street into a scene from a nuclear winter, destroyed the environment in downtown Manhattan, and subjected us to horrors that haunt us still. It was an act of aggression that was to plunge the United States into what President George W. Bush called the "War on Terror", the consequences of which would reverberate around the world for years to come.

I had arrived in New York as *Irish Times* international business editor nine months earlier. I thought I was leaving a lifetime of reporting wars and conflicts behind me. In January 2001, my wife Zhanna and I found an apartment and office in Tribeca Pointe Building in Battery Park City. It was right on the edge of the Hudson River, and three blocks north of the World Trade Center. It was a truly delightful place to live. The river esplanade had lawns, curving paths, basketball courts, slides, swings and sculptures. In summer it had a Mediterranean feel, with yachts sailing by and sunbathers stretched out on the grass.

It was a safe place for parents with kids, and for roller-blading, which I took up to keep fit. In the evenings people promenaded along the edge of the Hudson, and lingered at the harbour plaza of the World Financial Center, where champagne parties were held on balmy evenings aboard luxury yachts from as far away as the Cayman Islands. So many people patronised the open-air restaurants and bars there, most of them workers from the banks and brokerages of the twin towers, that in the evenings it became as noisy as an Italian piazza in the hour after dinner.

Most people think of the World Trade Center as the two soaring towers rising up 110 storeys into the sky, containing the offices of bankers, traders, shippers, commodity brokers, insurance agents and lawyers. Actually it was a complex of seven buildings on sixteen acres. It had a broad shopping and service concourse underneath. It was not just a place where 30,000 people came to work every day but a village, with its own zip code, 10048.

To enter this village, we would first walk through the park to the Winter Gardens in the World Financial Center, pass beneath the tall palm trees imported from the Mojave Desert, then climb the wide marble staircase, where wedding couples from Chinatown posed for album pictures, before crossing over to the World Trade Center along a glass-enclosed walkway that straddled West Side Highway. The walkway was so wide it was able to stage the New York orchid show every year. On the other side, we rode elevators down into the heart of a vast concourse. Here beneath the twin towers there was a chocolatier, a hot-bread shop, a kitchenware store, several magazine kiosks, a cobbler's, a hair salon with a Russian stylist called Irina, and dozens of other outlets. There was also a big coffee bar near the escalators leading yet further underground to the New York subway system and the PATH trains to New Jersey, which was convenient for quick business meetings. There was a cavernous delicatessen full of exotic foods and a multi-storey Borders bookshop with deep armchairs for customers. There was a cosmetics store where I once bought a wooden-handled

London Fog umbrella (and still keep as a memento), a pen shop, a tobacconist's, a Sunglass Hut, a Starbucks and Johnny's Fish Grill. We went to the south tower to queue for discount Broadway theatre tickets and to the north tower to pick up airline tickets. We went to the plaza at the foot of the towers for free performances of jazz, country, rhythm and blues and classical music. We used this underground world to walk from Battery Park City to Church Street Post Office at the north-east corner, or to Century 21, the cheap clothing store on Broadway where you could pick up designer clothes for next to nothing. It was a great way to avoid the hot sun in summer, or the freezing winds that blew off the choppy Hudson waters in winter. Occasionally we took visitors to the special elevator in the south tower that whisked us up to a height of 400 metres for a panoramic view of New York City.

On weekdays the area below the towers teemed with office workers like a Tokyo railway station, but at weekends the complex belonged to us, the Battery Park City residents. On Saturday mornings we would sometimes wander over and sample rugelach pastries with coffee in the adjoining Amish Market, a tiled deli with hanging hams and health-food buffet staffed by Turkish immigrants, situated next to the tiny St Nicholas Greek Orthodox Church that stood in the shadow of the south tower.

The evening of 10 September was warm and still. Aoife Keane, a twenty-year-old Dublin psychology student, the daughter of my friend Michael Keane, former editor of the *Sunday Press*, arrived to stay with us for a few days. It was her first time in New York. We went out onto our little balcony and she gazed up in wonder at the lights of the twin towers high above us. The building was constructed without light switches and the lights were never extinguished, day or night. She said, "I am going to go to the top tomorrow morning."

Aoife was still asleep the next day in the guest room, and Zhanna had gone to her office uptown, where she worked as director of development for the Geneva-based International Baccalaureate, when American Airlines Flight 11 crashed into the north tower at 8.46 a.m., laden with 10,000 gallons of fuel. The plane had flown past my apartment block, but downtown Manhattan is a very noisy place and I don't remember hearing it as I worked on an article on how the economic downturn was affecting New York's restaurants. When the bang shook our building, I thought, from years of monitoring the sound of explosions, that it was a bomb. I jumped up and saw a gaping hole near the top of the north tower, the nearest of the two towers, with flames and black smoke pouring out. I made several quick telephone calls, to my news desk, to my *Irish Times* colleague Paddy Smyth in Washington DC, and to Zhanna. I also called RTÉ, to which I often gave interviews, to alert them to what had happened. It was almost two o'clock in the afternoon in Ireland. They asked me to go on air immediately. Just before the broadcast I heard the RTÉ announcer report a newsflash about an aircraft hitting the World Trade Center. Only then did I realise what it was.

I woke Aoife after the interview. "Get up, something terrible has happened," I said. At this stage I didn't know if it was an accident or an attack. From the living-room window I trained my old pair of Russian military binoculars on a man at a window of the north tower. He was standing on a window ledge of the ninety-second or ninety-third floor, hanging out above Vesey Street 300 metres below. There was black smoke pouring from the row of narrow, vestry-like windows beside and above him. He was waving a white cloth. It looked like his shirt. He was in his thirties, I would say, and a little overweight.

Then Aoife said with a gasp, "There's another plane!" United Flight 175 skimmed over the Hudson River to our right and smashed into the south tower between the seventy-eighth and eighty-fourth floors, creating a huge orange and black fireball and showering Broadway with flaming debris. There was no doubt now that this was an act of war and I recall thinking that there would be terrible retribution. We watched helplessly as dozens of heart-wrenching individual tragedies were enacted within our gaze. More people appeared at upper-storey windows crying soundlessly for assistance. We saw five fall to their deaths in a short space of time. Flames began to leap from the side of the nearby Marriott hotel, drenched with burning fuel. About two dozen fire engines came wailing down West Side Highway and screeched to a halt outside the north tower. Scores of firemen ran into the buildings laden down with gear.

After a few minutes I decided to go to the twin towers myself, and took the lift to the ground floor forty-two storeys below. As I passed through the lobby of my building, a woman was in hysterics; her husband worked in the World Trade Center (he survived). I went to the corner of Vesey Street and West Side Highway. People were running in panic away from the burning towers. Others stood in shock, hands over open mouths, heads craning upwards. A security man pushed me back. Someone screamed, "Oh my God, people are jumping!" More bodies were falling onto Vesey Street and onto the plaza between the towers. Some fell with arms extended, as if for a crucifixion, taking what seemed like ten seconds to reach the ground. I thought I had better get back to my office. Frankly I was scared that the towers would collapse on top of me or that I would be hit by falling debris. Also, police officers were closing off the streets and evacuating apartment buildings. I was worried that I would not be allowed back to my office and I felt responsible for Aoife, who, on her own, was witnessing scenes of unimaginable horror on her first morning in New York. I made it back minutes before police ordered all residents of the building to leave. I only found out later that the building manager, Rosie Rosenstein, a friend with whom I would occasionally sit on a bench outside and marvel at our good fortune to live in such a wonderful neighbourhood, decided not to mention my presence to the police, because he knew how important it was for me to continue reporting.

Back at my vantage point I noticed a helicopter buzzing low over the north tower. I thought: why doesn't it take people off the roof, or lower a rope to the windows? I couldn't know that the doors to the roof were locked and the pilots could not approach because of the heat. Just before ten o'clock, I saw office workers who had been milling around the lawns of Battery Park suddenly turn and run as fast as they could. The south tower had started to fall. The top seemed to tilt over towards the river, and then crush the whole building beneath it. Jagged pieces of the tower the size of suburban houses crashed onto two fire engines, and engulfed rescue workers on the roadway. A huge cloud of dust and ash rose from the impact, enveloping the Embassy Suites Hotel below and the fifty-storey buildings of the World Financial Center.

I was by now completely numb, working on my reflexes, typing and making calls at high speed. The story was so enormous, I just had to keep my emotions in check, because my responsibilities to my newspaper were so great.

As the dust cleared, I scanned the windows of the still-standing north tower for the man who had been waving an hour before. Incredibly, he was still there, holding desperately on to a pillar between two of the narrow windows, as smoke poured out past him. He most likely worked for the Marsh & McLennan insurance company, which had offices on several floors at that level. I will never know. As I watched, two bodies fell past him from the higher floors, then two more, and I saw that the tower was shuddering violently. Much has been written about people "jumping". I believe that many were clinging desperately to life, but at that moment were simply unable to hold on. Intense smoke and heat and the shaking gave people little choice. They could not breathe and had to crowd onto the window ledges. About 200 people fell to their death that morning, most from the north tower. None were ever classified as "jumpers", i.e. people who deliberately commit suicide.

The north tower was now in its death throes. The end came at 10.28 a.m. The 110-storey tower imploded floor by floor, spewing out clouds of debris and atomised flesh. The man I was watching descended into the roaring blackness as if on a down elevator. I felt a connection with him. I had been watching him, on and off, and somehow felt he had been looking back at me. It left me with a feeling of guilt in the pit of my stomach, an awful sense of inadequacy and helplessness at not being able to do anything for him. My feelings about that day often come down to that one person and how he suffered.

As the yellow-brown cloud billowed out, rescue workers fled towards the river. Some jumped in and were pulled on board ferry boats. The dense mass of dust approached our apartment until we could almost reach out and touch it. Then it stopped, and retreated slowly, pushed back by a steady breeze from the Hudson. It left a thick layer of ash and dust coating the streets and parks below. It covered the broken bodies on Vesey Street like a shroud. The grey of the landscape was broken by orange-red flames licking up from cars at Vesey and West Side Highway which had been set on fire by the burning debris. More cars were alight on Greenwich Street. The wide walkway across West Side Highway from the Winter Gardens lay broken on the highway. Beyond it, the Greek Orthodox Church had been crushed out of existence. Thousands of scraps of paper floated in the air like giant snowflakes. Some firemen stood in Greenwich Street, stunned, coated from head to foot in dust.

The local telephone lines were cut when the towers collapsed, and the mobile telephone network was overwhelmed, so I could not contact anyone in New York after that. But the long-distance service and broadband still worked. I was able to call my family, keep up contact with my office in Dublin, send digital photographs, and do more radio interviews throughout the afternoon. People who have forgotten anything I ever wrote tell me they recall these broadcasts. I always avoided emotion in radio interviews, but that day, when describing events on RTÉ, I remember involuntarily saying "Oh my God, this is terrible" as I saw more bodies falling to the pavement below.

All afternoon I struggled to match the drama and awfulness of the occasion in my reports. Aoife had a shower around three o'clock. For months afterwards it bothered her, irrationally, that she had done that, while so many people had died outside the windows. Throughout this time a fire raged through No. 7 World Trade Center, a forty-seven-storey building that housed the diesel fuel tanks of the city's emergency command centre, inexplicably located in this likely terrorist target by Mayor Rudolph Giuliani against the advice of his officials, though he would deny that later. At 5.20 p.m. it collapsed, falling straight down onto Greenwich Street. On its own, such an event would have made world headlines. In falling, it smashed an electricity sub-station and cut off the electricity to our building. It was time to leave.

Carrying computer and overnight bags, we stumbled down forty-one flights of concrete emergency stairs in the dark. I kept thinking what it must have been like for those fleeing down the stairwells in the World Trade Center. I found Zhanna at a police barrier outside; I hadn't been able to get through to her all afternoon and she had managed to make her way downtown past several roadblocks. The three of us trudged north through streets clogged with emergency vehicles and exhausted firemen. Beyond the outer police cordon, groups of residents stood looking in stupefaction towards the smoking ruins. A car driven by Chris Coyne, a worker from St Vincent's Hospital, stopped and took us as far as Greenwich Village. They had been prepared for mass casualties, he said, but few were admitted. People either died or escaped.

Though within walking distance of the gigantic pyre, a few people were dining at open-air wine bars in 10th Street in the heart of Greenwich Village, as if nothing had happened. We met up with *Irish Times* stringer, Elaine Lafferty, for a kerbside meal at a tiny restaurant called The Place. The actress Helen Hunt and another woman were at the next table. Here a rather surreal event took place, given the day that was in it. A fight broke out between a waiter and another diner, which spilled past us onto the pavement. We abandoned our table and Helen Hunt disappeared along the narrow street as chairs and bottles flew through the air. Someone said, "Get the cops," as if there would be any available police to tackle a minor fracas, which in any event ended almost as soon as it had begun.

We got another ride uptown and managed to find rooms in the W Hotel on Lexington Avenue in midtown Manhattan. I thought we might be able to return to our apartment the next day but we were to spend ten days there. I turned our room into the temporary *Irish Times* office. After a week, a bill was slipped under the door asking for immediate payment, since the amount exceeded $5,000, mainly owing to the frequent use of the international line to which I had hooked my computer. I went to see the manager in the lobby, explained my situation, and asked if he could cut a deal on the telephone charges. He beckoned me to sit down. "I'm not going to allow you to leave this hotel . . ." he said (my heart sank), ". . . until we both agree on a reasonable charge for the telephone." He was as good as his word. When we were allowed back to Battery Park City, he cut the bill almost in half.

The attack on the United States happened on a Tuesday. On the Thursday I got a call from my colleague Paddy Smyth. "You are not going to believe this," he said. "There is no paper tomorrow." The Taoiseach, Bertie Ahern, had declared a state of mourning in Ireland for Friday, 14 September. Shops, supermarkets, banks, schools and pubs were asked to close for the day. It was an impulsive, emotional and understandable gesture, but misguided. No other country in the world closed for a day of mourning, not even the United States, where a mood of defiance engendered a business-as-usual attitude. The big American companies in

Ireland declined to take part. On that Thursday *The Irish Times* at first stated that the paper would be published as usual the next day, "to keep readers informed of news developments". But late that evening it issued a statement saying it would not, after all, publish on Friday. The reason given by managing director Nick Chapman was that the majority of newsagents around the country would be closed. The editor of *The Irish Times*, Conor Brady, was stranded in California where he had been attending a wedding, and was not consulted. His fury when he found out about this crass commercial decision matched my own. Even at the height of the 1916 Rising, *The Irish Times* had continued publication. No other newspaper closed for the day of mourning in Ireland, or anywhere in the world. I was the only staff reporter for any Irish media in New York covering one of the biggest stories of modern times, and had spent the day at Ground Zero in torrential rain collecting vivid and moving updates on the disaster, only to be informed that I might as well have gone to the cinema. Paddy Smyth had been gathering information on the fast-moving political developments in Washington, and he too was furious. Conor Brady told me afterwards that if he had been in Dublin he would have sold newspapers himself at street corners, rather than not publish. I would have too. It was a shameful day for *The Irish Times*, about which I am still angry.

To my relief, I learned that none of the many reporters whom I had got to know in New York were killed or injured covering the attack, though some had near escapes. Bill Biggart was the only journalist to lose his life in the collapse of the twin towers. The Irish-American photographer had worked in several trouble-spots, including Northern Ireland, and among the thousands of prints in his riverside studio were several of Gerry Adams and of Belfast kids. When the first plane hit the north tower, Biggart grabbed his cameras and started walking the three kilometres to the site, snapping pictures as he went. His wife, Wendy Doremus, called her husband on his mobile shortly afterwards. "Bill, this is an attack, one of the towers collapsed and the Pentagon's been hit," she said. He replied: "I'm okay, I'm with the firemen. I'll meet you in twenty minutes." He was killed instantly when the second tower collapsed. Wendy waited for him in the studio for a few hours. "I kept trying to call but I never got through after that first call," she told me later. The ringing of mobile phones among the debris was one of the most distressing sounds for the rescue workers. Wendy looked for Bill for days, calling at hospitals and handing out his picture. On Saturday afternoon they found his body, and his cameras. His last pictures, taken as the tower was falling onto him, showed that there was no panic among the firemen on debris-strewn West Side Highway. They didn't know that death was imminent.

We were allowed back to our apartment in Tribeca Pointe Building on 21 September. The rubble of the twin towers, extending thirty metres below ground in places, was still belching forth enormous columns of black smoke like a volcano, and producing an acrid smell. Steel beams were being pulled from the depths, still glowing red at one end. When the towers collapsed, their great mass obliterated practically everything within and beneath them, and left a mountain of rubble and metal weighing an estimated 1.2 million tons. The giant structures contained 192,000 tons of structural steel, one million square metres of concrete floors and half a million square metres of masonry walls. The towers had 254 elevators with individual electric motors as big as sports utility vehicles, and 43,600 windows. Mixed up with all this were the contents of thousands of offices, including cupboards, shelves, desks, chairs, couches, carpets, computers, televisions, fax machines, printers, telephones, files, potted plants, pictures, books and many tons of paper. Now, tall cranes swung back and forth, and lines of diggers with clam-shell grabbers climbed high to lift loads of twisted mesh, crushed glass and pulverised concrete onto trucks, and specialists in white protective suits and masks picked through the debris for personal possessions and human remains.

The inconvenience endured by residents of downtown Manhattan like us was of course inconsequential compared with the suffering of the relatives of the 2,603 listed as killed and twenty-four still missing. But the emotional impact affected us all deeply, especially as the search for bodies stretched on to the end of the year and into the following spring.

Before 11 September, Battery Park City residents had been typical New Yorkers. We kept much to ourselves, led our own lives and pursued our own interests. At first, when we returned, everything was different. We found ourselves hugging the concierge, grasping the hands of neighbours we had only nodded to before, and inviting strangers in for coffee. We compared notes about missing acquaintances and scanned messages on the Battery Park City website, such as, "Tony, no one is able to locate you, your brother has been frantically looking for you," or simply, "Susan and Howard, are you okay?" We were fortunate that our building suffered little contamination. In Gateway Plaza, the apartment block nearest the epicentre, people came back to find sofas coated with debris and doors kicked in by rescue workers. Watches, cameras, bicycles and, curiously, a dining-table, had been stolen. Our only material loss was spoiled food and lifeless house plants. We measured our social and spiritual depreciation in other ways. For us all, it was paradise lost.

The situation was more serious for those whose livelihoods were intimately bound up with the towers, like the owners and staff of the thousands of small businesses that had been damaged or destroyed. Bobby Concister of Le Pet Spa in Rector Place reopened on 2 October and found that twenty per cent of his clients had died and half of the rest were moving away. Ray Tahlov, a Russian Jewish barber on Chambers Street, told me as he cut my hair that trade was down by sixty per cent. What made it worse, he said, was that he recognised the faces of some of his regular customers in the pictures of the missing pasted up all along the street by despairing relatives.

In neighbouring Tribeca many fashionable restaurants were able to reopen after two weeks. We treated ourselves to a meal in the Tribeca Grill on Greenwich Street, part-owned by the film actor Robert De Niro, when it resumed business on 24 September, which happened to be my birthday. Normally one had to book days in advance: now we ate in a near-empty dining-room and the manager stopped by to compliment us. Mayor Giuliani appealed to New Yorkers to patronise the distressed downtown business community, and a week later when we went back to Tribeca Grill it was booked out. Through the window we saw Bill Clinton and comedian Jerry Seinfeld hogging what had been our table. For a brief period it became *the* thing to eat near the disaster site, and immaculately dressed people from the Upper East Side would work their way through Caesar salad and seared scallops at pavement tables within sight of the smoking rubble of No. 7 World Trade Center, which blocked the end of Greenwich Street.

But special promotions and token efforts by sympathetic New Yorkers could not detract from the fact that many of the people who had provided downtown establishments with their core day-to-day business were simply gone for good. Apart from those who died, tens of thousands more who worked for the 616 companies that had occupied the World Trade Center, or in neighbouring offices, were dispersed to other locations. So many banking and brokerage firms relocated across the Hudson that the waterside developments of Jersey City became known as Wall Street West. Some firms, like Cleary, Gottlieb, Steen & Hamilton, whose London office was destroyed by an IRA bomb in 1990, became virtual entities, with employees working from home. Even if they could, many staff did not want to return to lower Manhattan, where they had suffered the most traumatic event of their lives and lost friends and colleagues. The 1,200 traders of the New York Board of Trade at No. 4 World Financial Center – the location of the "pit" where Dan Aykroyd and Eddie Murphy bet on orange juice futures in the film *Trading Places* – moved to a warehouse in Queen's. Philip Marber, head of equities operations at Cantor Fitzgerald, which lost 677 out of 1,000 employees, spoke for many when he said simply, "We're not going back there."

A couple of weeks after 9/11, Paddy Moloney of The Chieftains came to New York and I took him to Ground Zero where he wanted to play a lament for the dead on his tin whistle. The Chieftains' founder performed alone in the remains of Liberty Plaza, with smoke rising from the smouldering rubble behind him. His only listeners were a small group of friends, a few New York police officers, and his daughter Aedin. The haunting strains of *Táimse Im' Chodladh* (I am asleep and don't wake me) and *Dóchas* (Hope) were almost drowned out in the harsh cacophony from mechanical diggers and cranes. The then Minister for Foreign Affairs Brian Cowen arrived in New York on 27 September and travelled with Irish officials to the site on a police patrol boat. They were stunned by the devastation and upset by the sight of a body being removed. On the way back along the Hudson River, Cowen led his small party in a recitation of a decade of the rosary for the victims.

The sense of communal togetherness we felt in the immediate aftermath of 9/11 eroded rapidly. By November, three out of ten tenants in our building had decided that they could not go on living beside the mass grave. They were sceptical about official assurances that there were no dangerous levels of asbestos in the acrid smoke that occasionally drifted up to our balcony. Some of our neighbours had lost their jobs and had no alternative but to move. Others couldn't stand the noise, as dozens of excavators loaded debris round the clock onto a fleet of Mazzochi flatbed trucks for transport to a landfill on Staten Island. The once-tranquil inlet of the Hudson River beneath our windows was clogged with an enormous floating dock where a crane squealed and banged as it lifted twisted metal pieces onto giant barges. Truth to tell, many residents were transient, like ourselves, and either on company accounts or pretty well off, and could choose where to live.

It took almost a year for all the debris at Ground Zero to be removed, and for the smashed Winter Gardens to be reconstructed. When it reopened, we found it a rather unsettling experience to enter the renovated steel and glass atrium with its new palm trees. It was like stepping into the pre-9/11 past. The sweeping staircase was there as before, only now it led not onto the walkway across West Side Highway, but to a roped-off viewing window overlooking the pit that was a metaphor for the hole in our lives. Every time I went there I saw the walkway in my mind, full of people hurrying to and fro, many of whom would have died on 9/11, their pulverised remains forming particles in the dust.

Our mood went up and down in the four years we lived in New York after 9/11. There were moments of gut-wrenching emotion, when bodies were brought out at dead of night from a scene like Dante's Inferno, with dazzling stadium lights silhouetting the skeleton of the towers and sparks cascading down from the acetylene torches of ironworkers, and there were times of exaltation, as when beams of light shone up into the clouds to mark the first anniversary of the attack. There were some good days; I particularly remember when the city block housing a sixteen-screen cinema and Lily's noodle restaurant reopened after a year's decontamination and refurnishing. We had missed Lily's scallion pancakes.

There were times too when resentment boiled up, especially when we learned two years later that we had been lied to by the Environment Protection Agency about the danger from air pollution. Its former administrator, Christine Todd Whitman, admitted that her officials had given unfounded assurances about indoor pollution and toxic dust from the asbestos used on the bottom thirty-four floors of the twin towers, because "we didn't want to scare people". In May 2008 the New York health department said that 360 of the responders and volunteers who dealt with the aftermath had died, 154 from cancer, and that it was examining whether the number of deaths had been "elevated" as a result of 9/11.

And there were times, even early on, when we could put 11 September out of our minds. The children of Battery Park City held their annual Halloween costume party six weeks later, led by Elmo and a bevy of princes, bear cubs and goblins, and in Greenwich Village the annual Halloween Parade went ahead as usual, except that the theme was changed from the Russian fairytale of Baba Yaga to the Phoenix, the bird of myth which is consumed by flames every 500 years but always rises in glory from the ashes.

For five years Ground Zero remained a pit. Construction of the World Trade Center Memorial and museum did not begin until March 2006. But even today, the building site is a place of pilgrimage for international tourists and camera-wielding Americans, drawn by a mixture of patriotism, curiosity and reverence. They talk in subdued tones as they walk around and read a display of pictures and historical references. The weekends around Ground Zero now belong, not to the residents, but to them.

2

The Great Game

Within weeks of the attack on the United States on 11 September 2001, American forces invaded Afghanistan. The perpetrator of 9/11, Osama bin Laden, and his al Qaeda organisation, were operating freely in Afghanistan, with the sanction of the Taliban government. For the Afghans, it was the second invasion by a superpower in a quarter of century. The Soviet armed forces had been and gone in the 1980s. Now it was America's turn to send its soldiers into one of the most inhospitable terrains in the world.

Afghanistan has a long tradition of overcoming foreign domination after a deceptively easy conquest. The British met little resistance when they arrived in Kabul in 1839 and placed their puppet, Shah Shuja, on the throne, but three years later the venture ended in the retreat and massacre of British forces. The Russians invaded in December 1979 and installed their communist ally Babrak Karmal in the People's Palace, but withdrew almost ten years later after suffering almost 15,000 killed and half a million wounded in action. The Americans now also found that taking Kabul was relatively easy, and soon their man, Hamid Karzai, was established as president.

Having been to Afghanistan a number of times, I had a good idea what the Americans would be up against. My first visit was in January 1980, a few days after the Soviet occupation. At the time I was based in Dublin, and when Douglas Gageby suggested that I go there to cover the invasion, I decided not to tell him that I had just seen a Reuters flash saying that the country was closed to foreign journalists. I would get in somehow. Three days later I arrived in the Pakistan city of Peshawar, and from there took a taxi for the thirty-kilometre trip to the Khyber Pass. Here I was prevented from entering Afghanistan by Pakistani border guards of the Khyber Rifles. I returned to Peshawar and wrote a story with a Khyber Pass by-line, then retreated to my room, wondering what I should do next. Such a by-line, however romantic, was good for one story only.

Then one of those things happened which proves that in journalism it always pays to help a colleague. A *New York Times* correspondent, Bill Borders, knocked on my door, having seen my name in the hotel register. I had first met Borders three weeks earlier, when he had turned up in Dublin and I had helped him compile a story on Anglo-Irish relations and brought him to dinner. He had been sent to Peshawar with the same mission as me, to get into Afghanistan, and he now told me that he had just been tipped off that the Afghan consulate in Peshawar would start issuing journalist visas the following morning. He had hired "the biggest goddam car" in Peshawar to drive to Kabul, he said, and would I like to come with him?

We became the first journalists to travel overland into Afghanistan since the Soviet invasion, though we had to leave behind the "biggest goddam car" at the Khyber Pass, and hire a pick-up truck and driver on the Afghanistan side for the remainder of the journey to Kabul. We were driven up through the narrow Khyber Gorge, where long icicles hung from precipitous rocks, and onto the vast Kabul plateau. There we were greeted by the extraordinary sight of thousands of Afghans running across a snowfield towards the fortress-like Puli Charkhi prison, from which the former regime's political prisoners were being released. We checked into the InterContinental Hotel, where my feeling of achievement was diminished somewhat on finding Pierce FitzGerald, brother of the then Fine Gael leader, Garret FitzGerald, and his daughter Pamela, having a quiet drink in the bar. They had been in Kabul for some weeks working on a World Bank project. Soon the bar got extremely busy as a second invasion got under way, this time by foreign correspondents arriving from all over the world.

There was a zest and innocence about reporting from Afghanistan in those days after the Soviet invasion. It was like our own Great Game. Few of us felt in any real danger. One day I even managed to walk into Puli Charkhi prison, ignoring the heavily armed Russian guards, and along with *Times* correspondent Robert Fisk, a colleague from Belfast days, I interviewed imprisoned members of the deposed Afghan royal family. The Russians, the Afghan communists and the *mujahidin* in the hills seemed to respect a convention that foreign correspondents should not be harmed. The representatives of the world's media were treated as a curiosity by turbaned tribesmen and Soviet soldiers in greatcoats. British journalists especially, some wearing Burton suits and Winstanley shoes, had fun retracing the path of the 1842 retreat of General Elphinstone and his ragged British Army, and reliving the days when the top-hatted Ulsterman, Sir William Hay Macnaghten, was the puppet-master of British Afghanistan, at least until his head, without the top hat, was paraded through Kabul by his assassins.

For Soviet journalists the mission was entirely different. The Afghan rebels hated them. They risked being killed outside Kabul simply because they were *shuravi*, as the Afghans called the Russians. They were also required to report propaganda rather than news. Some months later when I was visiting Moscow, I asked Vladimir Guncherov, foreign editor of the Soviet news agency TASS, what instructions he gave his reporters in Afghanistan. "We do not hide the fact that our sympathies are with the oppressed people of Afghanistan, just as they are with the oppressed Catholic population in Northern Ireland," he said. "Have you ever heard of our writer Mikhail Sholokhov, author of *And Quiet Flows the Don*? He put it well. He said, 'We write from our hearts and our hearts belong to the Party.'"

For the first few days in Kabul the telephones worked, but the lines went dead one afternoon, supposedly after a British tabloid reporter dictated a story to his office quoting a Russian soldier saying he did not know what country he had invaded (a Fleet Street favourite). The telex office remained open but we had to ply the operator with drink, a half-bottle to start and another half-bottle when the text was sent so he would not get too drunk, in which case his hand would not be steady enough to solder back the letter "h" that kept falling off his keyboard. Then the telex line was cut, and we had to find "pigeons" – outward-bound travellers – at the airport, who would take typed copy to news agencies abroad to "onsend" to our newspapers. These were the days before mobile and satellite phones and emails, when a reporter was only as good as his or her ability to find a way to transmit the story back home.

The Reuters man in Kabul left Afghanistan suddenly one day for India after what he called a "nasty scrap" with Afghan security officials, and he asked me to be their stringer until he was replaced. "You know the Reuters style," he wrote in a note giving me instructions, "boring but very complete, so please don't hesitate to send as much as possible if it's no trouble." He didn't know what the daily rate was, he confessed, but he was sure it was okay. "Basically we prefer losing out on a story rather than losing a correspondent, so please don't do anything on our account that would get you into hot water." I sent stories for two or three days by "pigeon" to the Reuters bureau in New Delhi. I never did find out what the daily rate was, because Reuters never paid me.

Rumour was rife and misinformation widespread in the early days after the Soviet invasion. I went with Bill Borders one day to a press briefing in the American embassy, but was ejected because it was for US reporters only. I learned afterwards that a piece of intelligence the diplomats peddled that morning was that the Salang Pass across the Hindu Kush to northern Afghanistan had been closed for several days. This was interesting news to me, since I had been able to drive with some colleagues across the Salang Pass the previous day, meeting only friendly Russian troops. At least they were friendly until the *Daily Telegraph* man tried to take pictures of gun emplacements from the back window of our car, whereupon we were held up at gun point and detained in their barracks for a few hours. Afghans too were suspect sources. "Are you sure this is true?" a BBC reporter asked an Afghan soldier who was describing to us in gory detail a bloody battle in a provincial town. "Yes, sure," came the reply. "I heard it on the BBC World Service."

It was only when I went back to Afghanistan six months later, this time illegally crossing the border from Pakistan in the guise of a *mujahidin*, that I came to appreciate fully the intensity of Islamic fundamentalism that motivated the Afghanistan fighters who had begun to give the Russians a hard time in the mountains. My journey started in the city of Quetta, capital of the tribal North West Frontier province of Baluchistan in southern Pakistan, in the company of Canadian freelance journalist Keith Leckie, and Mark August from *New Africa* magazine. We were guests of the Hisb-i-Islami (Islamic Party) rebel group, led by Gulbuddin Hekmatyar, which would receive millions of dollars' worth of military aid from the United States to fight its proxy war against the Red Army.

Two unlikely Afghan warriors, Jamal and Sherrifola, were assigned to take us across the Baluchistan desert and smuggle us into rebel-held Afghanistan. Jamal, who was taking blood-pressure tablets, had a habit of intoning "Oh my God" at every setback, of which there were many. Sherrifola was given in quiet moments to unwinding his cream-coloured, slightly scented turban, and scrutinising his handsome face in a pocket mirror. In Quetta we stocked up on essential gear for reporting from Afghanistan: sleeping bags, water filters, water bottles, water purifying tablets, antiseptic creams, antibiotic creams, tablets for dysentery, aspirins, anti-lice cream, mosquito repellents, salt tablets, lavatory paper, bandages, gauze, chewing-gum, boiled sweets, maps of Afghanistan, notebooks, binoculars and – most important of all – *Jane's Pocket Book of Armoured Vehicles*, for identifying Soviet and rebel vehicles.

We had to dress as *mujahidin* to avoid the attention of bandits and border guards on the journey. At six o'clock one morning, Jamal and Sherrifola took us to a courtyard, where several sleepy Afghans broke into grins at the sight of three foreigners awkwardly fitting on baggy trousers, cloaks and turbans. The jeep they provided to take us across the desert was an old canvas-covered Toyota with a cracked windscreen and leaking radiator. The bearings were gone in the nearside front wheel, so we had to splash it with water every thirty kilometres or so. We drove for hours, banging along riverbeds and wadis. Once when the jeep hit a boulder, the passenger windscreen fell into our laps. "Oh my God," wailed Jamal. We reached a yellow-coloured plateau where dust devils danced on the horizon, and near sunset came to a square stone building manned by Pakistan border guards, where a chain blocked the roadway. "Pretend you are asleep," ordered Jamal. We pulled thin shoulder blankets across our faces. A lone Pakistani policeman appeared. "*Mujahidin*," Jamal said, pointing to us. "Okay," he replied, lifting the chain. Inside Afghanistan, the jeep creaked and banged for an hour through jagged outcrops until, around a bend at about 9,000 feet, we came upon a green Islamic flag, and an outpost of the camp of Zafaruddin Khan, commander of the rebel forces of Zabul Province.

Some twenty rebels carrying Kalashnikov rifles emerged from a large tent to hug Jamal and Sherrifola and giggle at the sight of the foreigners in Afghan robes. We pitched our sleeping bags on the cockroach-infested blankets spread over the ground inside, and spent the evening listening to the fighters regale us with stories of "killing communists". A twenty-four-year-old assassin, Mahtat Hakim, boasted to me how he had killed seven communists in Kabul. "Do you want to know how I shoot them?" he asked. "I go up to them and I do this" – he violently shook his curly black beard and emitted a guttural howl – "then I do this." With his fingers he imitated the squeezing of a trigger. He had been with the *mujahidin* for two years, during which time he had not seen his wife or three-year-old son. "Do you miss them?" I enquired. "I am very happy here killing Russians for Allah," he replied. Later, he pulled my arm. "I don't know if my boy has any of these yet," he said, pointing to his teeth.

On the second night we were escorted in almost total darkness to the main camp. The Muslim guides went ahead singing religious songs. We were instructed to sing something to maintain voice contact. I obliged with the "Tantum Ergo" from the Latin mass, which seemed a good idea at the time. Zafaruddin Khan turned out to be an educated and mild-mannered twenty-five-year-old Afghan officer, with neatly trimmed moustache and manicured nails, and dressed in a fawn shirt and trousers and a tall astrakhan hat. A graduate of Kabul military college, he had led a successful mutiny at Zabul military base and claimed to have killed thirty-five communists. Despite his western appearance, Zafaruddin Khan's goal was not just to get rid of the Russians. It was deeply ideological. "When the Russians are defeated, and they will never succeed as long as there is one Muslim in Afghanistan, then we will have a pure Islamic state here," he said, sitting cross-legged in his tent hung with green Islamic banners. "All those who are disbelievers, we will not allow them in an Islamic Afghanistan." We were left in no doubt about the type of fundamentalist society to which this US-aided insurgency aspired: one where women would be prohibited from education or work outside the home, and would be required in public to wear the *burqa*, a society where public executions and floggings and the severing of limbs would be legalised, and popular music and television banned. "The Russians have come to destroy Islam, but we have the faith," he said. "We believe in holy religion. We will win." As the commander spoke, his eyes flickered up towards the tent roof. He signalled to me not to move. A scorpion was clinging to the canvas above me. An aide grabbed a towel and crushed the scorpion before it could drop onto my turbaned head.

Next day the commander organised a display of captured Soviet weaponry for our benefit. From a promontory in the valley we watched, *Jane's Pocket Book* in hand, as an array of military vehicles passed by, led by an eight-wheeled BTR 60 PK armoured personnel carrier and a large yellow Zil 164 troop-carrying truck. The *mujahidin* in the vehicles pointed fingers in the air and shouted "*Marg bar Shuravi*" as they passed, which Jamal translated as "Death to the bloody Russians". Their prize possession was an S60 automatic 57mm anti-aircraft gun installed in a bunker. The day before a Soviet Mig 21 had roared up the valley but had been caught in fire from the gun and crashed several kilometres away. While we watched the parade, three warriors came back triumphantly carrying the plane's heavy black 20mm cannon. Fearful of more air attacks, the *mujahidin* kept glancing nervously at the sky and after the parade was over we were quickly guided back to our tent. Next day we left. On the return journey to Quetta, the jeep finally broke down in the Baluchistan desert. We waited for an hour and fortunately a truck came along and took us the remainder of the journey.

In the next few years, the CIA provided a minimum of 500 stinger missiles – portable infra-red surface-to-air missiles with a range of 4,800 metres – to the warriors for Islam in the Afghanistan hills. And the next time I encountered the *mujahidin*, eight years later, in the city of Khost near Zafaruddin Khan's camp, they were firing at me.

This time I was a guest of the Soviet armed forces, as one of a group of Moscow correspondents invited to Afghanistan to testify to the success of Soviet troops in lifting a lengthy siege of the city of Khost, a dusty border town in a mountainous region of eastern Afghanistan. In the last phase of its occupation, the Soviet army had practically ceased offensive operations, but it had staged a successful sweep to open the road to Khost in order to demonstrate a Soviet victory before leaving the country.

We travelled first from Moscow to Kabul in an Afghan Air Ilyushin. As we spiralled down towards the airport, a Soviet helicopter gunship appeared and fired several magnesium flares, like tiny pieces of red-hot coal trailing white smoke, to deflect heat-seeking missiles that might be fired from the mountains. In eight years the Soviet occupation had made surprisingly little impact on the Afghan capital. In the hotel the signs were in English and Dari, though most of the guests were from the Soviet Union. The receptionist spoke a little English but feigned not to understand Russian. In the lobby kiosk, the paperback books on sale included *The Saint Meets His Match* by Leslie Charteris, *Alfred Hitchcock's Mystery Magazine 1973*, and *John F. Kennedy: A Political Profile* – but nothing in Russian. The shops and stalls were well stocked with western imports such as Toblerone chocolate, Old Spice shaving lotion and Marlboro cigarettes. Money-changers traded afghanis for American dollars. The Russian rouble was nowhere to be seen. Perhaps the reason for the lack of Soviet influence on Kabul, in contrast with the Americanisation of Saigon during the Vietnam War, was that the Russians had little spending money, and they could not mix socially with Afghans for fear of encountering assassins like my curly-bearded friend, Mahtat Hakim. Most Russian administrators and their families lived in apartment blocks inside a "green zone" outside town, and rarely ventured into Kabul.

The next day we boarded a propeller-driven Antonov-26 troop carrier for the hour-long flight to Khost. The road might have been opened for the military but it was still too dangerous for civilians. We landed at dawn on an earthen strip, where today there is a busy American air base. The only navigation light was a hand-held torch, and the plane took off again immediately to avoid incoming rocket fire. In the bustling town of 40,000 people, roosters crowed in back yards, donkeys and camels ambled by, and policemen in peaked hats with traffic indicators like table-tennis bats directed the occasional resident riding by on a Chinese-made bicycle. With a heavily armed escort, we walked down the narrow main street, where shashlik sellers were stoking up wood fires, and the warm air was heavy with the smells of cooking and manure, and went to sip tea with the local People's Democratic Party chairman, Saadat Gul Ahangar.

The Soviet army wanted not just to provide testimony of a last victory over the rebels, but to present the other side of the story: the case against the Muslim rebels. A rally was staged for our benefit at the bullet-scarred Palace of Culture, attended by a few dozen old men in turbans, a group of mawkish young soldiers, and dozens of pretty, brown-skinned children. We were addressed by twenty-seven-year-old Mahbyba, a slim woman with dark hair combed down to her eyelashes, who, with the passion of a young Bernadette Devlin, condemned the imperialists in the West for supplying weapons to the rebels. Chairwoman of the Women's Council of Khost, Mahbyba described the repression women could expect under Islamic law. They would be forced to wear the *burqa*, would be banned from working, and the girls taken out of schools. It was an uncomfortable experience for the foreign reporters there, who, with our western view of things, instinctively wanted to see the Soviet forces beaten. The people whose defeat the Americans were helping to bring about were the most westernised, secular and progressive elements in Afghanistan. The middle classes of Kabul and other urban centres were not wholly supportive of the

Russians. But they were faced with a terrible set of options. Having emerged from decades of feudalism, they knew that if the Islamic rebels won, modernisation of Afghanistan would be set back and the country would become a fundamentalist religious state. The intervention of the United States ensured that the movement for women's equality in Afghanistan, along with the advance of literacy, health care and the other benefits sought by a self-consciously developing nation, would be crushed.

The end of the young woman's speech was drowned out by a burst of outgoing rocket fire, which made everyone jump. It was time to leave, but we had to wait until darkness fell, when the Antonov could return and land. At the airstrip, as we trotted towards the taxiing aircraft, a rocket hit the ground some one hundred metres to our left. A second rocket exploded in a fountain of red streaks thirty metres to our right, and lumps of earth rained down on our heads. We stumbled up the ramp of the plane, which was immediately pulled up, and the Antonov roared across the baked mud and began climbing steeply. Hanging on to the parachute wire, Robin Lodge of Reuters and I peered out through the round windows and saw a third rocket landing on the spot where the plane had parked briefly to let us on. I wondered if those firing the rocket had been among the *mujahidin* who had entertained me a few years previously.

When the Soviet Army withdrew in 1989, and the Cold War came to an end two years later, both Russia and the United States left the war-ravaged nation to its own devices. The country slid into chaos. The Taliban evolved from the rival *mujahidin* groups and seized Kabul in 1996. By the end of 2000 the Taliban had imposed a very strict interpretation of Islamic law in most of the country. Women were repressed, popular music banned and thieves punished by amputation. Osama bin Laden, who had helped fight the *Shuravi*, established his camp in Khost district, from where he allegedly planned the 9/11 attacks on New York and Washington.

Gulbuddin Hekmatyar, head of the Hisb-i-Islami group, whose fighters I visited in the Afghan mountains, received a total of $600 million in US aid to fight the Russians. He was briefly prime minister during the civil war that followed the Soviet withdrawal. After 9/11 he backed the Taliban and claimed to have helped Osama bin Laden escape capture in the Tora Bora mountains. In 2003 the US State Department declared him to be a global terrorist. In May 2006 he released a video in which he said he was ready to fight alongside al Qaeda against United States forces. From October 2001, when coalition forces led by the US and Britain invaded Afghanistan, until mid-May 2008, an estimated 20,000 people, mainly Afghan civilians, were killed in the fighting. Of these, 742 were coalition forces, almost two-thirds of them Americans.

3

Saddam Pays My Expenses

After my first visit to Afghanistan in January 1980, I did not return directly home. I made a detour to Iran, where the initial phase of a long war between the United States and militant Islam was under way. The country was in turmoil in the wake of the Islamic Revolution the year previously, which had ousted the American-backed Shah. On 4 November 1979, Islamic students had seized the American embassy and taken sixty-six diplomats hostage in protest at the United States giving asylum to the Shah.

I was the only passenger to alight from the Ariana Airline Boeing 747 when it stopped in Tehran on the flight from Kabul to Amsterdam. In the terminal a young unshaven man in an olive green anorak snatched my passport from the immigration officer. "Tell me," he asked, as he leafed through it, "My wife is sick. She cannot get the proper medical attention here. Which European country should I send her to?" I said I would probably recommend Britain for its National Health Service. "You can go through," he said. Perhaps my reply satisfied him that I wasn't an American using an Irish passport.

I checked into the twelve-storey Intercontinental Hotel, a featureless grey building where the staff showed a distinct reserve towards western guests. As a group of American journalists was checking out, the cashier made a little speech in flawless English. "I am glad to see you leave. We don't like Americans. The day is past when Iranians can be bought by dollars."

The US embassy complex on Taleghani Avenue was so big it took me twenty minutes to walk around it. The red-brick exterior walls were plastered with slogans such as "CIA, Pentagon, Uncle Sam: Vietnam wounded you, Iran will bury you". The three main US television companies – CBS, NBC and ABC – had crews stationed at the gates. In the days before cable and satellite television, Americans got their television news from the three networks, and their reporters in Tehran were required to send daily bulletins for the prime-time evening broadcasts. They played a game of chicken, betting on which crew could hold back the longest from doing their daily "stand-up" report from the embassy gates, because as soon as one camera went into action, the Revolutionary Guards and their hangers-on would crowd round and shout anti-American slogans. The first to give in had to buy the others dinner that night in the Intercontinental Hotel. The game stopped shortly after I arrived when all American reporters were abruptly ordered out of the country, on the basis that the corrupt Shah's regime had never been subject to the same scathing media criticism as that aimed at Ayatollah Khomeini, and I found myself staying almost alone in the Intercontinental Hotel.

I went to the besieged embassy one morning and asked the Revolutionary Guards at the main gates if I could go inside. They took down the number of my hotel room. I was working in my room the next day when the telephone rang. A female voice said, "This is the den of espionage." It was a revolutionary student inside the US embassy. "Your appointment is for 9.30 on Friday morning," she said.

It was snowing heavily as I presented my press credentials at the embassy gate. I was taken into the compound by students with Kalashnikov rifles and led into an annex. A sign inside indicated that it had housed the State Department intelligence unit. Pictures of Ayatollah Khomeini were pinned to a large notice-board, and slogans were taped to the polystyrene wall tiles. On the floor lay a pile of embassy paperbacks. A gas fire hissed noisily in the centre of the room. Two unshaven students in zip-up sweaters and khaki windcheaters walked in and sat at a blanket-covered table, along with a woman translator in a white headscarf. In an hour and a half they did not smile once, as they responded to my questions with lengthy and mind-numbing revolutionary speeches, which the interpreter wrote in a legal pad and then read back to me word for word. One of the students named Rahim, who had a drooping moustache and deep brown eyes, accused US President Jimmy Carter of telling lies about the conditions of the hostages. Drumming his fingers on the table, he said, "We ask the American people and the dear peoples of Europe: listen only to the Muslim students. The hostages are treated well." In fact, when the last fifty-two hostages were released a year later, they described being held in solitary confinement. Rahim asked why Europeans were not supporting the overthrow of a cruel regime. "If the people of England knew of the crimes committed in their name in Northern Ireland, they would not allow the government to remain in power."

The students presented me with a "revolutionary pack" of embassy documents to prove that the CIA was still operating in Tehran. One document, dated August 1979, six months after the revolution, stated: "With regard for the great sensitivity locally to any hint of CIA activity, it is of the highest importance that cover is the best we can come up with. Hence there is no question as to the need for second and third secretary titles for these two officers, Kalp and Dougherty." Another document specified cover for a third agent, with the alias Paul Timmermans. It stated: "According to personal data in your passport, you are single, were born in Antwerp, Belgium 08 July '34, have blue eyes, have no distinguishing characteristics and are approximately 1.88 metres tall. Your occupation is that of a commercial business representative. Your Belgian passport was ostensibly issued in Jette [and] to enhance its validity the following back travel has been added, a trip to Madrid, Spain, in April 1977, a trip to Lisbon, Portugal, in August 1977, a trip to Helsinki, Finland, in 1978." Other embassy documents contained accounts of routine conversations with prominent Iranians, all of whom were subsequently banished from public life for their "collaboration". Diplomats in other western embassies, while sympathising with the Americans, told me privately how angry they were at their American counterparts for allowing such documents to be seized so easily. Their own contacts now declined to meet them.

The Iranian revolutionaries had good reason to be paranoiac about the CIA. In 1953, the US intelligence agency and MI6 had engineered a military coup to oust the democratically elected government of Prime Minister Mohammad Mossadegh, which had nationalised the oil fields of the Anglo-Iranian Oil Company, later known as British Petroleum (BP), and had installed a monarchy under which US and British corporations flourished and tens of thousands of Iranians were tortured and killed. Then – as now – American policy in the Middle East was about oil, in this case the huge oil resources on Iran's western border with Iraq, around the oil city of Abadan on the Persian Gulf.

After my encounter in the US embassy, I flew from Tehran to Abadan on a half-empty Boeing 727 to visit the oil fields. I was advised not to take Iran's domestic airlines, as it had been experiencing maintenance problems since the revolution, but I had no choice, because the roads were snow-bound. A Boeing 727, possibly the same plane which took me to Abadan, crashed outside Tehran four days later, killing all 127 people aboard.

Abadan airport terminal was festooned with revolutionary posters. Yasser Arafat's picture competed with a photograph of the despised UN Secretary General Kurt Waldheim kissing the hand of the deposed Empress Farah. It was a holiday – the anniversary of the Shah's departure from Iran a year previously. Young men strolled along the quays of the Shatt al-Arab waterway, some holding hands, shivering in leather jackets. A street photographer plied his trade. It could have been the banks of the Seine on a wintry Sunday afternoon but for the absence of young women. Here, in the Iranian province of Khuzestan, most of the population was Arab rather than Iranian. The revolution had been particularly bloody in the oil towns, which were surrounded by poverty-stricken Arab villages. Iraq's dictator, Saddam Hussein, coveted the oil fields of Khuzestan as part of his goal to make Iraq the dominant power in the Persian Gulf region. Tensions were rising at the prospect of an Iraqi invasion. The Shi'ite Iranian spiritual leader, Ayatollah Khomeini, who despised the secular regime of Saddam Hussein, a Sunni Muslim, added to the war fever by encouraging Shi'ite Arabs in southern Iraq to rise up against Baghdad's rule.

In the cool evening sunshine I joined a group of Arab youths watching a couple of moto-cross riders launch their Hondas into space over humps of black earth. One gripped my arm and pointed to a flat rooftop, where half-a-dozen figures squatted with rifles on their knees. They were Pasdarans, Guardians of the Revolution, he said. "We don't want them here, we fight them." The Pasdarans, who paradoxically honoured the Arab Palestinian leader, Yasser Arafat, as a revolutionary hero, had crushed an outburst of Arab unrest after the revolution. That night I listened to distant explosions as Arab saboteurs went about their work.

I took a taxi next day to the port city of Khorramshahr, ten kilometres north of Abadan, where twelve people had died in a bomb blast the previous week. In a back street I came across a little shop specialising in backgammon boxes and ornamental Persian scrolls depicting mildly erotic love scenes. The owner, a thin elderly man, was sitting on a small safe, in which he kept his dwindling supply of gold trinkets. Business was bad, he told me. He would dearly love to sell up and move abroad, perhaps to

England where he had a son, but he could not. He spread out his hands despairingly. He was not allowed to sell his property. He was a Jew. "Imagine how I feel when a poster goes up outside my door showing Yasser Arafat holding hands with Ayatollah Khomeini." He motioned me to silence as two men came in to rummage through the backgammon boxes. "Things are very bad," he whispered vehemently after they had gone. "Very bad, explosions every night."

The oil refinery in Abadan, the great prize in the Persian Gulf, was the largest in the world. It stretched for thousands of acres behind a gateway dominated by a five-metre-high portrait of the Ayatollah. In his yellow-brick offices, where a large relief map of Iran produced by "Aero Service Corp, Philadelphia, USA" took up one whole wall, the refinery manager, Parviz Shahideh, lit up a Winston cigarette as he explained how a revolutionary committee had taken over the refinery but had allowed the managers to stay in place. The committee had banned tea-drinking in the refinery canteens during daylight hours in the month of fasting; otherwise it was business as usual. However, breaking the hold of the US-based multinationals had crippled some of his operations, since spare parts were now difficult to get.

As I left, he pointed from the door of his building, across the seaward channel of the Tigris and Euphrates, to a palm grove one hundred metres away on the other side of the water. "That's Iraq," he said. "That's where all the trouble is coming from."

Nine months later I was in that Iraqi palm grove, in the company of Iraqi soldiers, watching as Parviz Shahideh's oil refinery at Abadan went up in flames. I had returned to the region, this time as a guest of Saddam Hussein, who had launched an invasion of Iran on 22 September 1980, with the aim of capturing the Shatt al-Arab waterway and the Abadan oil refinery, annexing Khuzestan and overthrowing Ayatollah Khomeini.

Saddam had invited foreign journalists from all over the world to come and witness, at Iraq's expense, what he believed would be victory over Iran after a great *blitzkrieg*. *The Irish Times* declined Iraq's offer of free air fare from Dublin, but when I arrived in Baghdad, I found that the 300-room, five-star Mansour Melia Hotel, where we were required to stay (what hardship!) had suspended charges for all foreign journalists. The dictator was picking up the tab for everything – rooms, restaurants, bars, laundry and international calls. The news was greeted with shock and awe by the expense-conscious journalists flying in from all over the world.

We know now that the mother of all invasions was the first in a series of military miscalculations by the Iraqi leader. But in the early days of what would become an eight-year war, Iraq was giddy with the prospect of victory. All along Al-Sadun Street in the city centre, where the air was filled with the smells of spices and cooking lamb, the sound of patriotic chanting and marching feet came from television sets in the shirt shops and kebab houses. Iraq's best singers had been recruited for duty, and the voice of Sadun Jaba, famous across the Arab world, could be heard all day against a backdrop of victorious Iraqi troops jogging past admiring onlookers. Every evening, however, the songs of victory ended in mid-chord as the electric power was cut to ensure total blackout.

The Iraqis had some initial victories. I was able to accompany the Iraqi military across a desert plain dotted with tanks to the captured Iranian border town of Qasr-e Shirin, an ancient provincial capital where the modern boundary between Iran and Iraq had been drawn up by the British in the nineteenth century. It was surrounded by Saddam's Soviet-made T54 and T62 tanks. Houses and shops had been systematically looted. Outside a two-storey villa, a white bridal veil and a small posy of artificial flowers lay discarded on the sun-baked ground, as if a wedding party had been abandoned. The electric clock on the wall inside had stopped at 2.47 p.m. on 27 September, the moment when Iraqi shells had cut off power. Papers, photographs, china ornaments and broken picture frames were scattered around the floors. In a children's bedroom a box of sequins had spilled over the white tiled floor, and in the kitchen broken glass lay ankle deep. In the Revolutionary Guards' headquarters, thousands of sugar lumps were trampled into the carpets amid blood stains. War invariably means death and the desecration of homes. But here I saw an act of kindness: when two very old men appeared, clutching each other's gnarled hands for support, Iraqi soldiers in metal helmets took their arms and found them chairs beside an empty fruit barrow.

Qasr-e Shirin was only a diversion. The real fighting was going on around the Shatt al-Arab. The Iraqi authorities supplied a blue Fiat touring bus to bring correspondents on the 400-kilometre journey from Baghdad, to see their successes around Abadan and Khorramshahr. Our Iraqi military escort took us to the palm grove on the waterway dividing the two countries – the same palm grove that Parviz Shahideh had pointed out to me from his refinery some months before. Several enormous fires were burning in the refinery complex, sending inky-black smoke billowing into the sky like a fast-moving thunderstorm. The soldiers told us not to go to the water's edge because there were snipers on the other side. As they and the other reporters took cover behind palm and eucalyptus trunks, a Norwegian correspondent whom I had befriended strode fearlessly out into the open to get a better view. I walked forward and joined him for a few moments. To this day I don't quite know why I did that. It was an act of irresponsibility, not bravery. Adrenalin, bravado and comradeship are a most dangerous mix, engendering a sense of daring and inviolability that has been fatal for many journalists.

As it was, there were risks enough in witnessing Saddam's war, whatever precautions we took. That evening in Basra, as I sipped thick black coffee with an Iraqi officer in the foyer of the Shatt al-Arab Hotel on the Shatt al-Arab waterway, there was a deafening roar as a jet plane flew low overhead, followed by four terrific bangs. Glass from the ornate fanlights and lumps of ceiling plaster fell on our heads. Both of us dived under the heavy coffee table, and then everyone got up and made a mad rush for the cellar. The hotel doubled as the control tower for Basra airfield, and I prayed that it was not on the target list of Iran's US-made F-4 Phantom jets. I thought I might be safer outside. There I found an Iraqi oil supply ship blazing furiously from end to end. A policeman was beating back excited sightseers with a multi-thonged whip, as sailors with blood streaming from head wounds staggered along the quayside. Thirty minutes later, as I hammered out a story on the telex machine by an open window on the hotel's third floor, the jets returned, flying past the window – so low I could see the pilots – through a hail of ack-ack fire to bomb targets in Basra centre.

We didn't get to Khorramshahr, which was resisting fiercely, though we were allowed close enough to see the Iraqi flag flying over outlying buildings. I wondered what new hell the frightened old Jewish shopkeeper in the backgammon shop was going through.

It was becoming clear even then, two weeks after the invasion, that the war was not going Saddam Hussein's way. When we were bussed back to Baghdad after the trip to Basra, the mood in the capital had changed. There were nightly air raids now by Iranian planes. Dogs howled across the blacked-out city as the explosions got closer. Then the planes started coming in daylight. I was standing at the entrance to the Mansour Melia Hotel one day when four Phantom jets roared overhead, so low I could clearly see the cockpits and the green, brown and yellow camouflage markings. A loud cracking sound came from the anti-aircraft guns on the roof of the broadcasting station across the road. Little spurts of water rose from the ornamental fountain in front of the hotel where the shell casings fell. There was a tremendous explosion as one of its bombs hit oil storage tanks not far away.

Saddam soon became less enamoured of his guests from the world's media. The free meals and drink stopped. Waiters began demanding the full menu price in the restaurants and bars. We were told that we would have to pay for our rooms and telephone calls. That's when we knew for certain that things were going badly wrong for the Iraqi dictator.

Just over a year after his invasion, Khorramshahr was liberated by Iranian fighters, the Iraqis were driven back from Abadan and Qasr-e Shirin, and it was Iran that was invading Iraq. The Americans came to Saddam Hussein's aid. Donald Rumsfeld, special envoy for President Ronald Reagan and future US Secretary of Defence, paid two visits to Baghdad to meet Saddam Hussein and discuss efforts to defeat Iran. One was on 24 March 1984, the day the UN reported that Iraq had used mustard gas and tabun nerve agent against Iranian troops. The *New York Times* reported that American diplomats pronounced themselves satisfied with the meeting and that "normal diplomatic ties have been established in all but name". US Vice-President George H.W. Bush subsequently ensured that, throughout the mid-1980s, Iraq received American financing, intelligence and military help. Before the Iran–Iraq war ended in stalemate in 1988, over a million soldiers and civilians died.

4

Small Potatoes

My reporting from Afghanistan and Iraq, which carried implicit criticisms of American foreign policy in the region, may have had something to do with the alleged contents of the file on me in the American embassy in Dublin in the early 1980s. I was described as "Northern Ireland Catholic, charming, politically unreliable". At least that was what a tired and rather emotional US embassy official told an equally tired and emotional Irish guest at a party, who later passed it on to me, so maybe something was lost in translation. Well, I didn't like him much either. Whatever about the first two characterisations, the third was fairly accurate from the American point of view. I was "politically unreliable", certainly as regards my critical attitude towards US policy in many parts of the world at that time, about which I made no secret when I lunched with American diplomats in Dublin.

One American envoy whose company I did enjoy in the early 1980s was the embassy press attaché, Robin Berrington, a slight, charming man in his early forties, whom I suspect had his own reservations about American foreign policy. I would occasionally lunch with Berrington, and listen to his complaints about the poor state of opera and ballet in Ireland. A lover of the arts, he didn't like his posting in Ireland very much. He would much prefer to have been sent to Japan, where he had been a student in the 1960s.

In December 1980, Robin Berrington made the mistake of expressing his mixed feeling about Ireland and its people in a round-robin "Happy New Year" letter, which he photocopied for posting to his numerous contacts in the State Department in Washington. One evening three weeks later, my colleague John Armstrong came to me at the *Irish Times* news desk, where I was on duty, with a copy of Berrington's letter. He had found it inserted into a brochure the US embassy had sent out to reporters and editors about the newly elected US President, Ronald Reagan. For a diplomat, it contained some very undiplomatic comments.

Ireland was "pretty small potatoes" compared to the other countries of Europe, Berrington informed his colleagues. "No great issues burn up the wires between Dublin and Washington. The country has food and climate well matched for each other – dull . . . The one bright spot is the people, but after two and a half years, they remain enigmatic and unpredictable despite their easy approachability and charm . . . The high cost of goods, their unavailability, the dreary urbanscapes, the constant strikes and the long, dark and damp winters combine to gnaw away at one's enthusiasm for being here. The troubles up north are a constant depression as well and there is no end in sight for that complex, senseless tragedy . . . The hottest item now seems to be the question of whether or not Ronald Reagan's ancestors really do come from County Tipperary."

After some sideswipes at "wild-eyed" Irish republicans and the Anglo-Irish set – "who speak as if they had marbles in their mouths" – Berrington proceeded to categorise the Irish in general as "a people with too much human nature – violent and compassionate – for their own good". Almost as an afterthought, he described a visit to Britain where he found the English "insufferable . . . Whatever reservations I may have about Ireland, at least the Irish are warm, lively human beings."

I rang the editor Douglas Gageby at home and read the letter to him. "We have to publish it," I argued. "It is a briefing for other

American diplomats and that makes it of public interest. Besides, the *Irish Press* and the *Independent* might also have it." "All right," said Gageby, "but promise me that Berrington won't be fired in the morning." I promised. The story ran on the bottom of page one, under the headline "Warm Irish But Dull Country". The rival newspapers didn't have it. Gageby wrote a leader praising Berrington as a rare diplomat who spoke his mind and who restored "one's faith in the humanity of diplomats". In a later editorial he said the letter "was worth a dozen speeches to Rotary or Chambers of Commerce. It was fresh, critical but with a good deal of feeling. Any Irishman couldn't have done better. He deserves to be promoted."

Berrington wasn't promoted, however. Far from it. The next morning he was sent back to Washington for "consultations". He found a note on his desk from the Ambassador, William Shannon, ordering him to leave the country within forty-eight hours. Shannon was too busy apologising for him to bemused Irish members of his staff to tell Berrington personally. Hearing that he had been "fired", and feeling somewhat guilty about not warning him beforehand, I drove round to Berrington's house in Ballsbridge, and found him packing his bags. "It was my decision to publish," I told him. "I'm desperately sorry you have been ordered home." "Don't expect me to thank you," he said, "but I appreciate your telling me."

At first it looked bad for Berrington. In the United States he was confronted with negative news stories about his undiplomatic observations. The *New York Times* suggested he should have been left to "cook in the Irish stew he created". The *Washington Star* headlined its account of the scandal, "Small Potatoes Line Irks Irish". *Time* magazine made his "small potatoes" remark a quote of the week, noting that it had "outraged the Irish".

In fact, the Berrington letter had not outraged the Irish at all. If anything, there was resentment that Ambassador Shannon, a former journalist and member of the *New York Times* editorial board, had not stood by his man. Certainly I was annoyed by what Shannon did, though this was more to do with my promise to Gageby that Berrington would not be fired. Seventeen Irish journalists sent a telegram to the State Department demanding that the unfair decision be reversed. Gay Byrne, presenter of Ireland's most popular morning radio show, praised Berrington for telling the truth. Opinion swung behind the diplomat. The *New York Times* did a follow-up story reporting that Berrington was actually winning praise from many Irish for his frank comments and that several writers to *The Irish Times* had suggested that he become the next ambassador to Ireland. The *Washington Star* reversed itself and said Bord Fáilte should hire Berrington as a consultant.

There was much speculation around Dublin about who might have slipped the letter into the brochures, and whether or not someone inside the embassy was out to get the press attaché. To this day Berrington will not speculate publicly. Years later William Shannon's widow, Elizabeth, wrote a book about her time in Ireland in which she said she could not blame the news editor who decided to publish the letter.

Berrington in the end kept his job in the diplomatic service. He was told to lie low until a few months later when his next posting became due – to his beloved Japan. Any concern that he would not be welcome there, because of the *contretemps* in Dublin, was dismissed by the American Ambassador to Tokyo, Mike Mansfield, who sent word to the State Department: "I could use anyone who could write a letter like that; I like his style." Berrington spent many happy years in Japan, writing the Ambassador's speeches and escorting visiting dignitaries such as Hillary Clinton around town, and standing in as an extra for visiting ballet and opera companies that needed western faces to fill costumes on stage. He was then transferred to London as press attaché, which was very big potatoes, and where great issues did burn up the wires between there and Washington.

The publication of his letter became a defining moment in Berrington's career. "People forever attach something like that to you," he told me one day many years later, after he had retired to live in Washington. "I would be in a bar, and I would mention that I worked in the embassy in Dublin, and I would be asked, 'Were you there when that guy wrote the nasty letter?'" But he also got a "boxload" of letters and telegrams from Irish people praising him for being forthright about the state of the nation.

Ironically, Ambassador William Shannon also left Ireland under something of a cloud. He caused some controversy during the Irish general election in June 1980, by seeming to display a preference for opposition party leader, Garret FitzGerald. The envoy was photographed sitting beside FitzGerald on a campaign bus in County Wicklow, and Shannon was criticised by the outgoing Taoiseach, Charles J. Haughey, for "putting his foot in it". The Ambassador denied any favouritism. Just as Berrington is remembered for his letter, Shannon is still associated in Ireland with that bus trip.

In 2003 Robin Berrington again put his name to a controversial letter. He was one of eighty former American diplomats who signed a petition to US President George W. Bush, slamming him for costing the United States its "credibility, prestige and friends" through a one-sided Middle East policy. Perhaps his time lunching with Irish journalists wasn't all wasted.

Having brought an American diplomat's career perilously close to extinction, I then succeeded in offending a prominent observer of the Irish scene from the other side of the Iron Curtain. During the Berrington controversy, and in the interests of journalistic balance, I thought it would be a good idea to publish what someone from the rival superpower thought of Ireland and its people. I already had material to hand, in the form of a Russian language paperback about Ireland written by the former TASS correspondent to Dublin, Yuri Ustimenko, which I had picked up in Moscow.

The Russian commentator went much further than Berrington. He criticised the food, the weather, the poor service in the shops and our "peculiar conversational habits". Food was not a pleasure but a severe necessity, he wrote. Mushrooms were "soaked and tormented beyond recognition". Ignorance of a subject was never a hindrance to conversation. Snowfalls were considered a natural disaster and brought the country to a halt, because the Irish had "never heard of a snow plough". Newspapers were full of vacuous discussion, while "every statement coming from the Vatican is assiduously published". One met priests more frequently on the Dublin streets than the slow-moving buses, and "in the city centre, pious monks are on duty shaking coins in tin boxes; this money goes to the upkeep of countless orders of missionaries abroad, while just close by on O'Connell Street Bridge, on the cold asphalt, sit beggars with outstretched hands". Ustimenko recalled how he could tell Protestants from Catholics at his south Dublin dinner parties: the Protestants would leave to go to bed early, but the Catholics stayed until two or three in the morning. He made the observation (without disclosing his research methods) that the "arctic temperatures in Irish bedrooms impart a unique flush to a woman's face and to no small degree assist in the growth in population".

The Irish Times published these quotations in the same place as the Berrington letter – bottom of page one. International news agencies picked up the Russian's comments, and they were transmitted around the world, so the story came to Yuri's attention in Moscow. He was furious. He wrote an angry response in the Russian newspaper *Literaturnaya Gazeta*. The extracts had been printed by *The Irish Times* for "unseemly political purposes", he fumed. "It is connected with the following. Some time ago the Irish newspaper printed remarks by Robin Berrington, a press attaché at the US Embassy in Dublin, about Ireland and

Irishmen. With a frankness rarely permitted themselves by diplomats, he displayed a very rude attitude to his host country. The publication of Robin Berrington's revelations caused a stormy reaction in Ireland. The newspapers started getting angry letters from readers. The hapless press attaché was soon recalled home and *The Irish Times* suddenly found itself in a role that is obviously unfit for it. The impression was created that it was undermining the good old relations between Dublin and Washington. The paper's leadership decided to mend its ways, and several days later *The Irish Times* printed an article containing separate phrases arbitrarily taken from my book." In fact, wrote Ustimenko, "Ireland leaves no one indifferent. And when you come to know it more, you definitely will love it with all your heart."

"I devoted a special place in my book to the newspaper, *Irish Times*," complained Ustimenko. "I wrote that 'it stands out among other newspapers as one of the most objective sources of information'. It appears that I was wrong."

5

Nous sommes amis

While American diplomats in Ireland might have had
reservations about my coverage of events in the Middle East,
Israeli envoys monitoring the articles I filed were distinctly
unhappy with some of my material, particularly when I reported
on 17 May 1979, in an article on the front page of *The Irish
Times*, that Israel was lobbing shells into an area of south
Lebanon where Irish peace-keeping forces were deployed. I cited
as my authority the United Nations Commander in south
Lebanon, Major-General Emmanuel Erskine. An Israeli diplomat
came to Dublin from London – there was no Israeli embassy in
Dublin then – and told RTÉ Radio that they had checked with
the general and that he had said no such thing. In other words,
that I had manufactured the report.

My interview with General Erskine had taken place in the
Lebanese coastal town of Naqora, which served as base
headquarters of the United Nations Interim Force in Lebanon
(UNIFIL). The Ghanaian officer commanded contingents from
ten countries, including Ireland, which had been sent to south
Lebanon in 1978 in the wake of a short-lived Israeli invasion,
sparked by a Palestinian massacre of thirty-seven civilians in an
attack on Israel from the sea.

The United Nations had mandated the peace-keeping force to confirm Israel's withdrawal from Lebanon, set up a buffer zone between guerrillas of the Palestine Liberation Organisation (PLO) in south Lebanon and the Israeli border, and restore normality in the strip of dusty, overcrowded, hilltop villages that had been abandoned during the invasion. The Irish had deployed an infantry battalion of 580 personnel in the town of Tibnin, with responsibility for an area of one hundred square kilometres, where they operated patrols, manned observation posts and checkpoints, and rendered humanitarian assistance to the local population.

The UN operation had, however, been hampered by a second buffer zone created simultaneously by Israel alongside the Israeli border, nominally controlled by a few hundred members of an Israeli-armed Christian militia, mostly recruited from a small number of Maronite Catholic villages, and led by a former Lebanese army major, Saad Haddad, whom the Irish officers regarded as a devious, unpredictable and violent puppet of Israel. From this zone, roughly sixteen kilometres wide and one hundred kilometres long, stretching from the humid Mediterranean coast to the cool slopes of Mount Hermon, the Christian militia frequently shelled UN-controlled villages, partly to counter Palestinian infiltration and ultimately to expand its control. This had been the cause of several protests by UNIFIL member countries. But shellfire into UN-controlled areas from within Israel itself, which endangered the lives of residents and peace-keeping forces alike, was a much more serious matter.

I had made a number of trips to south Lebanon to report on the Irish army's deployment and had heard the allegations of Israeli shellfire from Irish officers in Tibnin, a hill town dominated by a 900-year-old castle where once dwelled Saladin, the sultan of Egypt who had recaptured Jerusalem from the Crusaders. On 16 May 1979, I hired a car for the one-hundred kilometre drive from Beirut to Naqora, to inquire of General

Erskine if the claims were true. An NBC stringer in Beirut, Andy Murphy, came along for the ride.

General Erskine, wearing a blue UN beret and sporting a military moustache, received us in his office, poured us tea, and confirmed what the Irish officers had said: that shellfire was coming into their battalion areas from within Israel. This had been established from the back-trajectory of the missiles. The general also claimed that ninety per cent of the harassment of UNIFIL forces in the Christian-controlled zone was being orchestrated by Israeli officers. What was needed, he said, was political pressure on Israel from Ireland and other contributing countries to cease the harassment. I took notes rapidly, because my tape recorder batteries had died. Climbing back into the car, Andy handed me a cassette from his own recorder. "Here, keep this as a souvenir," he said. The interview appeared in *The Irish Times* the next day.

Four weeks later, back in Dublin, I turned on the lunch-time RTÉ news, and heard the minister plenipotentiary from the Israeli embassy in London, Yoav Biran, deny what I had written. Israel had checked with General Erskine himself, said Biran, who had come to Dublin after the Irish Department of Foreign Affairs had asked for "clarification" of my *Irish Times* report. He insisted that the UN commander had not said what I had reported he had said, and insisted that Israeli guns had not shelled Irish positions from within Israel.

I remembered the tape recording that Andy Murphy had given me "as a souvenir". I called RTÉ and the head of news agreed to play the recording on the next news bulletin at 6.30 p.m. It contained the following exchange between me and General Erskine about the charge that Israel was firing on UN-controlled villages. I started off by asking him about shell fire into the Irish area.

"Can you confirm that some of the shelling has come from inside Israel?"

"Well, we have confirmed that some of the shelling has come from Israeli positions."

"Israeli positions on the other side [of the border]?"

"On the other side, that's right."

"Into the Irish area?"

"Well, into all of the areas some of the time."

"Does this occur frequently, shelling from Israel?"

"From time to time it does happen."

The Israelis were unfazed by this direct contradiction of their assertions. Some months later an Israeli brigadier general visited the *Irish Times* building in Dublin to lobby for more favourable coverage of the Israeli side. In the editor's office we played him the tape recording. Indignantly, and with a straight face, he repeated the assertion that Israel had not, and would not, direct artillery fire into the UNIFIL area.

Whether fired by Israelis or their client Christian militias, Israeli guns had constantly shelled the UNIFIL strip in its first year of operation. In the six months before the Erskine interview, the "Irishbatt" area was shelled 500 times, with Irish posts coming under specific attack seventy-two times. The explosives aimed at UN outposts almost invariably landed where the gunners wanted – beside, not on, the target. Much of the fire was designed to intimidate pro-Palestinian Shi'ite villagers from supporting the guerrillas, or to force them to flee, thus reducing the chance of PLO infiltration. But the shelling could be murderous at times, as I saw on the afternoon of 11 May 1979, when the Christian militia opened fire on the village of Bra-shit in the Irish zone of operations.

From the Irish battalion headquarters in Tibnin, we had a grandstand view of the shelling of Bra-shit, perched on a hill two kilometres distant. The leader of the Christian militia, Saad Haddad, had sent a messenger with a ten-minute warning for the villagers to get out before he opened fire. Between three and five o'clock that afternoon, a total of thirty-three shells dropped on the village. Of these, twenty-eight appeared to be regular 122 Howitzer missiles, but the other five sent secondary explosive devices flying in a spectacular shower of blue streaks.

We went to Bra-shit after the firing stopped. An elderly Muslim couple and a Christian friend, aged seventy, seventy-five and ninety-six, who had been sitting beneath an almond tree, seemingly unaware of the ultimatum or too old to flee, were killed outright by a shell. Their remains, along with those of a pet sheep and branches sheared from their almond and olive trees, were scattered among the roses and flowering cacti of the garden. As Lieutenant Colonel Vincent Savino and Commandant Gerry McMahon examined the garden wall, where multiple pockmarks indicated that the five devices were US-made cluster bombs – supplied by the US to Israel on condition that they would not be used against civilians – we heard the shellfire start up again in the distance, and we ran for our lives into a stone hut, in case their guns had not been realigned. This time, however, they were firing towards the Irish observation post in another part of the village, dropping the shells fifty metres away to intimidate the Irish soldiers inside.

The Christian militia did not like the western media and harassed us if we came too close. Once they briefly took me prisoner. I accepted a lift from Beirut to Naqora with a British reporter, Charles Devereux. On a deserted stretch of the road along the Mediterranean coast we found our way blocked by half a dozen pro-Israeli militiamen in assorted uniforms. They searched the car and found a PLO press release in the boot. This infuriated them. They pulled us out and made us sit by the roadside with our hands over our heads. One of them drove off in Charles's car. A couple of hours passed, during which the only vehicle to come by was a two-truck convoy of Nigerian UNIFIL troops. Devereux shouted for help but they didn't hear and drove on. The militiamen threw empty Coca-Cola cans onto the beach a few metres below and fired bursts of automatic fire at them. The noise was terrifying. They refused to talk to us. One of them derived some amusement from making me touch the hot barrel of his gun. Dizzy with thirst in the hot sunshine, I asked for a drink. A whisky bottle was produced. I took a slug, smiled, and the atmosphere relaxed a little. Shortly afterwards, the car was brought back, followed by a Mercedes driven by a "militia commander", who looked and sounded very like an Israeli officer. He lectured us about carrying PLO literature and then let us have the car back and we proceeded to Naqora. Before leaving I took the opportunity to ask for an interview with Saad Haddad. "Go in from the other side," he said, meaning Israel.

I took him at his word. On my next trip to the Middle East shortly afterwards, I flew to Tel Aviv, and got permission to cross into the Christian enclave through the northern Israeli town of Metula. I was escorted by an Israeli Army intelligence officer, Lieutenant-Colonel Yoram Hamizrachi, and his wife Beate, a German-born freelance reporter. Hamizrachi, a large, bearded figure given to wearing pop-art shirts and a shoulder pistol, was a regular visitor to the enclave. The Irish had given him the nickname of "Fiddler on the Roof" because of his resemblance to Topol, the actor in the 1971 musical film. After dark, they drove me through a gap in the border fence and eight kilometres along a narrow road, pitted with shell holes, into the heart of the Christian-controlled territory. We arrived in Marjayoun, a mountain town of stone houses and arched doorways on a hill facing Mount Hermon. Saad Haddad lived in a small house at the top of a terraced street. Two militiamen sat on broken-down armchairs outside the door, with rifles on their knees. On the plaster wall of the living-room inside hung a small metal Madonna and child, and on the TV set there was a photograph of Saad Haddad with the Israeli Prime Minister, signed by Menachim Begin.

A thin, balding man with moustache and dressed in trousers and a vest, Haddad had been watching *The Streets of San*

51

Francisco on Jordanian TV before we arrived. He had a deep saucer-shaped wound on his right shoulder from an operation to combat the cancer that would kill him five years later. He seemed uneasy about being interviewed. "Why do I shell the Irish? I have nothing against the Irish," he protested, as his dark-haired teenage daughter handed round marzipan sweets and Arabic coffee. "I fire at the PLO, who are using the UN lines as cover." We debated back and forth about this. He exaggerated wildly, claiming that the PLO had 150 armed men in Bra-shit. I told him I had never seen armed men on a number of visits to Bra-shit, but I had seen dead elderly civilians. If there were casualties from his shelling, well, they weren't intended, he said. He expressed contempt for the UN and its Secretary General Kurt Waldheim, "who is always for the terrorists". He contradicted himself. UNIFIL was "better than nothing", then "good for nothing". The Irish were his friends, he assured me: "they are Christians like us". (Twenty-four hours after I had gone, he announced that he was planning "fierce attacks" on the Irish.)

The next day Saad Haddad's men took me to the "front line", a roadblock where half a dozen armed militia, some wearing suede shoes, bandoliers and cowboy hats, were taunting three crew-cut Irish soldiers, who were blocking the narrow road with their Panhard armoured car. The soldiers were nervous and exhausted, and angry to see an Irish reporter accompanying the "enemy". During the night their Panhard had been momentarily engulfed in flames by RPG7 rockets aimed at the militia by the PLO. Convinced they would die, they had shaken hands and blessed themselves.

I could only watch as a heavily bearded militia officer called Louis Hasrouni mockingly offered cigars to the Irish soldiers. "*Nous sommes amis, Libanais et Irlandais,*" he cried, rubbing together two forefingers adorned with heavy gold rings. He produced an over-sized bottle of Johnny Walker. Cups and bottle tops brimming with whiskey were pressed on the three soldiers.

"You are our friends," they shouted. A squat man built like the Hollywood actor Edward G Robinson, who called himself Major Abu Ariel, appeared with an expensive-looking camera. He took pictures of grinning militiamen throwing their arms round the Irish soldiers, while holding the whisky bottle high. Here was evidence to discredit them with the PLO, by making them out to be collaborators with the pro-Israeli militia.

I could not cross over to the Irish side of this "front line" and enter the Irishbatt area, because I had no entry stamp for Lebanon, which would cause serious problems if I tried to leave the country via Beirut. I had to return to Israel, with the "Fiddler on the Roof", and leave the way I had come, through Tel Aviv.

Haddad succeeded in poisoning relations between the Irish and the PLO. On one occasion when Irish officers, in an attempt to defuse a dangerous confrontation, escorted Israeli soldiers to the locations of an alleged PLO base to show there was nothing there, he used this to claim publicly that the Irish had co-operated with the Israelis. In Beirut the left-wing *As-Safir* newspaper reported that Irish soldiers had escorted Israeli troops in house-to-house searches. This was dangerous for the Irish, who were already antagonising the PLO by preventing them from operating freely in the UNIFIL area. On 27 April 1981, Private Hugh Doherty and Private Kevin Joyce were kidnapped by a PLO faction led by a Lebanese killer named Abu Amin Dayk. Doherty was found dead, shot three times in the back. Joyce's remains were never located.

Previously the PLO had seen the Irish as comrades-in-arms in a struggle against imperialism. At a heavily fortified PLO refugee camp at Sabra in west Beirut – which in 1982 would become the scene of a massacre by Israeli-backed Christian Phalangist militiamen – a Palestinian colonel told *Irish Times* photographer Pat Langan and me that they had trained a small number of IRA men in the use of explosives. "We consider their struggle is similar to ours," he said.

Relations between the Irish and the Israelis were marked by open contempt on the Israeli side. I had a heated encounter with several Israeli commanders in the Israeli border town of Kiryat Shmona. "If twenty Irish cooks, fishermen, old ladies came to Lebanon, they would be just as effective as soldiers who are not allowed to shoot," said one. Another said, angrily, "Haddad tells the Irish that Bra-shit is full of armed men, and to tell the village to get rid of those bastards, but they don't." A third commented, "I saw an Irish soldier who had come under fire and he was crying." (This referred to a militia attack at Naqora, during which an Irish soldier lost a leg.) Hamizrachi told me that he had to break up a fight among drunken Irish, a charge – denied by the Irish – that he delighted in telling every visitor to the area. The Israelis were also incensed at a statement by the then Irish Minister for Foreign Affairs, Brian Lenihan, when visiting Bahrain in February 1980, that the Palestinians had the right to self-determination and to a Palestinian state – a position that caused outrage at the time in Israel, but has since been adopted by both Israel and the United States.

On 12 April 1980, Haddad's militia attacked an Irish checkpoint at the village of At-Tiri, in an unsuccessful attempt to extend its enclave. In what was possibly the most serious battle in the twenty-three-year history of the Irish battalion in UNIFIL, the Irish fired several 90 mm shells from their Panhards and scored a direct hit on a militia vehicle. Dutch and Fijian troops joined in the fighting, during which Private Stephen Griffin from Galway was killed. Six days later Privates Thomas Barrett and Derek Smallhorn were abducted by Haddad's militia and driven off in a Peugeot car to an isolated spot and shot in the head, a deed allegedly assisted by an Israeli intelligence officer code-named "Abu Shawki". A joint UN-Garda investigation established that the soldiers were killed by Mohammed Bazi, the brother of a militiaman shot dead in the battle for At-Tiri. Despite UN demands that he be held to account, Bazi was allowed to emigrate to the United States where he was later reported to be living in Detroit, selling ice-cream.

Two days after the deaths of Barrett and Smallhorn in 1980, Shlomo Argov, the Israeli Ambassador to the United Kingdom and Ireland, condemned the killings on RTÉ. He found it incredible, however, that "people in Dublin, of all places, should be so insensitive to the plight of a Christian minority". He responded to Irish criticism of Israeli tactics by saying, ". . . you sit there all so smugly in Dublin, and pass judgement on things that are happening on the other side of the moon, on the other side of the world, without any real feel for the situation."

For the next twenty years, Irish battalions rotated in and out of Lebanon. Their positions were periodically overrun as Israeli forces made incursions, in 1982, 1993 and 1996. In 2000, Israel finally disengaged from the zone. The pro-Israeli militia melted away, and many of its members fled to Israel and the United States. Altogether forty-seven Irish soldiers lost their lives in Lebanon, before most of the Irish force was withdrawn in 2001.

6

Travels with the Pope

I got a break from the wars and conflicts of the Middle East when I was sent to Rome in September 1979 to report on preparations for the historic visit of Pope John Paul II to Ireland, due a week later, and then to accompany him on the flight to Dublin and afterwards on the second leg of his journey, to the United States. The Italian media got very excited, however, about going with the Pope to "war-torn" Ireland. *Corriere della Sera* warned that the Holy Father was venturing into an armed camp where Catholics attacked Protestants as heretics, and Protestants attacked Catholics as papists, with streets patrolled by armoured cars and roadblocks at every corner. *La Stampa* expressed the fear that the Pontiff was about to plunge into "an Irish volcano with many craters, a deadly mixture which divides Protestants and Catholics".

The Vatican press office was hopeless at countering these misconceptions – the Pope was not even going to set foot in Northern Ireland – or dispensing any newsworthy information. I spent the few days in Rome trying to persuade various clerics to talk, without much success. The Pope's secretary, Father John Magee, from my own county, Down, declined to meet any Irish reporters. The Bishop of Down and Connor, Cahal Daly, was also in Rome, working with Vatican officials on drafts of the speech the Pope would deliver on violence in Northern Ireland, but he was never one to socialise with the media. It fitted a pattern in journalism: the more infallibility assumed by a leader, the less communicative are the apparatchiks down the line.

I teamed up with Donncha Ó Dúlaing of RTÉ Radio to try to manufacture some news stories. He was accompanied by an RTÉ producer. Donncha was well known for his Irish republican sentiments. One evening during a spaghetti dinner in a restaurant on the Piazza Navona, when his colleague had gone to the bathroom, Donncha confided that the producer had been sent by RTÉ just to make sure he did not express overtly republican sentiments in his broadcasts. When Donncha excused himself, the producer leaned over the table and said, "Do you know, the only reason I'm here . . ."

Sure enough, on the Sunday before the Pontiff was due to fly to Dublin, when Donncha and I went to St Peter's Square to join a throng of pilgrims from all over the world, and he saw a group from St Joseph's Parish in Limerick carrying tricolours, I heard him say into his tape recorder that he had spotted Irish pilgrims waving "the flag of the thirty-two counties". I never found out if the "thirty-two counties" comment survived the editing process, but I doubt it.

The Pope also celebrated Mass that day in St Peter's Basilica, where one of the arc lights burst with a loud bang as he mounted the altar, causing brief panic among the security guards and giving a jolt of adrenalin to the media crushed in at the back, where we couldn't see what was going on.

Father Lambert Greenan, editor of the English language edition of the Vatican newspaper *L'Osservatore Romano*, dismissed worries about the Pope's security in the "Irish volcano", telling us that "as far as the Vatican is concerned, the Pope is more vulnerable here in Rome; if someone wanted to harm him it would be relatively easy to do so any Sunday in St Peter's Square." (His words were prophetic: the Pope was unharmed in Ireland, but two years later was shot in St Peter's Square by Mehmet Ali Agca from Turkey.) Nevertheless, the Vatican was so concerned by the blustering of the Reverend Ian Paisley against a visit by "Old Red Socks" to Armagh, the pontifical see in Ireland, that it had cancelled initial plans for the Pope to cross the border into Northern Ireland. I wanted to ask His Holiness about that, but did not hold out much hope of getting close enough, and he never gave interviews.

Aer Lingus, the national airline, brought the pride of its fleet, a Boeing 747 named the *St Patrick*, to Fiumicino airport in Rome, to convey the Pope to Dublin. The Pope arrived by helicopter at the airport and was ushered into the first-class cabin, where he was put under the protection of two senior members of the Garda Síochána, Detective Inspector Myles Hawkshaw from the special detective unit in Dublin, and Detective Superintendent Hubert Reynolds of Garda Headquarters. I was assigned seat 47B in economy class, which was filled with 170 other members of the travelling media. After we took off, the chief air hostess, Catherine Nash, announced: "Holy Father, distinguished visitors, you may now smoke if you wish." The economy class lit up, while the Pope engaged in an activity perhaps even more dangerous to his health, tucking into an Irish fry with bacon, egg, sausage and black pudding.

As the *St Patrick* made its stately way through French air space, the Aer Lingus press officer, Captain Jack Miller, announced that the Pope would pay us a visit in tourist class. He would walk down the left side, cross over at the back and return along the right side so we would all get a chance to greet him. "So would you please stay in your seats."

However, when the Pope, dressed in white coat and skullcap, appeared theatrically from behind the first-class curtain, he was besieged by reporters and photographers who jumped from their seats and shoved cameras, notebooks, tape recorders and microphones into his face. Italian paparazzi and normally dignified religious affairs correspondents elbowed each other as they climbed over the seats. The huge aircraft tilted perceptibly as its human cargo shifted to one side. The pilot quickly righted the 747, Hawkshaw and Reynolds restored some order, and the Pope was able to set out slowly on his scheduled route. Through a mass of microphones and cameras I heard the religious affairs correspondent of the *Evening Herald*, which had up to one million potential readers gathering in the Phoenix Park in Dublin, get in a question: "Holy Father, will you bless this picture?" The Holy Father obliged. I managed to push my head in under the microphone of RTÉ's northern editor Jim Dougal, to ask the Pope about not visiting Northern Ireland. "It is a sadness," he said. "It was my intention to go there, especially to go there to Armagh." Peace in Ireland, he added, was his constant prayer. And that was it. After twenty minutes he retreated to first class. By then the plane was entering Irish air space, escorted by four Air Corps jets. Pilot Tom McKeown brought it down to 400 metres and passed over the Phoenix Park, where we could see the huge crowds of people making their way in brilliant sunshine to the papal mass. Everyone on the ground stopped moving and waved wildly. It was not a volcano but a crowd that erupted in excitement at the arrival of the Pope in Ireland.

Normal life in the Republic came to a standstill as an estimated two-thirds of the population crowded into various venues to see Pope John Paul II. The nearest he got to Northern Ireland was Drogheda, where he recited the most quoted line from the speech drafted by Bishop Cahal Daly, "On my bended knees I beg you to return to the ways of peace." Commentators were quick to point out that he was sitting at the time. The plea was rejected by the IRA, and many northern nationalists saw it as one-sided. But the Pope also appealed to those in authority not to "cause or condone conditions which give excuse or pretext for violence".

Before he left, the Pope celebrated a youth mass for 200,000 people on Galway Race Course at Ballybrit. The ceremonies were organised by Bishop Eamon Casey and the crowd was entertained by the "singing priest", Father Michael Cleary, who was well known for his lectures to Irish people on their morals in a regular radio programme.

After three days in Ireland, the papal entourage and the travelling press boarded the *St Patrick* for the seven-hour transatlantic flight to Boston in the United States. Chicago-born Cardinal Paul Marcinkus, president of the Vatican Bank, who had checked out the papal sites in Ireland and who during the visit used his two-metre height and burly physique to elbow undesirables – like reporters – out of the Pope's way, informed us that this time the Holy Father would not be coming to economy class to greet the media. Or as he put it, cigar in mouth, after the Pope retired to the specially installed bed on the *St Patrick* with Irish tweed covers, "Guys, he ain't talking!" Before we landed, the Pope did come on the intercom to say "God bless you all. I bless all your families and your work and your religious objects you have with you."

When we arrived in the United States, it became evident that Ireland had been but a curtain-raiser for this more important destination. About one in four Americans professed the Catholic faith, making it the biggest congregation outside of Brazil and Mexico. Unlike the Irish at the time, American Catholics were in open revolt against some of the conservative tenets of Catholicism, such as the ban on contraception and women priests. The immense crowds in Dublin gave the Pope an enhanced moral authority with which to launch verbal assaults in the United States against abortion, divorce, contraception and the material selfishness that threatened family life.

In Boston, New York and Philadelphia, the scenes of enthusiasm and affection that had marked the visit to Ireland were repeated, if on a smaller scale. But in Philadelphia, especially, the effort to halt liberal trends in the Catholic Church in North America became evident. The Pope reaffirmed that women could not become priests, and that the automatic granting of laicisation to priests who wanted to return to secular life would cease. He spoke out against the trend since Vatican II of an increasing number of American priests putting social involvement before evangelisation. He also condemned sexual permissiveness in strong terms. He followed this up in Chicago, where he reaffirmed the Vatican ruling against contraception as an unnatural act and stressed that homosexual activity was morally wrong. In Washington he returned to the theme of abortion, telling a quarter of a million people that "when the sacredness of life before birth is attacked, we will stand up and proclaim that no one ever has the authority to destroy unborn life".

It was the last day of his visit before anyone stood up to challenge the Pope's conservatism. Many American nuns had begun to wear civilian clothes when working with lay people. The Pope had spoken out against this practice. Sister Theresa Kane, a Sister of Mercy and president of the US Leadership Conference of Women Religious, whose mother had emigrated to the United States from Galway, confronted the Holy Father when welcoming him to the Basilica of the National Shrine of the Immaculate Conception in north-east Washington. Wearing a plain grey suit, she urged him that women be included "in all ministries of the Church". The Pope was visibly annoyed. He raised his hands slightly to stop the prolonged applause from hundreds of religious sisters. In his address at the Basilica, the Pope pointedly urged nuns once again to wear their habits, rather than "civilian" clothes. This is the desire of the Church, he said.

His plea was ignored. A quarter of a century later in the United States I noticed that most American nuns were continuing to wear "civilian" dress and that Sister Theresa Kane was still fighting, without any success, for the right of women to become priests. "I'd do it again," she said in a radio interview about her confrontation with the Pope, "but this time with more urgency and passion."

I got one break during the Pope's US visit that, if I were less agnostic, I might classify as a minor miracle. I had been included on a pool of reporters allowed to accompany the Pope to a remote Midwest parish called Irish Settlement. That day *The Irish Times* told readers that my full report of the visit would appear the next morning. The Pope arrived in Irish Settlement at three o'clock in the afternoon, which was nine o'clock in the evening in Ireland, giving me just enough time to write and file a colourful story about the Pontiff greeting descendants of Famine emigrants in a tiny white church with a tapering rectangular tower, set among vast fields of corn and bluegrass. But, unexpectedly, there were no telephones provided for the media. This was in the days before mobile telephones or laptops with broadband connection. The nearest house with a telephone was half a mile away – and almost certainly locked up, because the family would be inside the church with the Pope. Disconsolate, I wandered off into a grove of maple trees, and there spotted, nestling among surface roots, a telephone handset. I followed the connecting cord with my eye. It snaked through the branches, looped to the next tree and disappeared off into the distance. Its rotating dial had been secured with a tiny lock. A note attached said the phone was the property of Reuters. The Reuters correspondent, in a comradely gesture, unlocked the dial and allowed me to use it to make a collect call to Dublin. God is good.

Pope John Paul II made the long journey back to Rome on a TWA flight. The *St Patrick* returned to Dublin and was then leased out for three months to take pilgrims from Algiers to Mecca. The first-class section was stripped out to fit in several rows of economy seats for the pilgrims. The space where the Pope slept was taken up with fervent Muslims, many of them peasants fulfilling their religious duty to visit Mecca before they died. Some of them nearly didn't make it. The plane became "sick", as one crew member described it to me. Things started to go wrong. When taking off from Algiers towards the sea one day, a flock of birds flew into an engine, setting it on fire. It failed to gain height and barely managed to "hedge-hop" back to the airport. If it had been headed towards the mountains, it would have crashed. There were some people in Aer Lingus who speculated that perhaps it was not a good idea to use a papal plane, named after a Christian saint, to carry Muslims to Mecca.

The huge and enthusiastic turnout for the Pope's visit to Ireland created much speculation that it would regenerate the Irish Catholic Church. The welcome was, however, as much an expression of appreciation for the international recognition that Pope John Paul II gave to the relatively young Republic of Ireland as it was an outpouring of religious fervour. It was the first papal visit to the country that had suffered for its Catholicism in the past, and only the second foreign trip by a pope who was to visit almost every Catholic country in the world thereafter. It was an endorsement of the culture of a mass-going nation and a high point for the Irish Catholic Church. But the slow secularisation of Ireland was already under way and would accelerate with the greater prosperity brought about by the consumer-driven Celtic Tiger. Many recalled the Pope's visit in later years for the fact that the two most prominent and supposedly celibate clerics at the Galway Mass, Bishop Casey and Father Cleary, became the centre of scandals for the way they conducted themselves after secretly fathering children, and how the Holy Father's constant companion in Ireland, Cardinal Marcinkus, later became involved in shady financial dealings that led to the collapse of an Italian bank and the suspicious death of two Italian bankers. And in the 1990s the nation learned with horror of the terrible, cruel sexual abuse of children in Ireland by some Catholic clergy, which continued unabated long after the Pope had been and gone.

7

Allegro non troppo

My life as a full-time, rather than an occasional, foreign correspondent started, strictly speaking, in London, where I had two overseas postings, one in the mid-1970s and one in the mid-1980s, totalling five years. London technically qualifies as a "foreign" assignment for an Irish correspondent. It is the capital city of another country, after all. But much of our reporting – from the House of Commons in particular – concerned Irish-related issues and appeared on the Home News pages. Correspondents from the Dublin media did not join the Foreign Press Association, like other foreign correspondents in London. We were treated as representatives of the British *provincial* press and, however offensive to our national sensibilities, this gave us privileges which no Irish reporter would want to give up. As *Irish Times* London editor, for example, I was welcomed into the Newspaper Society, a club comprised of London editors from the provincial media, which held monthly lunches with cabinet ministers. I was also admitted to the Lobby, the otherwise exclusive preserve of British political reporters, which was established in 1884, and whose members thought it would be unsporting to expel the unionist *Irish Times* in 1921 when Ireland became a "foreign" country. Lobby members got a pass which admitted them into the actual lobby adjoining the chamber of the House of Commons, and to off-the-record briefings with the prime minister's spokesman, held in a tiny attic room reached by a warren of corridors and stairways. When Margaret Thatcher was Prime Minister, the lobby briefings were conducted by Bernard Ingram, a gruff Yorkshireman with bushy eyebrows, who was inclined to regard my questions about policy on Ireland as rather impertinent. He seldom divulged any worthwhile information.

I gained a great deal of useful information, however, from another journalistic institution much honoured in London: the long lunch, where the game of leaking was played, and which usually served the purposes of both parties. The expense was borne with considerable tolerance by British and Irish editors – and sometimes abused. A British diplomatic correspondent was once allegedly asked by his foreign editor to explain the fact that the Soviet Embassy had denied the existence of the "Ivan Ivanov" for whom the correspondent was claiming regular luncheon expenses, to which he responded, "Ivan Ivanov is clearly an imposter. I shall cease entertaining him forthwith." Nevertheless real conversations conducted *sotto voce* over starched tablecloths were the source of many good stories, especially during secret negotiations between London and Dublin over Northern Ireland.

I had lunch one day, for example, in 1987 with the private secretary of a British cabinet minister who, over whitebait and Chablis, disclosed that Prime Minister Margaret Thatcher had written privately to the then Taoiseach Garret FitzGerald, to reject his proposal for three-judge courts in Belfast – a contentious issue between the two governments. Almost immediately after letting this cat out of the bag, my dining companion put his hand over his mouth and exclaimed, "Oh! I shouldn't have told you that." I changed the subject in case he felt obliged to add, "You mustn't print it." He didn't of course, because his minister wanted the news leaked to have the issue put to rest in British–Irish talks.

In such instances I was a willing conduit for information. I did not concern myself too much about serving anyone's agenda – in this case I could be accused of serving the interests of the Brits – so long as I was reasonably sure the story was accurate. The greatest professional satisfaction I could imagine was informing people of something that they didn't already know in the columns of my newspaper.

This isn't to say that I was never the unwitting conduit of a deliberately misleading story. During the negotiations for the Anglo-Irish Agreement, a high-ranking Irish official insisted to me, over dinner, that things were going so badly in the London–Dublin talks, that ministers had failed to set a date for the signing. I published the story, and subsequently found out that the date had in fact been set in stone many days before. In this case, I suspect I was used to put pressure on the British side to give in to last-minute Irish concerns.

Margaret Thatcher may have had her suspicions about me when on 14 November 1985, the day before the Agreement was signed, she heard me tell BBC Radio 4 that I believed it would give Dublin "oversight" over British policy in Northern Ireland. She was livid and, according to my British sources, she demanded at the morning cabinet meeting that Foreign Secretary Geoffrey Howe complain to the Irish government. I'm sure Mrs Thatcher thought that I was acting as the agent of Dublin. I wasn't. I just thought "oversight" was the best word to describe the new role of the Irish government in Northern Ireland affairs, which was to be "more than consultative but less than executive".

The business of lunching and leaking required careful handling. I managed to mishandle, in a spectacular fashion, a story passed on to me, which was very definitely designed to serve an Irish agenda. In 1976, journalists in Dublin and London were vying to be the first to report the ruling of the European Commission for Human Rights on a very serious charge brought by Ireland against the United Kingdom. This was that the five interrogation techniques used by British troops after the introduction of internment in Northern Ireland five years earlier – wall-standing, hooding, white noise, deprivation of food and deprivation of sleep – amounted to "torture".

On Thursday, 26 August 1976 one of my luncheon sources in London disclosed to me that the Commission's twelve-volume, 4,500-page report had been sent confidentially to the two prime ministers, and that they had agreed to keep its findings securely under wraps until they had had time to study it fully. It would not be made public for another week. My contact agreed to give me a photocopy of the report's summary, but on strict conditions: I must share it with *The Guardian* and I should not put my own name on the story. This was to obscure the source of the leak. *The Guardian* was not a direct competitor, so I agreed.

The report's findings were sensational. British security forces in the North were found to have breached article 3 of the European Convention on Human Rights, forbidding "torture and inhuman and degrading treatment", in their interrogation of internees in Northern Ireland in August 1971. My source, I realised, was motivated by a desire to have this in the public domain before the British government could somehow deflect international and domestic criticism away from itself and on to the Irish government for taking the case to Europe.

From the moment I got my hands on the report summary, late that Thursday afternoon, things started to go wrong. I rang news editor Donal Foley in Dublin, and told him that I had acquired the torture verdict exclusively. "But I can't put my name on it, and only you and the editor should know it's coming from me." Foley, a brilliant news editor, misinterpreted my message and announced at the editorial conference, attended by about two dozen senior staff members, "Conor O'Clery has got a great story but I can't tell you what it is."

Meanwhile I filed my story and, true to my promise, called Anne McHardy, the Belfast correspondent of *The Guardian*, around seven o'clock and read her out the details. Giving it to *The Guardian* that early was a major error. What I hadn't considered was that the first edition of *The Guardian* came out around ten o'clock in the evening in London, three hours before the Irish morning newspapers, and that the story, splashed on page one of *The Guardian*, would immediately be spotted and put on the wires by the Press Association, whose service was available to the rival *Irish Press* and *Irish Independent*. Which is what happened. In those days there was no cable TV news or Internet and getting the first break on a story in a morning newspaper was seen as a very big deal. Now every paper in Dublin had my great scoop for their first editions. Worse, because my unsigned account contained much more detail, officials in both governments immediately spotted that it was *The Irish Times* which had got the report, and anyone with their ears to the ground would know that I was the most likely suspect.

The publication caused a diplomatic uproar. The Taoiseach at the time, Liam Cosgrave, was furious at the leak, which 10 Downing Street would see as a grievous breach of trust. The government sent a superintendent of the Garda Síochána to London to interrogate Irish diplomats who had access to the report, and to carry out forensic tests to establish who, if anyone, in the embassy had it photocopied and given to *The Irish Times*. Nothing came of it. Meanwhile, an Irish diplomat – not my source – invited me for a drink and over glasses of lager tried, also unsuccessfully, to get me to admit authorship of the story, with unsubtle remarks such as: "Sure, everyone knows it was you," and "It must have been hard not to be able to put your name on such a big exclusive." I refused to confirm or deny anything, using the classic line, "If I tell you it wasn't me, then I am only narrowing the field and I'm not going to help you by doing that."

My informant's assumption about how the British would "spin" the report was well founded. The day before the official release, Merlyn Rees, then British Home Secretary, called in selected London journalists and accused Dublin of pandering to the IRA. "We regret the Irish government's persistence in thus raking over the events of five years ago," he declared. "The only people who can derive any satisfaction from all this are the terrorists." Fleet Street editors took their cue from Rees. Even the "liberal" *Guardian* stated, "Dublin will be guilty of torturing Northern Ireland if it goes on force-feeding the Provisionals with propaganda."

The Irish government had in fact taken the case to *weaken* support for the IRA, by showing nationalists in Northern Ireland that there was a legal remedy for their grievances and to ensure that the interrogation techniques would be outlawed in future.

The cap on a miserable week, professionally speaking, came on Saturday evening when I tuned in to Granada Television's weekly look at the newspapers, *What the Papers Say*. The presenter, Brian Inglis, who earlier in his career had worked for *The Irish Times* in Dublin, heaped praise on *The Guardian* for its "good old-fashioned scoop". The music that introduced the programme was *Allegro non troppo*, from Malcolm Arnold's "English Dances", which one could translate as, "Don't be too eager". That was a lesson I learned the hard way.

Another case which merited me proceeding "*allegro non troppo*" also concerned Merlyn Rees, when he was Secretary of State for Northern Ireland in the mid-1970s. Various attempts were being made to involve the IRA in ceasefire talks. I got a tip in confidence from Bishop Edward Daly in Derry that an initiative was about to be presented to the British Prime Minister, Harold Wilson, in which the bishops were involved. It envisaged a triumvirate of worthy persons – Nobel Prize-winning Republican Seán McBride, unionist lawyer Desmond Boal, and former British Liberal leader Joseph Grimond – coming together to engage in shuttle diplomacy among the Northern Ireland paramilitary groups and the British and Irish governments.

Some days later I interviewed Merlyn Rees about other matters. I couldn't resist asking, innocently, if Britain would be prepared to consider a triumvirate of some sort "including, let's say, a republican, a loyalist and a retired British politician to negotiate with all parties". There was a silence. "No," he said after a lengthy pause. "Not acceptable."

I telephoned Bishop Daly, who was at a conference of the Irish hierarchy in Maynooth, to tell him the plan was going nowhere and to ask his permission to run the story. By prior arrangement, we spoke in Italian, which I had studied briefly in university, to put off anyone who might have been eavesdropping. "Well, if that's the case," said Bishop Daly, "Go ahead." The story that Britain had rejected the idea was splashed on page one of *The Irish Times* the next day.

Some years later, Harold Wilson's press secretary, Joe Haines, disclosed in his memoirs, *The Politics of Power*, published by Cape, that the proposal was conveyed to Harold Wilson – by independent TD, Dr John O'Connell, on behalf of the bishops – only a week *after* I had announced that it had been rejected. I can only assume that Rees hadn't a notion of what I was talking about. Anyway, Wilson turned down the proposal, which meant that my story was correct, if premature, and nobody was ever the wiser.

One of the more shadowy figures in the murky underworld of British–Irish affairs was Colin Wallace, a smooth, prematurely bald County Antrim native who worked for the British Intelligence Services in Northern Ireland as a member of an ultra-secret Army Psychological Operations unit. Wallace tried to smear political and paramilitary figures on both sides with bogus stories and would later claim that in the early 1970s he was involved in discrediting Harold Wilson and members of his cabinet in an anti-Labour disinformation campaign by right-wing members of the security services known as "Clockwork Orange". He began leaking information about what was going on in intelligence operations, primarily to Robert Fisk of *The Times*, then based in Belfast. Wallace had to quit his job suddenly in early 1975 when a document meant for Fisk was intercepted and passed to the RUC. Wallace moved to England where he told confidants that the real reason for his ousting was his refusal to continue operating "Clockwork Orange".

In late October the following year, I got a call from Wallace in my London office to meet him on a platform at Greenwich railway station. There he presented me with an envelope and after a brief conversation disappeared into the crowd of commuters. It contained official documents showing that selected senior British civil servants were being required to attend courses on the techniques of psychological operations (psyops), including psychological warfare. One document marked "restricted" was the syllabus of the course, run by the Joint Warfare Establishment at Old Sarum in Wiltshire. This defined psyops as a flexible instrument for counter-insurgency which possibly could be used "in a friendly country". According to Wallace it had been applied in Northern Ireland, where there had been a head-on clash between the British Army and the Secretary of State over Merlyn Rees's rescinding of a psyops policy document. I took a taxi to the Department of Defence in Whitehall where a senior official confirmed for me that the documents were genuine. After *The Irish Times* published extracts, the Under Secretary for the Army, Robert Brown, admitted in the House of Commons that 262 senior civil servants had attended the courses at Old Sarum during the previous three years. There was much critical comment about this and Brown promised to take a party of MPs to see the Joint Warfare Establishment for themselves. The psyops course for civil servants was later abandoned.

Wallace, one of the first covert operatives to break ranks and accuse the intelligence services in Northern Ireland of collusion with loyalist paramilitaries, was convicted in 1980 of the manslaughter of a man with whose wife he was allegedly having an affair. The conviction was overturned in 1996 in the light of new evidence. The journalist Paul Foot, in his book *Who Framed Colin Wallace?*, published by Macmillan in 1989, suggested that Wallace was set up by British agents to discredit his most serious claims – that intelligence officials had attempted unsuccessfully to prevent Harold Wilson coming to power in the 1974 general election.

Some time later I was drawn back into the world of espionage. On 16 November 1979, Margaret Thatcher caused a sensation when she named Sir Anthony Blunt, an art adviser to Queen Elizabeth in Buckingham Palace, as the "Fourth Man" of the "Cambridge Five", an elite group of spies who worked for the Soviet Union from the 1930s to the 1950s. They were invariably members of the Apostles, a secret society at Cambridge devoted to Marxism. The first two, Guy Burgess and Donald Maclean, defected to Moscow in 1951, and the third, Harold "Kim" Philby, followed them in 1963. After being exposed, Blunt was hounded from public life – John Banville's 1997 novel *The Untouchable* is based on him – and speculation ran wild in the British media as to the identity of the "Fifth Man".

This was where I came in. Lord Killanin, president of the International Olympic Committee and a Cambridge friend of Burgess, tipped off Donal Foley that the "Fifth Man" was perhaps none other than the Seventh Baron Talbot of Malahide, a hereditary Irish peer who died in 1973. Foley asked me to look into this. There was, I found, much circumstantial evidence. Born in 1912, Milo (Miles) Talbot had studied at Trinity College Cambridge, where he came into contact with Blunt, Burgess and Philby, and joined the exclusive Apostles club. The political and homosexual atmosphere at Trinity in the 1930s lent itself, according to the writer and former British intelligence agent

Malcolm Muggeridge, whom I visited at his cottage in Sussex to inquire about Talbot, to "foolish fantasies", including flirtations with communism.

I drove to Cambridge and leafed through back editions of the *Trinity Magazine* in the archives, where I found articles praising Moscow's socialist experiments side-by-side with couplets and quatrains overladen with homosexual innuendo. There were sly references in particular to Burgess, and to Talbot, who according to contemporaries, was almost certainly the subject of doggerel verse with lines like, "I'm for Miles / I like his smiles."

Like Philby, Burgess and Maclean, Talbot joined the Foreign Office after graduation. In 1950 and 1951, he served as number two at the Foreign Office southern Europe desk, responsible for the Balkan countries, including Albania. It was during this time that MI6 helped organise the ill-fated "invasion" of communist Albania by Albanian exiles. The "invaders" were picked up as they infiltrated across the border because, it is believed, Philby betrayed them to his Soviet spy-master. Just one week before Burgess and Maclean, about to be unmasked, fled from London to Moscow in March 1951, Talbot was appointed deputy head of Foreign Office security, under George Carey Foster. In the aftermath of the defections, the Foreign Office was plunged into chaos, and all known associates of the Cambridge spies came under suspicion. Talbot later became head of Foreign Office security, then went *en disponibilité*, on leave without pay, as the investigations continued. Muggeridge, who had shared the same Marxist sympathies with the Cambridge spies, but had become disillusioned with communism after working as Moscow correspondent for *The Guardian* in the 1930s, assured me, on the basis of what I had ascertained, that Talbot was a prime suspect and that going on leave without pay meant he was being interrogated.

But I didn't reach the same conclusion myself. When I went to see George Carey Foster at his retirement home in west Cork, he dismissed any idea that Lord Malahide was the "Fifth Man". Talbot was friendly with Maclean but many Foreign Office officials were too, he said. "I don't think he had any communist leanings." The Lord of Malahide often went *en disponibilité*, he added, to look after his Malahide estate. Talbot had a 120-acre horticultural farm at Malahide where he employed seventeen people and assembled a collection of rare plants and seeds from all over the world. The identity of a "Fifth Man" was never definitely established, though it is now widely assumed to have been John Cairncross, another Apostle known to have passed information to the Soviets, who died in 1995.

The activities of "British intelligence" (which some people in Dublin like to refer to as an oxymoron) were inevitably directed towards Ireland. To secure communications in the run up to the 1973 Sunningdale negotiations, army technical experts travelled from Dublin to install a new teleprompter coding system at the Irish embassy at 17 Grosvenor Place in London. A few hours after they finished, a man claiming to be a telephone engineer arrived, uninvited, "to repair a fault". There was no fault. The deputy head of mission, Seán Gaynor, had the good sense to turn him away.

As a new round of sensitive, high-level negotiations between the British and Irish governments got under way prior to the 1985 Anglo-Irish Agreement, the Irish installed a new Swiss code machine in the embassy to send classified messages to Dublin, but soon became wary of using it, since it had been compromised. The evidence for this came when a coded message to Dublin from the embassy was intercepted by British Signals Intelligence, and the contents relayed to Margaret Thatcher. It conveyed the information that a junior British official had privately told an Irish embassy contact not to worry too much about a speech being made by a member of the British government, which could otherwise have caused upset in Dublin.

Within hours the junior minister was carpeted by a senior Whitehall official and told that Mrs Thatcher was rather cross to learn that the Irish were being tipped off in this cosy way. She would undoubtedly have been even less pleased to discover that the Irish were also tipped off about her reaction by an insider in the British government. Knowing that their embassy machine was not secure, the Irish subsequently used the system to convey only harmless intelligence or information they wanted the British to hear.

The diplomats also could not use an electric typewriter in the Irish embassy for confidential despatches, because they had been made aware that British intelligence had sophisticated listening devices capable of translating the sound patterns from the typewriter keys. The Irish officials had to resort to old fashioned methods of communication for important messages. An old typewriter was kept in the embassy to type up documents that rated a top-secret classification. A diplomat would fly with it to Dublin, or give it to an Aer Lingus pilot at Heathrow Airport, who would strap the message to his wrist and on arriving in Dublin hand it to an Army despatch rider for delivery to the Department of Foreign Affairs or the Taoiseach's office.

My story about all this in *The Irish Times* caused a flurry of speculation in the British media about a new crisis in British–Irish relations. Garret FitzGerald reacted stoically. He always worked on the assumption that bugging was taking place, he said. "Any Irish government that was simple-minded enough to assume that the intelligence services of the Soviet Union or the United States or Great Britain did not have the power to intercept messages would be taking risks with our national security."

A footnote to these stories of spies and espionage. One day in London I noticed that *The Irish Times* had made a mistake on its front page. Two stories appeared side by side, one about Richard Ingrams, the editor of the satirical magazine *Private Eye*, the other about the head of the Soviet spy agency, the KGB. The single-column photos had been mixed up, so Ingrams was labelled as the KGB chief and the KGB chief as Ingrams. I sent the page off to *Private Eye*, which delighted in highlighting newspaper boobs. It was rather disloyal of me, but this was too good for them not to have. Besides, they paid five pounds for every offering used. *Private Eye* published it prominently the following Thursday. That day when I arrived at *The Irish Times* office in Fleet Street, I found my colleague Maeve Binchy working on her weekly column. I asked her, "Did you see *Private Eye* this morning?" "Yes," she replied, with hardly a pause in her typing. "And I got my fiver in the post this morning too."

8

The Point of No Return

During my time in London, the South African embassy in Trafalgar Square was picketed around the clock by anti-apartheid demonstrators. I called in one afternoon in July 1985 to request a visa. Journalists often had to wait months for permission to report in apartheid South Africa but I was issued a work permit almost right away. The immigration official winked at me conspiratorially as if to say, "Tell it as it is." I planned to spend some weeks travelling around South Africa, reporting on the state of emergency that had just been imposed by the government in the face of widespread unrest, and assessing the mood and opinions of ordinary people, black, coloured and white.

Which is how I found myself not long afterwards sipping tea with Millie Kaiser, a kindly, grey-haired lady, a retired teacher like my own mother, who had emigrated to South Africa from Skerries in County Dublin in the 1940s and lived with her Afrikaans husband in a leafy avenue of a Transvaal town called Belfast, two hours' drive east of Johannesburg. She had invited me into the living-room of her pretty bungalow where we sat on big soft armchairs with starched antimacassars, and there she told me in all seriousness that the trouble was caused by agitators and that most blacks were not in favour of change.

As evidence of her claim, Mrs Kaiser brought her "boy" into the living-room. Her "boy" was fifty-four-year-old Samuel Sithole. Both he and his employer looked startled when I got up and shook his hand as he stood awkwardly by the door. "Samuel, do you like Bishop Tutu?" she asked. "No, Ma'am," he replied. "You like President Botha, don't you?" "Yes, Ma'am." Then he was dismissed.

Europeans like the Kaisers formed the backbone of the ruling National Party. They did not see themselves as unreasonable in their support of apartheid, and they felt that they treated their black workers well, which by their values they undoubtedly did. They paid Sam a little extra "pocket money" on Saturdays and said they clothed him and paid his bus fares and medical expenses.

The sublime racism that existed in this little town, with its 3,000 people of European extraction and 5,000 blacks, was common throughout white South Africa, and helped explain the resistance to change among supporters of the apartheid government. In the billiards room of the Belfast Hotel, retired Afrikaner farmer Solomon Kocoetzee said he was in favour of some reforms, but "it must stop at some point, otherwise I am afraid what will happen". As he lined up his cue to take a shot, his playing partner, farmer Vanlo Loggerenberg, said that if apartheid went it would be the end for whites. "When New York had to open up to the niggers, the whites had to go away," he said, matter-of-factly.

South Africa at this time was coming under increased internal and international pressure to end the system of separate existence for the races. The government had dug in its heels and enforced a state of emergency. The police and army had been authorised to use their weapons in response to protests or acts of defiance. In the following days I saw just what this meant. In Daveyton township outside Johannesburg I came across sixteen-year-old Dehisile Mbohani laid out in the back of a mini-bus, her eyes half open and glazed in death, shot by police as she and thousands of others defied a ban on funeral processions. In Zwide township outside Port Elizabeth I was shown the crumpled body of fifteen-year-old Zimesile Mapela, lying on the lambswool seat cover of a car, his arms folded over his yellow T-shirt and his legs dangling on the floor, with a small hole in his hip where a police bullet had passed through. I joined 2,500 young people as they defied a ban to attend a funeral of twelve victims of police shootings in the same township. Four V-shaped Casspir armoured cars, four police Land Rovers and six Buffel trucks filled with soldiers appeared at the perimeter of the vast burial ground and would, I believe, have opened fire on the crowd had it not been for the courage of a BBC camera crew that stood its ground in the middle. Nevertheless we all had to run, leaping over garden gates and ducking under wire fences, as the police and soldiers chased everyone away with *sjamboks*, heavy leather thongs that caught stragglers on the back and legs. In covering these events, I was struck by the lack of overt racism among the black population. I was greeted with smiles and revolutionary handshakes everywhere I went, and much laughter when they saw me running from the police whips like everyone else.

Desmond Tutu, then Anglican Bishop of Johannesburg, who had been awarded the Nobel Peace Prize the previous year for advocating peaceful means to resolve the conflict, told me in his office in Johannesburg that he had reached the point where he now fully backed the banned African National Congress (ANC), the national liberation movement, despite its espousal of revolutionary violence. "I do not support the method that it seeks to use," he said, "but I understand perfectly that a group of people who had tried to use peaceful means until 1960 when the leader of the organisation [Nelson Mandela] was detained, can perhaps say, 'We have no option but to use violence.'"

The situation was complicated by faction fights in Natal province between ANC supporters and Africans, mostly Zulus,

supporting Chief Mangosuthu Buthelezi, head of the Inkatha
Freedom Party and a collaborator of the white government. The
police and army had done little to stop violence that pitted black
against black, and black against Indian, in the townships around
the city of Durban on the east coast during that August.

I travelled to Durban and arranged an interview with
Professor Fatima Meer, the head of the Institute of Black
Research at the University of Natal, who had frequently been
arrested for her anti-apartheid activities. Just before I arrived in
a rented car at her suburban bungalow in Durban, along with
fellow Irish journalist Emily O'Reilly (now Ireland's Ombudsman)
who was reporting for the *Sunday Tribune*, the grey-haired Indian
professor had received word that the multi-racial Gandhi
settlement about twenty-five kilometres north of Durban, which
she helped to run, was being attacked by Inkatha supporters. It
was a target because it was identified with the ANC. The news
had been brought to her by fifty-four-year-old Dorothy Nyembe,
a leading ANC activist, who had fled that morning as the
assailants arrived. Known throughout the movement at "Mam
D", she had just been released from prison after fifteen years, and
had moved into one of the houses at the Gandhi Settlement.
"Please take us there to see what is going on," said Professor
Meer.

We drove the two women to the settlement, which lay off a
highway several kilometres outside Durban. It contained a
cluster of about fifty houses constructed from wood and tin,
among them the shack where Mahatma Gandhi had lived until
1911. They were situated around a brick museum, dedicated to
the Indian leader who had led the early struggle against racism
and prejudice in South Africa, and a schoolhouse with five
classrooms. The museum was intact but smoke was pouring from
the windows of the schoolhouse.

About sixty Africans, some armed with sticks, were strolling
leisurely among the dwellings, setting fires and looting chairs,

mattresses, cushions and clothing. One woman had a table on her head. Dorothy Nyembe slumped down in the back of the car and watched expressionless as she saw her wooden house being stripped of its contents.

Fatima Meer was frantically worried about the Gandhi memorabilia in the museum, which included his desk, swivel chair, books, photographs, papers and cloth he had spun himself, but she judged it too dangerous to get out of the car to remonstrate with the looters. "I think you should turn around slowly and drive back," she said as some men gathered around us rather menacingly. I edged through them in low gear, and drove back towards the highway. There we saw a dozen young residents of the settlement hiding behind a wall. Professor Meer invited one of them to come back with us to Durban to fetch a pick-up truck and rescue the Gandhi mementos. She first established that he had a driving licence, though there were no police on the highways that day. The violence in the townships suited the purposes of the government, she maintained. "It appears to the world that it is racial – black against Indian – but it is not just that. All the black shops have been burned too, and there are thugs on both sides."

A spasm of violence was taking hundreds of lives in Natal. It had started with the murder two weeks earlier of Victoria Mxenge, a civil rights lawyer and a thorn in the side of the apartheid South African government. The attackers were suspected to be followers of Chief Buthelezi. Inkatha supporters armed with spears and knives had then attacked mourners at a memorial service for Mrs Mxenge. Fighting and looting had spread throughout the townships.

In Durban we pulled up at a garage where the Indian owner unquestioningly handed the professor the keys of a pick-up truck. The youth drove it back towards the settlement. We went to Professor Meer's bungalow from where she telephoned the chief fire officer, Superintendent Constant. He told her the police had instructed them not to go to the Gandhi Settlement, because of the "fighting" there. "There are no riots there now," she said. "This is a plea for help to save the Gandhi Settlement. Please listen to someone else, a foreign journalist." She handed the receiver to me. "I can confirm there was no rioting there half an hour ago," I said. "Just looters and arsonists." He promised to check with the police again. Four hours later the pick-up truck returned to Professor Meer's home. The young man and his friends had managed to rescue Gandhi's desk and chair and some photographs. The fire service had not turned up. "It is very important for the world to know that it was blacks who tried to rescue the precious possessions of Mahatma Gandhi," said Professor Meer.

We returned to the Gandhi Settlement the next day. It was utterly destroyed. The South African police and fire-fighters had not made any effort to save a site that was sacred to devotees of the great Indian leader. All that was left of the little houses were warped sheets of blackened tin. We clambered over rubble into the wrecked Gandhi Museum, past a brass inscription: "Opened by Harry Oppenheimer, January 28th 1970", and a blackened notice saying "Do not touch". Glass littered the museum floor. Gandhi's old metal printing machine, too heavy to carry away, had survived. We collected bits and pieces and cardboard inscriptions, so that the full damage could be catalogued. Gandhi's handloom and cloth had disappeared, as had the iconic wire-rimmed spectacles that had been displayed on his desk. The tin house where Gandhi evolved his philosophy of passive resistance had not been burned, but the roof had collapsed and the white-washed walls had been kicked in. A swarm of bees had settled on the debris inside, making it impossible to enter. The schoolhouse had been gutted.

Later that day we got a glimpse of the turmoil in the nearby township of Inanda, when we tagged on behind a military convoy. The township was a vast hillside of tin shacks where impoverished Indians and blacks had lived together until that week. Almost all the homes of more than four thousand Indian residents and scores of black-owned shanties had been burned or looted, and over sixty residents had been killed in a week of fighting. All "people of colour" who worked in Durban, a port city on the Indian Ocean first developed by English settlers in the nineteenth century, were required, with a few exceptions, to reside in such townships. Disfranchised by the apartheid system, they had to carry a pass and they could not vote in South African elections.

White citizens, by contrast, lived in quiet avenues in the suburbs, with curved swimming pools and shaded gardens. As the Gandhi Settlement burned that weekend, many of them were making their way into the centre of Durban to hear President P.W. Botha address the Natal congress of the ruling National Party about how he proposed to deal with the nationwide unrest. They saw none of the destruction, because the worst affected townships, Umlazi, Kwa Mashu and Inanda, were set well back from the main highways. Little disturbed their tranquil existence. In the stores and restaurants of Durban, the black and Indian workers whom the white residents encountered were friendly and courteous. On the seafront, elderly white men and women, wearing identical white fedoras, played bowls on manicured greens. A large sign on the wide, sandy beach stated, in English, Afrikaans and Zulu: "Under Section 37 of the Durban beach by-laws, this bathing area is reserved for the sole use of members of the white race group." Out at sea, scores of tanned surfers rode the Indian Ocean waves in a warm north-easterly wind.

Listening to South African radio and watching television news that week in Durban, it was evident that the white population knew little of what was going on. SABC, the South African Broadcasting Corporation, from which seventy per cent of whites got their news, played down the unrest as the work of hooligans. It did not report the political assassination of Victoria Mxenge which had ignited the violence, but credited Buthelezi's Inkatha mobs for restoring "law and order" in the townships. On

SABC television, the only TV news channel available, the "necklacing" – killing with a blazing tyre – of an alleged informer, twenty-four-year-old Roseline Skosanna, was shown over and over, but there was no mention of a court case in Klerksdorp where four whites were being tried for incinerating a black girl in the boot of a car after raping her. The name of the imprisoned ANC leader Nelson Mandela was never mentioned on radio or television or in the print media. His picture appeared that week in the American magazine *Newsweek*, but South African government censors had carefully blacked out his face with felt pens in all copies on sale in Durban newsagents. "White South Africa knows less about what is going on than people in Europe," Allister Sparks, former editor of the *Rand Daily Mail* and an outspoken critic of apartheid, told me. "They only realise that something is going on if they are directly affected, like if the maid doesn't show up."

President P.W. Botha was due to deliver his address in Durban Town Hall, a replica of the Edwardian City Hall in Belfast, Northern Ireland. As I entered, a policeman asked me politely for my gun. I didn't have one, but all around me middle-aged women in twin sets and pearls were digging pistols from their handbags, and men were pulling guns from their belts and depositing them on shelves for collection later. The South African President entered the hall to rapturous applause. A balding man with large glasses and the countenance of a banker, he grabbed the sides of the podium as he spoke, his eyes darting from side to side. His chin quivered slightly when he got angry, as he did when several white members of the anti-apartheid women's Black Sash movement – who demonstrated proof of white resistance to apartheid and were frequently ostracised in their own communities – heckled him from the balcony. "I can't hear you; you are a voice in the wilderness," he jibed back. In his speech Botha blamed the unrest on "barbaric communist agitators and murderers" and, looking at the press seats, he declared he would not release Nelson Mandela, as many foreign governments were demanding. "That is the end of the story," he said. If he did release Mandela and had to re-arrest him, "then what would I do?" he cried. "Hang him," someone shouted.

After the event several delegates went to the Malibu Hotel on Marine Parade for a "wake" for the All Blacks rugby tour, cancelled because of a ruling by the New Zealand High Court that the New Zealand Rugby Union could not field a team that excluded Maori players, as required by the South Africans. There were free cigarettes and drinks, and videos of previous All Blacks–Springbok games were shown. Downstairs the men-only bar staged a strip show. A white girl went among the drinkers, sitting on their laps wearing only a g-string and tassels. She finished her act with a snake.

As this was going on, some 300 black schoolgirls and about 100 adults, of whom twenty or so were white, were taking their places on plastic chairs in Durban's Methodist Hall on West Street for a memorial service for Victoria Mxenge. There arose a low sound of despair, more a sigh than a murmur, interspersed with the clicks of the Zulu tongue, as they heard Anne Colgan of Black Sash, a woman of Irish descent with permed ginger hair and sleeveless frock, tell how the lawyer was murdered. Four black men had rushed out of the darkness and shot her as she was being left home to her bungalow by the Rev. Mcebisi Xundu, the leader of the United Democratic Front (UDF), the umbrella group for all the anti-apartheid groups that regarded Nelson Mandela as their leader. At the time Victoria Mxenge was one of the defence lawyers for sixteen members of the UDF in a treason trial. As the hall stood for a moment's silence, Colgan, standing beside Archbishop Denis Hurley of Durban, raised her freckled arm in a clenched fist salute. Afterwards the Archbishop told me, despairingly, "People are prepared to sacrifice their lives to bring about change. We have reached that point." As we left the hall two plain-clothes policemen, leaning casually against the metal pillars of the Durban History Museum, snapped our pictures, using cameras fitted with zoom lenses.

I left South Africa with the feeling that things would get worse before they would get better, but that a point of no return had been reached, and that the defiance of the victims of apartheid, combined with international pressure, would sooner or later bring about the end of an immoral system of government.

It wasn't until five years later, after P.W. Botha had stepped down owing to a stroke, that the National Party government under F.W. de Klerk took the first step towards democracy by lifting the ban on the African National Congress and releasing Nelson Mandela from prison. Apartheid laws were gradually scrapped and the first multi-racial elections held in 1994, giving the ANC an overwhelming majority. Among the ANC candidates elected to parliament was Dorothy Nyembe. "Mam D" became one of the "founding mothers" of the South Africa democratic constitution. The Inkatha party won a majority in KwaZulu-Natal and, in the interests of national reconciliation, Chief Buthelezi was appointed Minister of Home Affairs in the first post-apartheid government. Bishop Tutu, who became the first black Anglican Archbishop of Cape Town and primate of the Anglican Church of Southern Africa, headed the new government's Truth and Reconciliation Commission. P.W. Botha spurned requests to apologise for apartheid, declined to testify at the Truth and Reconciliation Commission, and was fined and given a suspended jail sentence for his refusal to answer charges about human rights violations.

The Gandhi Settlement was rebuilt, and Gandhi's house and museum were reconstructed, with the help of funding from the government of India. It was reopened on 27 February 2000 by President Thabo Mbeki, as a beacon of reconciliation and peace in the new South Africa.

9

An Irishman in Moscow

In December 1986, Conor Brady was appointed editor of *The Irish Times* and asked me to open a staff bureau in Moscow and chronicle the changes stirring in the communist world. I didn't hesitate. I had been to the Soviet Union three times on assignment since 1979 and longed to go back. It was becoming evident that a political springtime had arrived in Russia, and we sensed the first tremors of the convulsions that were about to shake Soviet society, and in a few years bring down the iron curtain and end the Cold War.

I was always fascinated by Russia. As a teenager I read classic Russian novels such as Dostoevsky's *Crime and Punishment* and Tolstoy's *War and Peace*. I managed to save half a crown a week, for five weeks, to secure a first edition of Boris Pasternak's *Dr Zhivago* in the Belfast bookshop Erskine Mayne. Winston Churchill once described Russia as a riddle wrapped in a mystery inside an enigma, and the prospect of the opening up of a secretive totalitarian society created enormous interest throughout the world. The previous year, the Soviet Communist Party Politburo had appointed Mikhail Sergeyevich Gorbachev as General Secretary. In contrast to his hardline predecessors, Gorbachev was personable, articulate and a reformer. He introduced *glasnost* (openness) and *perestroika* (restructuring), to try to revive the moribund Soviet economy. People in the west were seized with a great curiosity about life in a vast, hostile superpower that had failed to keep up with the modern world's technology and consumer advances.

In those days it took several months to get permission to work as a permanent correspondent in the Soviet Union, and it wasn't until 23 March 1987 that I arrived in Moscow, my suitcase weighed down with the *Cambridge Encyclopedia of Russia*. I registered my presence with Mikhail Gorbachev's press secretary, Gennady Gerasimov, a tall, smooth diplomat, to whom I offered a bottle of Bushmills as a token of Irish–Soviet friendship. "Aha! A small corruption. I'll take it," he said cheerfully, putting it in his desk drawer. I told Gerasimov that I would not put a question to him at his regular bilingual briefings for foreign correspondents – who invariably addressed him in English – until I could ask something in Russian. I memorised a question and addressed it to him soon afterwards, earning disapproving glances from some colleagues who thought I was showing off.

As Soviet society opened up, however, competence in Russian became essential, and I spent many hours memorising nouns and verbs. My early attempts at speaking Russian led to some embarrassing moments. At a party a Russian lawyer peppered me with simple questions in Russian that I could understand – such as "Do you like Russia?" – to each one of which I responded with the answer "*Da*" (yes). Then he asked me something I didn't understand, and when I tentatively ventured another "*Da*", he burst out laughing. He had apparently asked me, "Am I boring you with all these questions?" But soon enough I was able to bore people with my own questions in Russian.

In the early stages of Gorbachev's rule, the control of society by the Communist Party and the KGB remained absolute. Foreign journalists were subject to Cold War restrictions. We had to apply for permission to make journeys out of Moscow, and many cities remained closed to outsiders. The foreign community in Moscow was largely confined to a dozen diplomatic compounds guarded by militiamen in sentry huts. Not surprisingly the western press corps tended to be paranoiac and insular. A correspondent for United Press International told me that he was under instructions not to file any human-interest stories about Russians, adding, "Hell, they never write anything nice about Americans."

The Foreign Ministry assigned me a tiny apartment on the top floor of a hideous new seventeen-storey apartment block at 1 Marksistskaya Street, a kilometre south of the Kremlin, with an adjoining single-room flat for an office. The lift sometimes didn't work and there were frequent power cuts. I had to install a telex machine on which I hammered out news copy, leaving my knuckles out of shape to this day. At least it was reliable. International telephone calls were sometimes delayed for hours. There were so few calls made between Dublin and Moscow at that time – the Irish community amounted to about a dozen misfits like myself and a few diplomats – that I was soon on first name terms with the international operators in Dublin. Garret FitzGerald tried to ring me once, and asked the Irish operator for my Moscow number, without saying who he was or whom he was calling. As Dr FitzGerald tells it, the operator replied: "Oh, Garret, Conor is out at the moment but he'll be back in an hour."

By opening a bureau in Moscow, *The Irish Times* became the first Irish company formally to register its presence in Russia. The first Dáil in 1920 had recognised the Soviet Union and sent a small cash donation, but after that Ireland's attitude had been characterised more by prayers for the conversion of Russians than by any meaningful contacts.

With the excitement created by Gorbachev's reforms, it now became a fashionable destination for Irish visitors of all kinds, many of them delegates to conferences sponsored by Soviet institutions to discuss peace and disarmament. Bibi Baskin arrived to record her weekly RTÉ chat show, during which she asked me on air what I missed most. "Marmalade," I said. "You can't get it here." In the next couple of months I received several jars of marmalade brought by sympathetic Irish tourists.

Dick Spring, then head of the Irish Labour Party, arrived in Moscow as a delegate to a meeting of the Socialist International Disarmament Advisory Council. I took him for dinner with Patrick Cockburn, then Moscow correspondent for the *Financial Times*, and afterwards set out to drive him back to his hotel in the *Irish Times* Lada. Halfway there I was stopped by traffic militiamen and fined thirty-two roubles (about thirty Irish pounds) for a traffic misdemeanour. I then got totally lost in Moscow's darkened streets, at one point stalling on tramlines as a tram approached, until a helpful citizen called Grigor climbed into the car and guided us to the hotel.

The Russian poet Joseph Brodsky once said that the Russians were like the Irish "in their poverty, their spiritual intensity, their strong personal relationships and their sentimentality". These attributes undoubtedly created an affinity between the Russians and the Irish, two peoples who could name, and often recite, their national poets. Boris Pasternak was revered by Russians, not for *Dr Zhivago*, but for his poetry. Devotees of Pasternak would gather every weekend at his grave in a cemetery in the village of Peredelkino, south of Moscow, to recite his verses. Among them was an elderly Jewish man, Emanuel Libschitz, his shoes cracked and his suit worn and shiny, who once launched into W.B. Yeats's "The Second Coming" in Russian when I brought Irish visitors to see the grave.

Cultural affinity, and the mutual enjoyment of drink and *craic*, helped Ireland secure one of the first, and at the time one of the biggest, joint enterprises between Soviet Russia and a foreign country. Among the reforms Gorbachev introduced was the establishment of joint business ventures with foreign partners. The first of these was an Indian restaurant opened in July 1987, run jointly by Moscow Council and the Indian Tourist Board. Six months after I arrived, Aer Rianta, the Irish Airports Authority, began negotiations with Aeroflot officials on a joint-enterprise duty-free shop at Moscow's international airport, Sheremetyevo 2. At the time there were no duty-free shops anywhere in the Soviet Union. The only retail opportunity for passengers passing through Sheremetyevo 2 was a *Berioshka* (Silver Birch) store, selling Russian dolls, vodka and outsized art books for foreign currency only.

Aer Rianta faced stiff competition, particularly from the US airline Pan American, which on 16 December 1987 put in a $120 million bid for the concession. A Pan Am team of executives flew into Moscow and established itself on a whole floor of a city-centre hotel where it expected to conduct formal negotiations. Aer Rianta executives, however, had a better sense of the psychology of the Russians, with whom they had been doing business since the mid-1970s, when Aeroflot began shipping its own fuel to Shannon as barter for maintenance and landing fees. Aer Rianta officials came regularly to Moscow, spent weekends at Aeroflot *dachas* and drank vodka and shared communal steam baths with their Russian counterparts. As a state enterprise, Aeroflot also found it more congenial to deal with a semi-state body like Aer Rianta, rather than a capitalist concern like Pan Am. Aeroflot had another reason for preferring the Irish. In 1983, when airports across the world banned Aeroflot flights for several days in protest against the shooting-down of an off-course South Korean airliner by a Soviet fighter plane, Shannon Airport had stayed open to refuel transatlantic Aeroflot flights. A top Aeroflot official told me that they had never forgotten that.

Within three weeks Pan Am conceded victory to the Irish. On 16 February 1988, Martin Dully and Liam Skelly of Aer Rianta signed a contract with their Russian friends in Moscow's main Aeroflot office. The Irish undertook to build and operate a duty-free store in record time, and also provide and maintain ground-handling equipment and a de-icing facility. The two sides agreed on a logo: a combination of the shamrock with the spires of St Basil's Cathedral in Moscow. Several Irish companies got involved in spin-off contracts. Modern Display Artists designed the stores at each end of Sheremetyevo 2 and brought over the fixtures and fittings from Ireland in a fleet of twelve trucks. Part of the airport hotel was refurbished by the firm of Jim Woods from Newmarket-on-Fergus. I came across Irish bricklayers at the airport laying cement blocks flown in from the west of Ireland. Carpet-layers came from Ennis and electricians from Sixmilebridge. At Shannon Airport, Andrew Bromfield, a fluent Russian speaker who had lectured at Limerick Institute of Higher Education, gave rudimentary lessons in Russian to store assistants before they left for Moscow.

The duty-free store was opened on 12 May, less than three months after the joint venture was signed, and – something Aer Rianta executives like to boast about – almost two years before the first McDonald's opened in Moscow. Irish goods took pride of place on the shelves, including Jameson whiskey, Bailey's Irish Cream, Carroll's cigarettes, Waterford Glass, Henry White cashmere coats and Irish linen, smoked salmon, bacon and sausages. T-shirts with USSR emblems were supplied by O'Neill's of Dublin. (A plan to print T-shirts with the letters KGB was dropped when the spy agency demanded a ten per cent cut.)

In the following months Aer Rianta opened a second duty-free shop in Leningrad. A third was established on the Russian–Finnish border on the road between Leningrad and Helsinki, where the Irish tricolour and the Soviet flag fluttered side by side against a backdrop of razor wire and tank traps. As a grim-faced Russian customs officer searched my car before I crossed into Finland one day, I asked if he knew Michael Cashin, the Aer Rianta official who had organised the joint venture. "Mikhail Kashin – he is my very good friend," cried the customs man, banging the boot shut and waving me on. Aer Rianta's investment would survive the fall of the Soviet Union, and in 2008 it was the largest airport retailer in Russia, employing 1,000 people across the three Moscow airports, including twenty Irish staff.

The new openness brought about a cultural thaw in Russia, and the communist world became a popular destination for western singers, rock stars, orchestras and theatrical groups. The former TASS correspondent to Dublin, Yuri Ustimenko, wrote in his 1970s' book on Ireland that "to visit Moscow is a dream that never leaves the Abbey Theatre Company". As Irish interest and excitement in Gorbachev's Russia grew, the Abbey Theatre decided to make this dream come true, and take what actor Eamon Kelly described as "a steppe in the left direction".

In February 1988 a forty-member Abbey troupe arrived in Leningrad, now St Petersburg, accompanied by seven journalists. The Red Army helped transport the props sent from Dublin, including 100 Irish spuds for a potato-gathering scene. The Abbey brought two plays. One was *The Great Hunger*, an adaptation by Tom Mac Intyre of Patrick Kavanagh's poem about spiritual hunger in rural Ireland. Directed by Patrick Mason, it presented the tragedy of a middle-aged bachelor, Paddy Maguire, played by Tom Hickey, in a grotesque characterisation of country life in the 1940s. The other was John B. Keane's *The Field*, directed by Ben Barnes, with Niall Tobin playing the part of the Bull McCabe. Theatre-goers in the Soviet Union who hoped that the Abbey would bring a classic Irish drama, such as a Sean O'Casey play, for its first Russian performance were disappointed. The plays were first shown in Dublin to Vladimir Chernyaev of the Soviet Ministry of Culture, who confessed to me in Moscow afterwards that he was very worried about how Russian theatre-goers might react to *The Great Hunger*.

I enjoyed *The Great Hunger* and sat through all four performances, two in Leningrad and two in Moscow. But I noted that a few members of the audience, perplexed by the black humour and the parody of religious practice, didn't return after the interval. A Soviet expert on Irish theatre, Valentina Ryabolova, said, "To me, all these people on the stage were very strange. I didn't feel empathy with any of them." I quoted in my report a comment by Niall Tobin to me and two other journalists about the mixed reception for the play, "I don't even think it should be staged. It's not theatre at all. It's a lot of wasted effort and I don't mind saying so." (In his 1995 memoir, *Smile and be a Villain*, Tobin wrote that an actor sometimes relaxed and forgot that a journalist is "never off-duty till he's dead".) Patrick Mason defended the choice of *The Great Hunger*, arguing that the Abbey Theatre was not a museum theatre but was dedicated to new Irish works. The controversy over *The Great Hunger* caused considerable strain between the Abbey touring group and the Irish reporters, with both sides seeing the other as having a "great obsession" about its merits or demerits. Mason accused me at a dinner hosted by the Irish Ambassador in Moscow of trying to split the Abbey group. (*The Great Hunger* later got a similar reception months later in New York where *Irish Times* theatre critic David Nowlan reported "walk-outs" and general bewilderment about what the play was about.) *The Field*, however, got an enthusiastic reception in Russia. In Leningrad an interpreter earned a place in Abbey folklore for her comment about trying to squeeze extra people into the back of the theatre. "Have you seen all the people out front! We can't stand some of them."

I took on an acting role myself in Moscow some time later, when the poet Yevgeny Yevtushenko appealed for volunteers for a crowd scene in a film he was directing called *Stalin's Funeral*. I dressed up in 1950s' gear and ran up and down a boulevard for an afternoon with hundreds of Muscovite extras, as he shouted directions through a bullhorn. I made the cut, but only for half a second, as a face in the crowd.

Back home for a holiday in the summer of 1987, I was plied with questions about Russia. In County Leitrim, where I was holidaying on the Shannon, I was made fully aware of just how closely events in the USSR were being followed in Ireland when I fell into conversation with an elderly farmer, unshaven, with his trousers tied with cord. He ascertained that I worked in Moscow. He fell silent, then asked me, "Is it true that collectivisation is fucked?" I assured him it was. He went on to explain that he had been taught in school in the 1930s that the Ukraine was the bread basket of Europe and he couldn't understand why agriculture had failed in the modern Soviet Union.

A goal of foreign correspondents in those early days of reform was to get an interview with Mikhail Gorbachev. He had a practice of meeting personally with one reporter from a country he was about to visit. When Gorbachev announced that he would stop off in Ireland in February 1988, on his way to a summit meeting in Washington with US President Ronald Reagan, I applied for an interview. I was turned down. The visit to Ireland was not important enough: it was just a two-hour lay-over at Shannon airport while Gorbachev's plane was being refuelled – an event that he tactfully insisted was not a "stop-over" but a "milestone" in relations between the two countries. However, the Soviet Foreign Ministry told me that, as I was travelling with the Moscow press corps, Gorbachev would expect, and answer, a question from me at a photo opportunity at Shannon Airport. I duly asked a question, on Soviet attitudes to Northern Ireland, which elicited the rather surprising response from Gorbachev, given Russia's critical reporting of the British role there at the time, that Northern Ireland was "the internal business of Great Britain". In putting my question, I addressed the Soviet leader as "Mikhail Sergeyevich", using his first name and patronymic, which is the formal style in Russian. Afterwards an Irish colleague complimented me for being on such close terms with Gorbachev that I could call him by his first name.

The red flag fluttered over the airport terminal that day, the first time it had been raised in the west of Ireland since the short-lived Limerick Soviet of 1919. Limerick TD Jim Kemmy, leader of the Democratic Socialist Party and a life-long socialist, said, "I never thought I'd see the day – and not an anti-communist bleat out of anyone."

The next stop-over by a Russian leader at Shannon was less auspicious. In 1994 Boris Yeltsin failed to get off the plane when returning to Moscow from Washington, leaving Taoiseach Albert Reynolds, members of his cabinet and the band of the Southern Command, standing on the tarmac. Only in March 2008 was it confirmed, by the Russian Ambassador at the time, that an incapacitated Yeltsin had been restrained by an aide from leaving the plane, and that a "high-ranking Irishman" had complained that the non-appearance "insulted us to the depth of our souls and showed a small country like Ireland wasn't worth reckoning with".

10

The Day After

On 26 April 1986, reactor No 4 at the Chernobyl nuclear power station suffered a steam explosion, resulting in a nuclear meltdown and the spread of radioactive particles high into the atmosphere. It wasn't until two days later, after employees at Sweden's Forsmark nuclear plant found abnormally high readings on their radiation monitors, that the world became aware that a catastrophe had happened. Over the following months, correspondents were forbidden to visit the stricken areas of Ukraine and Byelorussia, and it was impossible to get a first-hand account of the effect on people and the environment. But there was one country where the devastation caused by the accident could be witnessed and measured. That was Sweden itself.

Five months after the explosion, I flew to Umeå, a university town on the Gulf of Bothnia in central Sweden and drove inland to the Lapp village of Klimpfiall, where the first snows of winter had sprinkled the heather and bog cotton of the low mountains bordering on Norway. It was mid-September, the time of year when the reindeer herds were culled for their meat and the Lapps, known in Sweden as the *Sami* people, made their annual income through selling the meat on the market. Smoked strips of reindeer meat served with sour cream and blackcurrants was a popular Swedish dish. September was also the time of abundance in the Scandinavian forests. There were elk, hares and woodcock and, in the rivers and lakes, trout, char, salmon and carp. The forest floor was ankle deep in blueberry, cloudberry and wild raspberry, and mushrooms grew among pale patches of reindeer moss.

At Klimpfiall they were coming to terms with the fact that the land and the forests for hundreds of kilometres around had been blighted by the nuclear fallout. The radioactivity in the Chernobyl nuclear cloud had been washed out of the sky by heavy rains over central Sweden. A vast area of Lapland suffered the biggest increase in radiation level in Scandinavia. Much of the wildlife, fish and forest foods had been rendered unfit for consumption. The lichen moss on which the reindeer fed had soaked up the radioactive rain like a sponge and had retained large amounts of cancer-inducing caesium with a half-life of thirty years. The reindeer had become contaminated and their meat inedible. The last nomadic tribe in Europe found its lifestyle threatened by something that had occurred many hundreds of kilometres away.

"We don't take from nature but it is we who are paying the price," said Anna Blind, a small, cheerful woman with delicate oriental features, whose husband Per Anders and son Jon Olov were helping neighbours to herd the reindeer, using motorbikes and Land Rovers. The Swedish government had decreed that any food with more than 300 becquerel (bq) per kilogramme of contamination – the unit for measuring radioactive caesium particles – could not be eaten because of the cancer risk. Everyone in the district was now talking about becquerel levels. Roland Olofsson, owner of the reindeer meat plant at the small town of Vilhelmina, told me that a stray reindeer found nearby had registered 15,000 bq. The reindeer would be slaughtered as normal but the meat would be delivered to mink farms because it was unfit for human consumption, and would be for many years. Olofsson, a burly Swede in jeans and check shirt, got a regular government bulletin giving readings all over Sweden. Together we leafed through its closely typed pages in the factory canteen. Cattle were below 300 bq everywhere and sheep between fifty and 2,000. The levels for fish varied widely, and because of their feeding cycle they were still picking up radioactivity. In one lake a perch had registered 137 bq, in another 5,523. On Lillorsjon Lake a small salmon had registered 13,770 bq. Many trout had 6,000 to 20,000 bq. Berries were just above the limit, but mushrooms had absorbed a lot of caesium and one picked outside Lycksele, a nearby town, had 4,984 bq.

The elk hunting season, a national pastime in Sweden, had just begun. The Umeå daily newspaper, *Västerbottens-Kuriren*, showed a photograph of a contaminated elk calf being buried in a shallow pit in Nordmaling County, sixty kilometres south of Umeå. It had a reading of 2,400 bq. An old man in hunting cap and gun told me as he set out into the woods, "What you can't see won't hurt you." His younger friend remarked, "It's all right for him. But I don't want cancer ten years from now. I'm shooting for sport only."

It was fourteen months before the Kremlin permitted foreign correspondents to visit the site of the nuclear accident itself. The culture of secrecy was so embedded in Soviet society that nothing was published in Moscow about becquerel levels or on how to measure contamination. I could find no information in the Russian media about the source of vegetables, meat, poultry and fish being sold to the public. The authorities had banned the sale of food from an exclusion zone around the stricken power plant, but little account had been taken of wind or rainfall that might have affected crops and animals in other regions.

When the media ban was lifted, I was driven with nine other correspondents from the Ukrainian capital, Kiev, to Chernobyl in June 1987. The thirty-kilometre exclusion area around the power plant was like a war zone. No civilians were allowed to enter without an escort. The only traffic consisted of lorries and buses carrying soldiers wearing white face-masks and water trucks that patrolled the roads day and night to keep down the dust. The gardens and orchards of abandoned villages were overgrown and unpaved side streets were choked with grass and dandelions. In open country the grain crop had reseeded, producing vast expanses of waist-high spring wheat mixed with weeds. All 135,000 people in the zone had been evacuated. A hose pipe continuously flooded the steps at the entrance to the single-storey Communist Party headquarters in Chernobyl, eighteen kilometres from the plant. Here an official instructed us not to use air-conditioning in our mini-bus, nor to enter the forest, nor to drink spring water. He also warned us to avoid smoking, even as he lit up a Kosmos cigarette with nicotine-stained fingers and inhaled deeply.

The workers' town of Pripet beside the power plant had been abandoned and resembled a scene from *The Day After*, the 1983 American TV film showing the after-effects of nuclear war on a town in Kansas. All 50,000 inhabitants had been evacuated in a fleet of 1,200 buses in two hours on the afternoon of 28 April 1986, two days after the explosion, apart from two old women, aged seventy-two and eighty-five, who remained hidden for six weeks living on tinned food. The evacuees were told they would be able to return in three days, so they had left everything behind. Radioactive dust had contaminated trees, grass, soil, cars, bicycles, prams, swings, slides, washing still on the line, chairs, beds, kettles, picture frames, books – everything in contact with the air. Not a single item could be taken away. On the balcony of a second-floor apartment, a vest, two shirts, a sheet and two pairs of socks were hanging on a line where they had been drying for 412 days. Nothing stirred around the empty Prometheus Cinema, the Forest Glade Hotel or the huge red portrait of Lenin in the main square, except for little eddies of sand spiralling across the asphalt in the hot breeze and drifting against the kerbstones. All the topsoil in the parks had been trucked away and replaced with sand. Three-hundred dust-covered Lada, Moskvich and Volga cars and dozens of Minsk and Yava motorcycles were parked along a side road. The pine trees that shaded them were brown and withered, killed by the radioactivity. In a government greenhouse, however, Professor Nikolai Arkhipov had established that heavy fertilising with calcium enabled him to grow uncontaminated cucumbers and strawberries. We trustingly ate a couple of strawberries he offered us.

The Chernobyl nuclear power station, with its hundreds of electricity pylons, stood in the centre of a vast man-made desert of imported sand. At the entrance to the plant, where two reactors were still working, pop music was playing. A poster showed a nuclear missile crushed by a huge fist, and the words, "We say no to nuclear madness". We were allowed to observe, from a distance of 500 metres, and only for a few minutes, the stricken reactor No. 4, entombed in concrete and black metal, and resembling the hulk of an upturned ocean liner. A Foreign Ministry official with me switched on his Geiger counter. He told me it was registering 12.8 millirems of radioactivity, one hundred times that in the town of Chernobyl, meaning we were standing on a "hot spot". We moved quickly away. We were not wearing any protective clothing. Officials advised us to get rid of our shoes when we returned to Moscow. (I packed them in plastic and tossed them down the rubbish chute in my apartment, there being no other way to dispose of radioactive material.)

As I gazed at the black tomb that day, I recalled the words of Bessmertny, a character in a play about Chernobyl written by Vladimir Gubaryev, the science editor of *Pravda*, who had given me a copy of his text. "Tens of thousands of years ahead, none of us will be here . . . Even the pyramids of Egypt will be just a handful of dust, yet the sarcophagus around this reactor of yours will still be standing. That's some monument to leave our descendants, isn't it?" The fact that an editor of *Pravda*, the official organ of the Communist Party, could pen such challenging lines, indicated the extent of disaffection, even in the controlled Soviet media, with the inept party leadership. Chernobyl compounded the sense of crisis in a society that in so many other ways was failing its citizens.

No one knows exactly how many people lost their lives because of the Chernobyl disaster. In 2005 the Chernobyl Forum, led by the International Atomic Energy Agency and World Health Organisation, attributed fifty-six direct deaths and a possible further 4,000 deaths due to cancer caused by radioactivity. Using data from the Belarus National Academy of Sciences, Greenpeace estimated that 270,000 people in the affected region would develop cancer, of whom 93,000 would die. The exclusion zone, much smaller now, has become a haven for wildlife.

In Sweden, caesium levels remain high in mushrooms and freshwater fish, though reindeer meat can be eaten again. In contrast with 1986, there is much improved co-operation with the Russians on an international emergency warning system. If there ever is to be a next time, it will be Russian scientists who alert Sweden, not the other way around.

11

The End of History

In January 1987, Mikhail Gorbachev released the former nuclear scientist Andrei Sakharov from internal exile in the closed city of Gorky, now Nizhny Novgorod, where he had been confined since 1980 for his opposition to the occupation of Afghanistan. It was the first crack in the totalitarian system Gorbachev had inherited as General Secretary of the Communist Party. From then on we could measure the pace of change in the Soviet Union by the steps taken towards Sakharov's full rehabilitation.

Unsure how far it could go, the official media at first continued to treat Sakharov as a non-person. Then in mid-1987 *Moscow News* carried his comments on a daring human rights play. In November it published an interview with Sakharov about Stalin's crimes, a hitherto taboo subject. This caused a minor sensation. In December, *Moscow News* went further, calling, in an editorial, for the release of all political prisoners. Finally, on 3 June 1988, the Foreign Ministry hosted a press conference for Sakharov to allow him to cope with requests for access from scores of American correspondents who had arrived in Moscow for a visit by President Ronald Reagan. The balding, bespectacled scientist told us, "Mikhail Gorbachev, an outstanding statesman, deserves trust and should be given a chance. From the bottom of my heart I wish him luck." The Soviet journalists at the press conference applauded loudly. Gorbachev had won over the highly respected Nobel Prize winner as his ally in his struggle to strengthen socialism and give it a more human face.

Gorbachev at that time was at the height of his power and authority. He and his elegant, attractive wife, Raisa, were treated as celebrities abroad. Margaret Thatcher, who famously said she could do business with him, came to Moscow and enthused about making a better world together. She also entertained Sakharov and his wife Yelena Bonner to lunch in the British embassy and visited the Monastery of St Sergius in Zagorsk, where during a rather chaotic walkabout I found myself chatting with the Iron Lady while Soviet officials slammed a gate behind us in the face of the British Foreign Secretary, Sir Geoffrey Howe, whom they did not recognise.

We foreign correspondents hung on Gorbachev's every word, checking his speeches for new information on how the wind was blowing. But there were signs that his popularity among ordinary people was waning. Nothing on the ground improved. One day, when I enthused about his latest speech, a Russian friend retorted dismissively, "*Mnogo slov!*" – "A lot of words!" People suspected that Gorbachev was not really serious about radical reform, and that in any case his many decrees were being ignored by the entrenched bureaucracy and party apparatchiks.

At that time the Soviet Union was teetering on the brink of economic collapse. Chronic shortages in government stores were growing worse, mainly because of the inefficiency of state factories and badly run collective farms. The industrial and agricultural infrastructure was practically beyond repair after decades of neglect and lack of investment. State control of commerce had sucked energy and initiative from the economy. There was little incentive to make money because there was practically nothing to buy. Almost everything was *deficit*. People came from the neglected provinces to shop in Moscow, only to find that here, too, goods were in short supply. A popular anecdote told of a country visitor asking a Muscovite for directions to a shop called "Principle" and being told that there was no such store. He insisted there was, saying he had heard that "in Moscow, in Principle, there's everything". Another described a woman going into a shop and asking "Have you no meat?" and being told, "No, here we have no fish; next door they have no meat." If it wasn't for the fact that most Russians stored fruit and vegetables harvested from garden plots there would have been real hunger in winter. A cut-back on vodka production to combat alcoholism also increased popular frustration. It led to long queues, profiteering and the home production of illicit and sometimes lethal spirits known as *samagon*, which used up scarce sugar supplies.

The shortages got steadily worse. Just after I arrived I counted seventy items in my local supermarket. Three years later I found only three products for sale: matches, cooking oil and sausage (inedible). Things got so bad that many western governments organised food parcels. I went out with a Red Cross worker visiting bereft pensioners in the Moscow suburbs. The most wretched scene I witnessed was a bed-ridden woman in her eighties, weeping after she opened a package from Germany. "And to think we were the victors," she said. The parcel contained marzipan bars and cigarettes.

Foreigners in Moscow, on the other hand, could buy fruit, meat, vegetables, beer and spirits in a half-dozen foreign currency stores. Soviet citizens were not allowed to hold foreign currency, and this created a humiliating apartheid for them.

Another simmering cause of discontent was the continuing suppression of religion. Russia was a land of both physical and spiritual devastation. All across the country, once-beautiful churches with the typical five domes and Greek crosses had been transformed into storage rooms, or lay empty and vandalised. Tolgsky Convent of the Entry into Jerusalem, for example, situated on the Volga, 250 kilometres north of Moscow, which had been one of the finest centres of pre-revolutionary art, had been turned into a juvenile prison camp. I found the biggest church in the complex, the Vidyensky Cathedral, had been flooded and used as a swimming pool and a smaller church converted into a cinema. One of the first things Gorbachev did was restore such properties to the Russian Orthodox Church. In July 1990, the Tolgsky convent became operational again, with over 100 nuns in residence and its own farm, poultry-yard, greenhouses and an apiary.

The first person inside the party leadership to challenge Gorbachev to move more quickly was Boris Yeltsin, a heavily built, somewhat ponderous Siberian with pig-like eyes and a strong-boned face. As party boss in Sverdlovsk, now Yekaterinburg, he had been a typical *apparatchik*, lacking charisma and given to wooden oratory. When I went to Sverdlovsk to research his background, local people took me to see the ruined site of Ipatiev House where the last Russian tsar had been killed by the Red Army, and which Yeltsin had ordered destroyed to prevent it becoming a place of royalist pilgrimage. They also complained that he had used public funds to erect a monstrosity of a party headquarters, known as the "White Tooth". However, Yeltsin was able to galvanise people and get things done and Gorbachev promoted him in 1985 to Moscow party chief and member of the Politburo of the Communist Party, the "cabinet" of a dozen or so top comrades who effectively ruled the Soviet Union.

Yeltsin surprised his new comrades by breaking some leadership conventions. Instead of barrelling through the city in a Zil limousine with darkened windows, he rode on the metro and asked people in stores how they lived. He took the idea of reform seriously, declaring at a party conference that communism had failed to feed and clothe the people with decency. In the summer of 1987 he encouraged informal political groups to come together to discuss *perestroika*, and he ensured

The north tower of the World Trade Center, just after the first plane struck, as seen from the *Irish Times* New York office, on 11 September 2001

The scene on 9/11 on the cover of *The Economist*; the *Irish Times* office was at the top of the tall shoreline building on the left

Thick dust coats my
neighbourhood after the
collapse of the second
tower on 9/11

View from *Irish Times*
New York office in the
days after 9/11

"Captured" by Russian invader, Afghanistan, 1980

With the Mujahidin and captured Russian rocket launcher in Afghanistan,
August 1980

Acting the tough guy with
Israeli army officer, on the
border with Lebanon, 1979

PHOTO: PAT LANGAN

Acting the tough guy again – this time with PLO officials in Beirut, 1979

PHOTO: PAT LANGAN

Popping a question to Pope John Paul II, en route to Ireland, September 1979

Escorting Margaret Thatcher, in Zagorsk, Russia, March 1987

Tolgsky Monastery, Russia, 1988, in transition from prison camp to convent

Pro-Yeltsin demonstration in Moscow, 1989

Former camp inmate,
Yuri Chernev, leading
1989 anti-Soviet rally
in Moscow

Organised resistance:
Latvian workers
barricade streets in
Riga against Soviet
troops, 1991

Below:
Rally for Lithuanian
independence, Vilnius,
January 1990

Above:
Demonstrators at 1990 rally in Vilnius, claiming that the Lithuanian independence movement was "Nazism"

Left:
Soviet minder Nikolai, with difficult journalist from the capitalist west, in Russia, 1980

Ararat, with family friend Lisa, shortly before he was assassinated in June 2003

they got premises for their meetings. It was unheard of before then to allow quasi political events to take place without party discipline. One foggy autumn evening I was smuggled into one of these meetings in a fifth-floor conference room of the Institute of Mathematics and Economics, by an Irish student, John Murray (who later became head of the Department of Russian and Slavonic Studies at Trinity College Dublin). It was chaotic. There were accusations that some speakers were spies for the KGB or the CIA, or both. But one demand was approved: that a memorial be erected for the victims of Stalin. This was going far beyond talk of simple "reconstruction".

On 21 October 1987 Yeltsin shocked a meeting of the party's Central Committee by delivering a scathing lecture on the failures of the revolution and criticising the routine sycophantic praise being heaped on the leadership. Gorbachev was furious. He asked Yeltsin if he was "so politically illiterate that he needed glasses" and accused him of "hypertrophied self-esteem". Yeltsin promptly resigned from the Politburo. Rumours swept the city about this confrontation. An official account of the meeting was leaked and I soon acquired a copy. It revealed that Yeltsin was on his own. A special meeting of the Moscow party was called, attended by Gorbachev, at which savage attacks were made on the troublesome Siberian, who was then forced out of his job as Moscow city boss.

While Yeltsin depicted Gorbachev as timid, autocratic and fond of half-measures, the social set around the Soviet leader in turn despised Yeltsin for pushing too quickly and crudely for change and for grandstanding to the crowd. A prominent member of the Soviet elite, Oleg Troyanovsky, who was Soviet Ambassador to China from 1986 to 1990, poured scorn on Yeltsin over dinner one evening at my home, calling him an ignorant bumpkin who disgraced Russia abroad. Many diplomats and correspondents at the time, dazzled by Gorbachev's oratory and impressed by his sophistication, shared this view.

The *narod*, the common people, saw Yeltsin differently. The largely passive Russians, intimidated and indoctrinated to support the Communist Party, had never shown much sympathy for dissidents, but they could rally behind a party figure who trumpeted their complaints and rejected privilege. Yeltsin articulated the suspicions of rank-and-file party members and factory employees that they were getting a raw deal, while an army of hated and corrupt bureaucrats led a comparatively comfortable, privileged life.

Yeltsin did not help his own case. He withdrew from public view, after being given the humiliating post of Deputy Minister for Construction. He attempted suicide, according to a close colleague, as *Pravda* led a smear campaign against him. The party newspaper reported that Yeltsin had been drunk during a lecture delivered in the United States (he clearly was). For months the issue of Yeltsin simmered on the surface of Russian political life. It was this, more than anything else, that in the spring and summer of 1988 turned the streets of Moscow, where unauthorised demonstrations were normally broken up, into a series of debating chambers. Small crowds began gathering regularly on the Old Arbat, the pedestrian walkway in the centre of Moscow, to join in swirling arguments about Yeltsin. These soon evolved to include "forbidden" topics such as the war in Afghanistan, shortages, Stalin, injustices and all the grievances for which citizens had no other outlet. People began losing their fear and wearing Yeltsin lapel badges. At a large informal gathering in Gorky Street (now Tverskaya Street) I once heard a young man in a leather jacket shout through a megaphone, "They got rid of Boris Yeltsin; they must be stopped." The crowd responded by shouting, "Yel-tsin, Yel-tsin".

Under pressure at home and abroad to end totalitarian rule, Gorbachev announced in 1988 that, as an experiment in democracy, the non-elected Supreme Soviet would be replaced by a Supreme Soviet chosen by a Congress of People's Deputies of 2,250 members, 1,500 of whom would be elected in multicandidate elections. What he didn't bargain for was that Yeltsin would be one of the candidates in the election. One day in the autumn of 1988 I got word that Yeltsin was making his first public appearance since his disgrace, at Moscow University on Gertsen Street near the Kremlin. When I reached the lecture hall, the students were so tightly packed around the entrance that I could hardly squeeze in, and I was unable to write down his words in the unbearable crush. Students fainted and were lifted over our heads by a forest of hands. It was the old Yeltsin, castigating party members who held to outdated dogmas. When the election campaign got under way, party hacks tried to keep him off the ballot, but were outmanoeuvred by pro-Yeltsin officials who were growing in number in the *apparat*.

On election day, 26 March 1989, Mikhail and Raisa Gorbachev arrived to vote at an old palace in Lenin Hills serving as a polling station. They strolled through the grounds accompanied only by a couple of security men. How easy it would have been to get a quick interview with him along the way, I thought. I positioned myself beside some bushes to snatch a few words on his way back. When he emerged, however, he gave a long press conference to my colleagues congregated outside the polling booth, while I stood in the rain on the empty path. When he finished and approached me, one of his two security men simply pushed me and my notebook into the bushes and the small party swept by. I rushed over to the Palace of Pioneers in Frunze district, where Yeltsin was voting. There was a such a scramble by journalists trying to interview him that one of the polling booths was knocked over. Yeltsin was trapped and reluctantly talked to us. His eyes intense and staring, he accused the party of dirty tricks against him. "One could write not a novel but a thriller about it," he said. He got six million votes, some ninety per cent of the greater Moscow turnout, a powerful endorsement of his criticism of the party elite. Andrei Sakharov was also elected a deputy, representing the Academy of Sciences.

On 25 May, when the Congress met in the concrete and glass Palace of Congresses inside the Kremlin walls, Russia experienced more democratic openness than at any time since before the Bolshevik Revolution. One of the most secretive institutions in the world suddenly became an open talking shop. There was free-wheeling debate matching the verbal anarchy of the streets, and, for the first time, open discussion about the "blank pages" of Soviet history, especially the murderous repression of the Stalin era and the secret protocols of the Hitler–Stalin pact annexing the Baltic states. We watched and participated in discussions in the vast lobby of the Palace of Congresses and in the Moscow Hotel, the grim concrete building just off Red Square where the deputies were staying and where late evening meetings were held in a haze of blue smoke from Russian cigarettes. We became familiar with the rhetoric of Russian political conversation, and especially the habit of ending a long dissertation with the words, "That's the first point, now the second point."

The Congress was a triumph for Gorbachev's policy of *glasnost*. He decreed that the debates be televised live throughout the USSR. Millions of watching citizens got a crash course in the Soviet Union's forbidden history – which had the unintended consequence of undermining the very legitimacy of the communist state. However, the Congress had what historian-deputy Yuri Afanasyev termed an "aggressive, obedient majority" who would support the party line, come what may. So, despite his huge Moscow vote, Yeltsin was at first excluded from the new Supreme Soviet, the 542-member working parliament elected by the Congress, though he was quickly given a place when thousands of demonstrators took to the streets outside the Kremlin in protest. Sakharov was constantly interrupted by cat-calls when he took the podium to call for an immediate end to the repressions under the Stalinist model. During his speech a visibly agitated Gorbachev switched off Sakharov's microphone.

People watching on television were outraged. Many never forgave Gorbachev this one arbitrary act of censorship.

Six months later, on 15 December 1989, Andrei Sakharov died in his tiny apartment at 48B Chkalov Street near Taganskaya Square where he had held court since his release from exile, dressed typically in a cardigan and slippers. Aged sixty-eight and worn out by his exertions, he suffered a heart attack while writing a speech for the second meeting of the Congress. By chance I arrived with *Irish Times* driver Valery Chervyakov just as his body was being taken from the apartment in a white station wagon with ambulance markings. Curious to know what was to become of the remains of the Soviet Union's most prominent and beloved dissident, we followed the ambulance through city-centre streets, where policemen on duty manipulated traffic lights to ensure that it did not have to stop. We drove along Kutuzovsky Prospect and out the Minsk Highway on to the Rublyovskoye Highway. The little convoy then spun right in a cloud of powder snow towards a white marble building and Sakharov's body, in a green bag, was taken inside on a stretcher. The building was the Kremlin's private morgue. The Nobel physicist, who never flagged in his fight for human rights, had become an icon not only to the people but to the establishment he had castigated. The next day Sakharov was taken from the morgue, where his brain had been removed for scientific inspection, to lie in state in Moscow's Youth Palace. Thousands of people queued for hours in driving snow to shuffle by the flower-strewn bier, where haunting movements by Brahms were played by a string quartet. A woman cried out as she passed the body, "Who killed Sakharov? Those who dictate and the usurpers of power!" She was gently urged to keep moving. Boris Yeltsin came and stood for ten minutes, wearing a black and red mourning band on his sleeve. Gorbachev and five Politburo members also arrived to say a last farewell.

Gorbachev moved steadily to the right in the following months, as the reform movement threatened to spin out of control and fatally erode Communist Party authority. He surrounded himself with old-style conservatives. This manifested itself in an even more dramatic Congress session in December 1990. Few paid much attention during the ten-day event to a nondescript neo-Stalinist deputy called Gennady Yanayev, with the rheumy eyes of a heavy drinker – until Gorbachev proposed him as his vice-president, only a heartbeat away from the presidency. Yanayev failed by thirty-one votes to get endorsed. Gorbachev could not disguise his anger. He told the deputies they would have to vote again and this time it would be a vote of confidence in him. They endorsed his nominee in the second vote. No one could understand why he did it.

It was at this Congress that things began to fall apart for Gorbachev. The reform-minded Foreign Minister, Eduard Shevardnadze, who was unpopular with the old guard for his role in dismantling the Soviet military structure in Eastern Europe, scrapped his planned speech and accused from the podium two colonel-deputies of waging a campaign to settle scores with him and like-minded ministers. "Reformers have taken to the hills," he told a silent hall. "A dictatorship is on the offensive . . . I cannot reconcile myself with what is happening. I am resigning." In the pandemonium in the lobby afterwards, I noticed Alexander Yakovlev, one of the top reformers still in Gorbachev's Politburo, quietly heading for a side door in his overcoat and flat cap. "Is it the end of *perestroika?*" I asked him. "Well it doesn't depend on one person, but there are signs that the extreme right is holding its head high and has a glint in its eye," he told me, before walking off into the darkness. In the centre of the foyer, the bald and bespectacled Colonel Nikolai Petroshenko, one of the extreme-right colonels named by Shevardnadze (and who reminded me of the actor Phil Silvers in his role as "Sergeant Bilko"), went from group to group in high excitement, claiming that the real dictatorships were not in

Moscow, but in the republics, where Russians were suffering under nationalist leaders rebelling against Moscow rule.

During these days of impending crisis, western leaders continued to place their faith in Gorbachev and to treat Boris Yeltsin as an uncouth *muzhik* from Siberia, even after Yeltsin was elected chairman of the Russian Federation, one of the fifteen Soviet Republics, in May 1990. In the spring of 1991, British Prime Minister John Major snubbed the Russian leader on a trip to Moscow, and the same year Yeltsin was introduced at a meeting of the Socialist Group in Brussels as a "demagogue". Few world figures recognised that Yeltsin was the political leader best able and most inclined to offer the Russian people a way out of the paralysis, chaos, inefficiency and despair brought about by the failed communist experiment that Gorbachev was trying to reform. Nor did they fully appreciate the significance of the fact that there had been a steady defection of the best and brightest reformers and intellectuals into the Yeltsin camp, leaving Gorbachev surrounded by, and accountable to, hardliners like interior minister Boris Pugo, defence minister Dmitri Yazov and KGB chief Vladimir Kryuchkov. The more democracy-minded members of the Russian intelligentsia knew the score better. With only a narrow base of support in the big cities, the intellectuals were drawn into the Yeltsin camp because they sensed that he rather than Gorbachev could carry them along to their goal of a democratic Russia. They alone could not hope to sway the masses or persuade the military to switch sides in a crisis and bring about the demise of communism.

While aligning himself with the right in defence of the integrity of the Soviet Union, Gorbachev still embraced *glasnost* as a way of easing internal tensions. In 1990 he restored citizenship to the writer Alexander Solzhenitsyn, who had once enraged the Kremlin with his searing books about Soviet prison camps and who was living in enforced exile in the United States. The response by the author of *The Gulag Archipelago*, that "the clock of communism has struck its final hour", was widely publicised in the Soviet media. During this flowering of *glasnost*, writers, musicians and poets who had been suppressed found publishers again, and practically all the Soviet newspapers became platforms for free-wheeling debate about previously forbidden topics.

As former exiles returned to Moscow, Gorbachev's culture minister, actor Nikolai Gubenko – like Gorbachev a reform-minded communist who today is a Communist Party deputy in Russia's Duma – organised one of the most emotional of homecomings, that of Mstislav Rostropovich. Banished from Russia in 1978 for his defence of Solzhenitsyn, the cellist and conductor was allowed to return in February 1990. Gubenko introduced the slight, balding musician to the press at the Foreign Ministry in Moscow. "When I left the Soviet Union, it was a big island of lies," said Rostropovich, "but now the Soviet Union is cleaning itself of lies." His wife, the Bolshoi opera singer Galina Vishnevskaya, her eyes flashing with anger, recalled the "barbarous act" of Leonid Brezhnev (who had once tried to seduce her) in revoking their passports.

The next night I joined hundreds of excited Muscovites, slipping and sliding over icy footpaths to crowd into the Moscow Conservatory to see Rostropovich take the stage. Every seat and aisle was crammed with music-lovers who erupted in cheering when he appeared. Leading the applause was Galina, seated in a box beside the stage, jewellery glittering defiantly on her black costume. Beside her, Raisa Gorbachev clapped enthusiastically. The last time Rostropovich had played here, in 1971, the high-ceilinged hall had tingled with electricity as the slight, bearded figure of Solzhenitsyn appeared in the audience. That evening, as we listened to Rostropovich perform Dvorák's Cello Concerto, the electricity sparked again across the auditorium, making it one of the most memorable moments in the struggle of freedom over totalitarianism in Russia.

Karl Marx, the father of communism, inspired the party over which Gorbachev presided with his famous prediction that communism was "the end of pre-history". Far from resuscitating socialism, Gorbachev now faced what the American writer Francis Fukuyama hailed in a 1989 essay as "the end of history" – the end point of mankind's ideological evolution, and the universalisation of western liberal democracy as the final form of human government. It was a common, if understandable, misconception on Gorbachev's part as the Cold War neared its end with the collapse of Soviet communism that the relentless advance of unfettered capitalism could be held in check by a kinder, gentler form of socialism.

12

Spoiled Forever

As the authority of the Kremlin waned, the forces of independence began to assert themselves in the Baltic republics of Estonia, Latvia and Lithuania, which had been annexed by Stalin in 1940. I began commuting by overnight train to Tallinn, the capital of Estonia, the smallest but initially the most rebellious of the three, equipped with a bottle of cognac and a pack of cards to pass the evening with colleagues. An attendant would wake us in the morning at Tallinn railway station with glasses of hot tea. We would get out and stretch our legs in the medieval streets and squares around the fourteenth-century town hall, which provided a glimpse of the Baltic city in bygone days.

By the late 1980s, the Central-European character of Tallinn was under serious threat. The Russian Orthodox cathedral of St Alexander Nevsky crowned a hill in the old town and Soviet-style apartment blocks dominated the suburbs. The railway station timetables were printed in Russian only. The city was policed by militiamen from all over the Soviet Union. The bills in the biggest hotel, the Viru, were made out in Russian, though most of the customers were Finns who came from Helsinki by ferry at weekends for the cheap booze. The Soviet Communist Party newspaper, *Pravda*, was, as required, placed on the top of the folded newspapers at every street kiosk. Russians were everywhere. The Russification of Estonia had been proceeding steadily since the end of the Second World War. By 1987 half the people living in Tallinn were Russian speakers from Russia, Ukraine, Byelorussia and other Soviet republics, compared to a third a decade earlier. There was much local animosity towards these newcomers. Once when I spoke in Russian to a shop assistant, she put her nose in the air and turned away. Most of the Russian immigrants were industrial workers, and many Estonians saw themselves as intellectually superior. Native Estonians dominated communications and the arts. When I went to give an interview on Tallinn radio, I found the cleaners were Russian women, and the editorial staff were all Estonian.

I enjoyed going to Tallinn because Estonians made a fuss of western reporters. We were their conduit to the outside world at a time when they sensed that Soviet power was weakening, and they sought every opportunity to make their case internationally for independence. Another attraction was the good coffee and delicious German-type pastries that were unavailable in Moscow. Here too, however, the chronic shortages afflicting the Soviet Union meant that shelves were often empty, and the restaurants sometimes ran out of drink, at least officially, allowing an underground economy to flourish.

One evening when I went with Rupert Cornwell of the London *Independent* to a restaurant where all liquid stocks had been exhausted, we had to buy a black-market bottle of vodka from the doorman, who warned us to keep it hidden. So we placed it under the table, occasionally sneaking a refill. We spotted other diners doing the same and, at one table, three men were enjoying a suspiciously clear liquid they poured from a teapot.

The Estonians were the most westernised of the Soviet nationalities, and being so close to Finland, and avid viewers of television programmes beamed from nearby Helsinki, they knew well how the consumer-driven world of the West was passing them by and how pro-democracy agitation in Moscow was weakening the Stalinist nature of Russian control.

If one man can be credited with being the first to seize the opportunity opened up by Gorbachev's reforms to lead his country out of the Soviet Union, it was Edgar Savisaar, the portly and bespectacled head of Estonia's state planning committee. Savisaar suggested in a television programme in the spring of 1988 that it would be a good idea to set up a "popular front", uniting all the different strands of Estonian society, including the Communist Party, the churches, the universities and the cultural organisations, with the aim of carrying out the reforms being encouraged by Gorbachev for the republics, such as *khozraschot*, or self-financing. The sixteen participants stayed on in the studio to work out a declaration incorporating this idea, which the leaders of the Estonian Communist Party, many of them closet subversives, approved the next day. It was sent to Moscow. It was a daring, even audacious, move as it subverted absolute Communist Party control, but Gorbachev could hardly object. Tens of thousands turned out for the first rally of the Estonian Popular Front in Tallinn's Pevcheskiy Field on 17 June that year.

The popularity of the movement, and the acquiescence of Moscow, emboldened civic leaders in the tiny republic. With a sophisticated, north European sense of political finesse, the Estonians kept pushing the door further open. Seven months later, on 24 February 1989, the anniversary of the day the tiny republic gained its short-lived independence between the two world wars, they symbolically raised the banner of freedom again. At precisely 8.33 a.m., as the sun rose above the horizon, the blue, black and white flag of independent Estonia, banned as an official emblem since the Soviet annexation of the republic in 1940, was hoisted over the Danish stone tower known as Pikk Hermann, to the cheers of tens of thousands of Estonians massed in a park below. The standard of Soviet Estonia, with its hammer and sickle, had been hauled down at dusk the previous evening and consigned to the city museum. Savisaar drew huge cheers that morning when he declared, "The flag taken down yesterday had no respect among Estonians . . . The raising of the Estonian flag shows we are masters in our own land. God Save Estonia."

It was a breathtaking act of defiance of Moscow and it had local Communist Party support. I saw the slim figure of Estonian Communist leader, Vaino Vajlas, among the men taking off their hats and fluttering them in the air. "Twenty years of independence spoiled us forever," Estonian radio broadcaster Maarika Saarna told me over the noise of cheering, explaining the desire to restore the freedom that Estonia, along with its Baltic neighbours, Latvia and Lithuania, had enjoyed before Stalin's tanks had rolled in. Celebrations of the flag-raising went on all day, culminating in an extravagant pageant in a Tallinn concert hall. Here I witnessed hundreds of members of the Estonian intelligentsia cheering and throwing flowers. A choir in evening dress sang, "I want to love you, Estonia, to my death". A colour guard of youths clenched their fists around the flag poles with a determination and anger that reminded me of young men at Provisional IRA ceremonial events in the 1970s.

On that day, Estonia psychologically left the Union of Soviet Socialist Republics and the whole artificial edifice of the Soviet Union began to unravel, though it would be nearly three years before it would finally fall apart.

The Russian population in Estonia remained passive during these nationalistic displays. There was no anti-Home Rule movement of the type seen in the north of Ireland a century earlier when Irish nationalism was on the rise, not even in the north-eastern Estonian city of Narva where most residents were Russian. Unlike Irish unionists, their roots in Estonia were shallow and they had no attachment to the land. The majority had come in living memory to work in the big industrial enterprises that Moscow had established on the Baltic coast, attracted by slightly better living conditions. Indeed, some welcomed the prospect of greater independence from Moscow. There was a popular anecdote at the time about a Russian who came to live in the Baltics in the hope that one day he would wake up abroad. What most concerned them was the prospect of having to learn Estonian. Russian workers, coming home exhausted after toiling in the factories, had little enthusiasm for studying a difficult foreign tongue with fourteen different case endings.

Latvians, too, yearned to get back the independence they had enjoyed between the wars after centuries of domination by Swedes, Germans and Russians. Time was not on their side. In 1940 Latvians constituted seventy-five per cent of the population of Latvia, but by 1989 this had fallen to just over fifty per cent. In the capital Riga, where a million people lived, only one in three was Latvian, the result of Soviet industrialisation and planned large-scale immigration.

The Latvians took their cue from Estonia, and founded their own popular front some weeks after the Estonians had founded theirs. Among the 1,000 people who turned out for its initial congress in Riga were former political prisoners intent on pushing towards independence, and Communist Party conservatives determined to hold it back. They were addressed by members of the Latvian intelligentsia, many of them passionate academics in goatee beards. Their often subversive debates were broadcast live to incredulous people in the city's cafés and barber shops.

Janis Rukshans, a long-haired member of the Latvian Communist Party with gaunt face and blazing eyes, brought cheering delegates to their feet with his accusation that the country had been occupied and the economy destroyed by criminals. To cries of "Get up!" the party First Secretary, Jan Vigris, and his colleagues, Russianised Latvians in identical grey suits, sheepishly rose from their seats to join the applause. Rukshans, I noticed, was wearing a tie with the initials NIDG – the Northern Ireland Daffodil Growers' association. He told me he got it on a visit to County Armagh to buy daffodil bulbs for his private flower business. I asked him how, as a party member, he could engage in capitalism. "This is Latvia, I'm a Latvian," cried Rukshans, who would later be recognised as a world authority on daffodils.

A doctor of philosophy at the Congress, Vilnis Zarens, told me, as we ate cream puffs during a break, "We want the same rights as independent nations; we don't want the destruction of our language and culture as happened in Ireland."

Historically there was always a Russian presence in Latvia but it was never very significant. Between the world wars the Russian community in Riga consisted of little more than a few embittered exiled aristocrats with no estates to go home to, as the Irish writer Hubert Butler put it in an essay, "Riga Strand in 1930". Many of these émigré Russians lived in near-poverty along Riga Strand, a thirty-three kilometre beach of white quartz sand backed by pine trees, which before the First World War had been the playground of wealthy overlords from tsarist Russia. During its inter-war independence, Latvians had taken over the Victorian-style stone villas and *dachas*. Men bathed nude before 10.00 a.m. and from then until noon the women had it to themselves. Butler described how holidaymakers came from Finland, Germany and Poland to enjoy the strand, and youths from the ten per cent Jewish population of Riga gathered to sing songs in the evenings around bonfires on the sand.

All that ended when Latvia was occupied by the Soviet Union in 1940 and invaded by Nazi Germany in 1941, and barbed wire replaced the beach umbrellas. A third of the Latvian population was exterminated under Hitler, or sent to the gulag by Stalin after Soviet power was restored in 1945. Only 1,000 Latvian Jews survived the war.

Eduard Berklavs remembered the Soviet tanks arriving at the start of the war. He was then twenty-four and a member of Latvia's pro-Soviet Communist Party. With other Latvian communists, he was summoned to the Soviet embassy and given the names of the new pro-Moscow government by the Soviet deputy commissar for foreign affairs, Andrei Vyshinsky, notorious for his prosecution of the Moscow show trials in the 1930s. Berklavs became Latvia's Communist Party boss in 1958. When he and other nationalist-minded communists tried to use their position to stop the influx of Russian immigrants and protect the language, he was stripped of power and exiled to the Russian town of Vladimir. Just after the Latvian Popular Front was formed, I went to meet the seventy-two-year-old Berklavs in the Latvia Hotel, a typical Soviet concrete tower deliberately built a metre higher than the thirteenth-century Church of St Peter, patron saint of Riga. Berklavs was, in his way, Eastern Europe's first Dubcek, and like the Czechoslovakian Communist Party leader, a reformer ahead of his time. Now, he told me, only independence could save Latvia for the Latvians.

Inspired by Butler's essay I went one cold March afternoon in 1990 to Riga Strand, taking the wide commuter train from Riga with its curved wooden benches like garden seats. I got out at Jurmala, one of seven holiday villages. Russian enterprises and trade unions had taken over the Victorian-style stone villas, and built concrete and glass sanatoria for the Russian proletariat. The Soviet Interior Minister, Boris Pugo, who was advocating in Moscow that the popular fronts be crushed by force, had a holiday mansion here. Retired Soviet officers and factory directors in trilby hats, with spouses in bulky overcoats, strolled along the water's edge far into the distance.

The wartime barbed wire had gone, but any holidaymakers who came to Riga that year were prisoners on the sands, because Soviet industries had made the sea too polluted for swimming.

Lithuania was the last of the three Baltic republics to revive its dream of independence. Here nationalism was intertwined with religion. Lithuania was a Roman Catholic country of three-and-a-half million people. Since its annexation in 1940, the Kremlin had tried to control the influence of the Vatican by imprisoning the most outspoken priests, and converting many places of worship into public halls and museums. The Church of St Kazimieras, located in a cobbled Vilnius street where women in black shawls sold medals beneath wrought-iron balconies overflowing with geraniums, was designated a museum of atheism. Inside I found a replica of the first manned space capsule, along with the words of astronaut Yuri Gagarin, "I didn't see any God up there."

The communist rulers of Lithuania monitored the clergy so closely that when I went to talk to Monsignor Juanas Tunaitas, secretary to the Lithuanian Catholic Church, early in 1988, a state official sat in on the conversation. The monsignor's reception room could have been the parlour of any parochial house in Ireland, with a picture of St Joseph on the wall, a potted aspidistra on the polished wooden floor and a crucifix over the sideboard. Monsignor Tunaitas was extremely careful when discussing church–state relations in front of the government representative. He acknowledged uneasily that several priests and bishops were in prison for "anti-Soviet activity". When I asked him about the museum of atheism, he gave a slight cough: "Everyone has the right to believe or not to believe."

On 23 October 1988, four months after Estonia showed the way, Lithuanians founded their own popular front, called *Sajudis*. The founding congress of *Sajudis* was marked that evening by the first Catholic mass in thirty-eight years in Vilnius Cathedral, a classic building with six Doric columns which in 1950 had been transformed under Soviet rule into an art gallery and concert hall. Tens of thousands of Lithuanians crowded into the cathedral square, and filled the darkened streets of the old city with flickering candles, as the ceremony was performed by Cardinal Vincentas Sladkevicius.

Afterwards I went to visit the diminutive, elderly cardinal – without any communist official present – in his mustard-coloured wooden cottage behind a little wicker fence in Kaisiadorys, forty kilometres from Vilnius, where he had up to then been forced to live in rural exile. The hamlet had elements of the world of Don Camillo, the fictional Italian village in Giovanni Guareschi's satirical tales, where life revolved around the communist mayor and the parish priest. The Lithuanian Communist Party leader, Algirdas Brazauskas, was a native of the village, and he often dropped into the cardinal's cottage for conversations about the country's future. The unique relationship between the two set the pace for change. Brazauskas was another Dubcek. It was he who decreed that the cathedral in Vilnius should be rededicated, and he also ordered that the Church of St Kazimieras be returned to the Catholic hierarchy.

The leader of Lithuania's Catholics was overjoyed by the changes but worried about the downside of freedom. "If the values of the permissive society are imported into Lithuania, they will do more harm than good," he said, slapping his hand on the table in disgust at the prospect of such things as gay and abortion rights. "We are thankful to God that we are isolated from bad influences."

The *Sajudis* movement paid lip service to Gorbachev's policies of *glasnost*, *perestroika* and democratisation, but soon demanded the restoration of Lithuanian as the official language, and public disclosure of the secret protocols of the 1939 Nazi/Soviet Pact, under which the Baltic republics were annexed by Moscow. This was an extremely sensitive subject at the time. We Moscow-based correspondents had to be careful how we described the Baltic states in our reports. The term "annexed" infuriated Soviet officials, so we used neutral phrases like "absorbed by" to avoid censure. (We had to get permission from the Soviet Foreign Ministry to travel outside Moscow and this could be refused.) In February 1989, *Sajudis* went a step further, declaring that Lithuania had been forcibly annexed by the Soviet Union, and that its goal was the restoration of independence.

Soon every one of the fifteen Soviet Republics had a popular front of one sort or another – even Russia itself. As the dominant power in the Soviet bloc, the Russian Popular Front was geared towards counter-revolution rather than independence. It was founded on 29 October 1988 in the city of Yaroslavl. There were only ninety-nine delegates and two foreign correspondents – I found a colleague from the *Financial Times* there as well – and it was a ragged, rancorous affair with much waving of tsarist and pre-revolutionary flags. But even this could only have been possible with approval from someone on high, such as Politburo member Alexander Yakovlev, who was born just outside Yaroslavl and was in favour of reform. It was a first step. One of the organisers was Yuri Chernev, a nondescript former camp inmate wearing a flat cap. The next time I saw him, a year later, he was leading 10,000 people through the streets in the first permitted anti-communist demonstration in Moscow since before the 1917 revolution.

On 11 March 1990, after *Sajudis* won a state election, Lithuania became the first Soviet republic actually to declare independence, just over a year after the Estonians symbolically raised their flag over Pikk Hermann. Nationalist workmen chiselled off the Soviet emblem from the parliament building and replaced it with a canvas depicting a knight with a sword in hand, the emblem of pre-war Lithuanian independence. The Russian language plaque at the music conservatory – home to the bearded music professor, Vytautas Landsbergis, leader of *Sajudis* – was unscrewed, leaving a rectangle of unweathered stone.

The conservatives in the communist leadership in Moscow were appalled. They argued that the time had come to stop the rot. Gorbachev himself never intended that his changes should go so far: he wanted to reform the Union of Soviet Socialist Republics, not bury it. He warned the Lithuanian parliament to submit to Soviet power, and imposed an economic blockade. Red

Army troops staged provocative parades in Vilnius. Military helicopters dropped leaflets over the city, urging the twenty per cent Russian and Polish minority to join pro-Soviet rallies. Some Lithuanians dependent on Soviet-related jobs joined them. The kindly face of an elderly Lithuanian woman, Mikalina Urbelita, contorted in fury when I asked her why she wanted the country to remain in the Soviet Union. "Before the war there were no factories, there were no pensions, there was unemployment," she said. "And we had a fascist government."

The manoeuvrings of Soviet troops brought back unwelcome memories to ninety-four-year-old Yousas Urbshis, the Foreign Minister of that government in pre-war Lithuania, who lived in a cramped first-floor apartment in the town of Kaunas. Frail and dignified, he told me how in October 1939, not knowing that the Soviet Union and Nazi Germany had secretly agreed on the division of Europe under the Molotov–Ribbentrop pact, he was invited to Moscow for "friendly negotiations". "The Lithuanian and Soviet flags were flying at the airport," he recalled. "It was ten o'clock in the evening when I was taken directly to the Kremlin. Stalin was there with Molotov. Stalin put a map of Europe on the table. On it was a line. He said the Soviet Union had agreed with Germany that Europe should be divided and that most of Lithuania would go to the Soviet Union." Then Stalin said that Lithuania must sign a treaty on mutual aid. "But the mutual aid treaty was a diktat. Under it we would have to allow 20,000 Soviet soldiers in garrisons on Lithuanian soil. I tried to argue. I said, 'Clearly this is the occupation of Lithuania.'" Stalin and Molotov just smirked. His government refused. Less than a year later Urbshis glanced out his window one morning and saw that his dacha was surrounded by Soviet soldiers. He and his wife Mariei were arrested. They spent the next thirteen years in various prisons in Russia, and were not allowed to return home until 1956. "I found I had lost my mother and father, my older brother and other family members," the old diplomat said, as tears welled up in his eyes. "They had been deported to Siberia and died there. I didn't know."

Early in 1991 the Stalinists in the Kremlin gained the upper hand. On 10 January Gorbachev issued an ultimatum threatening military intervention if Lithuania did not accept Soviet power within twenty-four hours. Next day paratroopers and Interior Ministry troops, acting in the name of a shadowy National Salvation Committee, seized several public buildings in Vilnius. Before dawn on 13 January a KGB commando unit attacked a crowd that had gathered to protect the television tower, killing fifteen people. In the aftermath Gorbachev, the champion of *glasnost*, proposed censorship measures to stop "anti-Soviet propaganda", but this caused uproar in the Supreme Soviet and he did not take it further.

The crackdown failed to intimidate the Lithuanians. Thousands of people rallied to protect the parliament building. Pro-democracy forces in Moscow joined in a world-wide outcry. Boris Yeltsin flew to Tallinn to calm both nationalist and Russian populations in the Baltics. He signed a protocol with the Baltic republics, and promised legal protection for soldiers who refused to take part in repressing the separatists. An army paratrooper unit in the Byelorussian city of Vitebsk refused to redeploy in Latvia. Those of us who attended Yeltsin's press conference when he returned to Moscow saw him at his best – sober, self-assured and confident. There was widespread anger in Moscow at the killings in Lithuania, with the most outspoken media calling the crackdown a last ditch stand by a regime in its death throes. The Politburo in Moscow lost its nerve. Caught between his own reform instincts and his desire to maintain Soviet borders, Gorbachev's half-hearted attempt at military intimidation of the Baltics failed.

In Riga thousands of Latvians, not knowing who would prevail in Moscow, took to the streets to protect their parliament building. They erected barricades in the cobbled alleyways. For several weeks, the smell of wood smoke from their bonfires filled the narrow streets. Many Russians, infected by the spirit of democracy in Moscow, showed that they too had had enough of totalitarian government. Some brought out the previously banned red, white and blue flags of independent Russia and helped man the barricades. In the Lutheran Cathedral in Riga, where volunteers slept at night, some of the nurses were Russian. "How do you get on together?" I asked a Latvian and a Russian nurse in a whisper one night, as hundreds slept on the pews. In response, they hugged each other.

13

Wars without End

When an empire falters, its smouldering internal conflicts, snuffed out by the weight of totalitarian control, are inevitably reignited. This was the case in the Caucasus, where scores of nationalities lived. The generation of foreign correspondents who arrived in Moscow in the mid-1980s as Kremlin watchers became by the end of the decade part-time war correspondents, chronicling a series of vicious conflicts which remain unresolved to this day.

Of all the republics and autonomous regions in the Caucasus, Chechnya was potentially the most unstable. Occupying an oil-rich territory roughly the size of Northern Ireland, the Chechens had first been subjugated by the Russians in the nineteenth century. In February 1944, on Stalin's orders, the entire Chechen population, along with the neighbouring Ingush, was deported east to Kazakhstan on allegations of collaboration with Nazi Germany, and the capital, Grozny, was left in the hands of a mostly Russian population. However, in 1957 Nikita Khrushchev allowed the Chechens to return, and many of the Russian residents left to seek a new life, mostly in the Baltic republics. In the three decades from then until 1991, Chechnya enjoyed relative peace as part of the autonomous republic of Chechen-Ingushetia.

Trouble began brewing in Grozny, a city of 360,000 people, in the summer of 1988, when spontaneous protests against the construction of a biochemical plant evolved into a "Union to Promote Perestroika", which in turn became a popular front. As in the Baltics, the popular front initially made modest demands but soon began forcibly ejecting ethnic Russians from party and government posts. On 27 November 1990 a Chechen National Congress was formed and declared sovereignty as its main goal. It elected General Dzhokhar Dudayev of the Soviet Air Force as its chairman. A small, neat dresser, with a pencil moustache, Dudayev was the highest-ranking Chechen in the Soviet military. He was based in Estonia and, significantly, refused to take part in military action against Baltic nationalists in early 1991. In the following weeks protesters tore down the plaque in the town centre honouring General Alexei Yermolov, the Russian general who had crushed the Chechens in the nineteenth century, and about whom Pushkin wrote the famous line: "Bow down, Caucasus, Yermolov is coming", and the airport was renamed Sheik Mansur, after a Chechen fighter who had slaughtered Russians in 1785.

I saw cars with pictures of Saddam Hussein in their back windows and at night heard gunshots echoing across the city when I arrived in June 1991. Nevertheless I was still able to enjoy a relatively trouble-free stay as guest of an Armenian family in a comfortable single-storey brick house on the outskirts of Grozny. They were relatives of my wife, Zhanna, who had lived until she was eleven in a house in Grozny built by her Russian-Armenian father, Stanislav Suvorov, on Pavel Musorov Street, before the family moved to Krasnoyarsk in Siberia. She remembers Chechen, Ingush, Russian, Ukrainian, Tatar and Jewish people coming by the house in the evenings, where her parents sewed clothes to make extra money. This was the sort of bourgeois activity that was frowned upon by the Communist Party but no one seemed to mind: Armenians were expected to make shoes and garments and sell them. The Suvorovs lived well. Their house had three bedrooms, a living-room and a formal dining-room hung with wall carpets, which boasted a black "Rostov-on-Don" piano and a walnut furniture set, and in the garden they had pear, apricot and plum trees. They owned a blue Volga sedan with a metal deer on the front in which they would go for picnics in the oak and beech groves of the hills, where wild asparagus and damsons grew, and for longer drives to the Black Sea coast in Georgia.

We had a festive lunch in the walled courtyard on our first day in Grozny, gathered around a long outdoor table laden with shashlik and dishes of fruit and vegetables, and shaded from the hot sun by a leafy vine. It was a memorable occasion, with many toasts of cognac in tiny glasses, but it was overshadowed by a deep foreboding. After living for two generations in Grozny, the family was making preparations to sell up and leave. They knew that when the Chechens decided to follow the Baltic republics and declare independence, as was inevitable, there would be war. Moscow regarded Chechnya as part of Russia proper, and a Muslim city in revolt was no place for Christian Armenians. Within a month they had sold the house with its garden of fruit trees and strawberry beds, and had fled to safer regions of southern Russia, along with most of the 26,000-member Armenian community in Grozny.

Events followed a similar course in Georgia, though with a different outcome. First annexed by tsarist Russia in 1810, Georgia had always seized historical opportunities to challenge Moscow's rule and it aspired to be recognised as a European country. Rustaveli Avenue, the long, narrow main street of the Georgian capital, Tbilisi, had a southern European feel, with fine low buildings housing cafés and art galleries and shaded by sycamore and plane trees. Named after the medieval Georgian poet, Shota Rustaveli, its most imposing edifice under Soviet rule was the House of Government, set back from the road in a small square.

It was here on 9 April 1989 that Soviet paratroopers gassed and hacked to death twenty people, nineteen of them women, when dispersing a demonstration in support of a hunger strike against Kremlin interference in Georgian affairs. Shortly afterwards, when I went for lunch with one of the organisers of the hunger strike, Merab Kostava, the waiters in the *khachapuri* restaurant overlooking the fast-flowing Kura River in Tbilisi rushed to get us a table. Everyone treated the stocky poet with thick white hair and moustache as a national hero. "We're seeing the break-up of the Soviet Union – every Georgian wants independence now," said Kostava, who had served ten years in a Siberian prison for advocating human rights. "We'll see independence in my generation."

Kostava was killed in a suspicious road accident six months later, and the independence movement was taken over by his comrade, Zviad Gamsakhurdia, a handsome, green-eyed university professor who, with Kostava, had led a campaign for human rights in the 1950s before controversially recanting. Gamsakhurdia lived in a red-brick mansion overlooking Tbilisi, guarded by several heavily built men and a ferocious black dog. In a cavernous room lined with sculptures and paintings, Gamsakhurdia boasted that his models for the independence struggle were the Irish heroes Roger Casement and Terence MacSwiney. People in Georgia knew that both had died to win freedom for their country, he said. In a famous open letter, written to Lenin in 1921, his father, the Georgian novelist, Konstantine Gamsakhurdia, declared that "Georgia was not as politically evolved as Ireland but that Georgia would have its Casements and MacSwineys until it gained full independence." These Irish heroes were in his mind when he helped organise the hunger strikes, said Gamsakhurdia. "That prophecy is being fulfilled today."

Georgia symbolically broke with the Soviet Union on the first anniversary of the 9 April killings. A huge rally was held in Tbilisi to mark the event, attended by sympathisers from other republics waving the independence flags of Azerbaijan, Ukraine,

Lithuania and Estonia. "We sometimes learn from others, like the Baltics," said Georgi Chanturia, another leader of the nationalist movement, "but maybe they can now learn something from us." The crimson, black and white flag of independent Georgia was flown from public buildings, and the lampposts along Rustaveli Avenue were strung with flickering electric candles. Well-wishers stood on every balcony overlooking the crowds. In the evening the deep tones of a fifty-strong ensemble of black-robed Georgians, with long moustaches and draped with bandoliers, throbbed through a powerful stereo system. I scribbled in my notebook the words of Irakli Tsereteli of the Independence Party: "We are more united now in our struggle with the empire."

If evidence was needed of the demise of communism in this part of the Soviet Union, it came from the ideological secretary of the Communist Party of Georgia. I asked him if Moscow would respond with force to Georgia's declaration of independence. He answered by crossing himself and replying, *"Dai Bog nyet"* – "God forbid."

Zviad Gamsakhurdia was declared President of Georgia, and the venue for our next meeting, about a year later, was his presidential office in the Georgian Parliament, beneath a blue and gold enamelled wall plate depicting St George armed with a lance, the symbol of independent Georgia. It was snowing outside and officials sat in their overcoats because electricity had been cut off owing to a Kremlin blockade. Moscow had not recognised Georgia's independence and still controlled overseas relations, a point brought home to Aer Rianta which, at the end of 1990, agreed a joint venture with a Georgian company to set up an international shop on Rustaveli Avenue, only to be forced to abandon it when Soviet officials refused an import licence for the contents of six forty-foot containers trucked all the way from West Germany to the Georgian border.

What most excited Gamsakhurdia's passions, however, was Moscow's military aid for South Ossetia, a region of Georgia bordering Russia where the 30,000 ethnic Ossetians had declared their intention to unite with North Ossetia inside Russian territory. His face contorted with anger as he fulminated against the "deceitful" and "treacherous" Ossetians. If Casement and MacSwiney were Gamsakhurdia's heroes, the South Ossetians were his Ulster Unionists.

A nasty little war had started around the main South Ossetian town of Tskhinvali, 100 kilometres north-west of Tbilisi. Georgian militia who had been driven out of the town manned a roadblock on a narrow approach road lined by poplar trees infested with magpies. As I waited with my companion, Jonathan Steele of *The Guardian*, for permission to pass through, a pot-bellied vigilante with a hunting rifle wrenched open the door of a car and pulled out a terrified young Ossetian by his scarf and roughed him up. We had to walk from there through deep snow to enter the town, along a road barricaded with shoulder-high sewage pipes and guarded by Soviet conscripts. All that was left of a street of a dozen houses where Georgians had lived were blackened gables. It was like Belfast in 1969. As sniper fire crackled out nearby, we ducked into a little store in the town centre with bullet holes in the ceiling, where we found five women sitting around a wood stove. They laughed when I said I was from Ireland. The Ossetians, they explained, called themselves "Ire" people and joked that "Ire-land" was their original homeland. Venturing farther into town we met the deputy town mayor, Gerasim Khogaev, who described the street-to-street fighting of a month before, when 3,000 Georgians were driven out, as "terrible, friend against friend". Hundreds of Ossetians forced out of nearby villages by Georgians milled around the town's council building. They protested that they were not dupes of the Kremlin. "We are a cultured people, not wild like Gamsakhurdia says," said Julietta Ostayeva, a bespectacled school teacher with white hair and wearing a tweed suit. Here the people clung to the security of the Soviet past.

Lenin's picture adorned the walls and the red flag flew from public buildings. Their allegiance was to Russia and they were preparing for a long war.

An even bloodier war was fought over a beautiful mountain region south of Georgia, about the size of County Kerry, comprising deep ravines, sheep pastures, mountain villages, vineyards and orchards of peaches, pears, apples and nuts. This was Nagorno-Karabakh, an Armenian-populated enclave inside the territory of the Republic of Azerbaijan. Stalin had arbitrarily assigned it to Azerbaijan in 1923. Encouraged by *perestroika* and *glasnost*, the region voted on 20 February 1988 to join neighbouring Armenia. This ignited a popular movement in Armenia and mass rallies were held in the Armenian capital, Yerevan, to demand unity with Nagorno-Karabakh and greater sovereignty for Armenia within the Soviet Union. As Armenia came to the brink of open revolt in the autumn of 1988, Soviet Army T-72 tanks were deployed at the five entrances to the main square in Yerevan, their long 125-millimetre guns pointing up the tree-lined avenues. The Armenians convinced themselves that Moscow had it in for them. In a barber's shop in Yerevan where I went for a haircut, people nodded knowingly when a waiting customer complained, mistakenly, that Raisa Gorbachev was a Muslim and that this made Mikhail Gorbachev hate Armenians.

Then the earthquake happened. On 7 December 1988, an enormous shock of 6.8 magnitude devastated several Armenian towns and killed an estimated 25,000 people, including four out of five doctors. Mikhail Gorbachev cut short a visit to the United States to go directly to the scene of the disaster. To his astonishment and fury, he found himself, amid the ruins of one of the most severe earthquakes of the twentieth century, arguing with crowds about Nagorno-Karabakh.

Hemmed in on three sides by hostile Muslim entities – to the east Azerbaijan, to the west Turkey and to the south Iran – and under the heel of the Soviet Union, the Christian Armenians tended to suffer from paranoia. Travelling around the stricken region, I found a widespread belief that the Kremlin had deliberately triggered the deadly earth tremors. In the devastated epicentre of Spitak an old man snapped as he hobbled by, "Earthquake? What earthquake? There was no earthquake here. They did it, to punish us for trying to get Nagorno-Karabakh." Even educated Armenians, like Gohash, a charming primary school teacher in Kirovakan, assured me that it was an underground explosion to punish Armenians. Many Armenians believed that the 20,000 Azeris who fled inter-communal violence in Kirovakan a week before the earthquake must have had advance knowledge.

The only Armenian body capable of rallying the demoralised and shocked Armenians for rescue efforts after the earthquake was the Karabakh Committee, the republic's variant of a popular front which had been formed to agitate for union with Nagorno-Karabakh. It began organising groups of volunteers. However, three days after the earthquake, fearing that the Karabakh Committee was usurping state authority, Soviet forces rounded up its main activists, including the leader, Levon Ter-Petrosyan. They were kept in prison until 31 May 1989, when the tanks were withdrawn from the streets under pressure from pro-democracy forces in Moscow and critical international opinion.

Like the leaders who emerged in so many other republics as the Soviet union broke up, Ter-Petrosyan was an academic and an intellectual. A forty-year-old expert on ancient manuscripts, he knew Armenian, Russian, Arabic, Hebrew, ancient Greek and Manchurian Chinese. He also spoke faultless English, as I found when I met him just after his release at the Karabakh Committee headquarters. This was located in an old merchant's palace with a winding marble staircase in the centre of Yerevan where debates and arguments raged all day among excited groups of people. Drawing on a Marlboro cigarette, Ter-Petrosyan explained how, in all the republics, at that moment in history,

136

there were optional centres of power. "The party has administrative power. We have power over the people. But we have always kept contact with the administrative organs." The Armenians had to tread carefully in their relations with Moscow, he explained. Russia had historically been seen as their protector of last resort against the Muslim world. Independence had its perils. Ter-Petrosyan favoured sovereignty within a Soviet federation. When later, in August 1989, he was elected head of the Supreme Soviet in Armenia, he maintained contact with the Kremlin. In January 1991, after Soviet troops clashed with pro-independence demonstrators in Lithuania, Gorbachev sent Ter-Petrosyan to lead a three-man delegation to Vilnius successfully to broker a peace deal between Soviet officers and the Lithuanian leader Vytautas Landsbergis.

The conflict around Nagorno-Karabakh degenerated into open warfare, with sniping, ambushes and shellfire. In May 1991, approaching the enclave from the Azerbaijani side through small, steep valleys with poppy-strewn vineyards and sheep pastures, I found the Soviet forces openly siding with the Azerbaijanis. On 19 January the previous year, Soviet troops had killed 137 Azerbaijani protesters in the Azerbaijan capital, Baku, but the republic had come back into the Soviet fold and, under its communist leader, Ayaz Mutallibov, had voted in a referendum in March 1991 to retain the Soviet Union. Moscow responded gratefully by helping Mutallibov's regime regain popular support, which it achieved by providing television pictures of Soviet forces attacking Armenian positions at his behest.

On both sides, little mountain hamlets had been emptied by shellfire. "The villagers used to be friendly with each other," said Faisal Aliev, an Azerbaijani stone-cutter, as we walked through the deserted settlement of Airu where the lane leading to the nearby Armenian village was blocked by a telegraph pole and a tree trunk. "We were like that" – he held his two forefingers together. "But not for the last three years." Armenians had in turn fled from Azeri villages, such as Dashbulag, where army units and Azerbaijani militia were busy destroying the Armenian church with explosives.

The war over Nagorno-Karabakh was like a "second Afghanistan" said Lieutenant Mikhail Kudreshov at a sand-bagged base in Airu, taking no notice of mortar blasts nearby. His conscript soldiers, from Russia, Kazakhstan, Estonia and Azerbaijan, wore the floppy beige hats I had seen on soldiers fighting the Afghan war. Here, however, unlike in Afghanistan, the Muslim forces were on their side – Azeri militants had painted Islamic slogans on their armoured personnel carriers. Next day, on the road outside the regional Azerbaijan capital of Agdam, I saw Azeri people putting flowers in the barrels of six tanks parked by the roadside. But Agdam was overlooked on three sides by Armenian positions, and its 160,000 residents were piling furniture on lorries and fleeing. It was evident that Armenian forces were winning.

In August 1991 events came to a head in Moscow which decided the fate of the Soviet Union and all its restless and rebellious constituents. Gorbachev agreed a new union treaty that envisaged a voluntary federation of the Soviet Union's republics, with the likely loss of the Baltic republics. This was too much for the old-style Communists, who staged a coup in Moscow on 19 August 1991, led by KGB chief Vladimir Kryuchkov and fronted by Gorbachev's hard-drinking vice-president, Gennady Yanayev. (With impeccable timing, I had moved from Russia to the United States just a month before and I had to watch events unfold from a yet-to-be-furnished house in the Washington suburb of Bethesda with only a TV set.) Gorbachev was put under house arrest at his dacha in the Crimea. The coup had no public support, however, and collapsed after Yeltsin defiantly climbed aboard a tank outside the Russian Supreme Soviet building, popularly known as the White House. One of the coup leaders, Boris Pugo, and his wife committed suicide. Gorbachev returned to Moscow to find that Yeltsin was the new power in the land.

Between 21 August and 22 September, Estonia, Latvia, Lithuania, Georgia, Armenia and Azerbaijan asserted their independence, along with Ukraine, Belarus, Moldova, Kyrgyzstan, Uzbekistan, Tajikistan and Turkmenistan. Gorbachev resigned on 25 December and the Soviet Union was formally dissolved the next day. Boris Yeltsin became President of Russia, a post he held until succeeded by Vladimir Putin in 1999.

Edgar Savisaar, who started the first popular front inside Soviet borders, became the first Prime Minister of independent Estonia. In Latvia the natives regained Riga Strand, where blue flags today signal clean water. In Lithuania, Vytautas Landsbergis became the first head of state until he was succeeded in 1992 by the former communist leader Algirdas Brazauskas. In 2004, Estonia, Latvia and Lithuania joined NATO and the European Union. The biggest problem facing the Baltic states today is not an influx of Russians, but an outflow of emigrants, tens of thousands from Latvia and Lithuania especially, to other EU countries, prominent among them Ireland, seeking a better life as their home countries try to catch up with a west European standard of living.

The failed coup in Moscow became the catalyst for what became known as the "Chechen Revolution". As soon as it occurred, General Dudayev called for mass resistance to Soviet occupation. In the following weeks armed nationalists seized public buildings. Some communist officials were killed. On 2 November 1991 the Chechen parliament proclaimed full independence. Boris Yeltsin, who had assumed command in Russia, found himself with the same dilemma Mikhail Gorbachev had faced in the Baltics. He was in favour of giving Soviet republics their independence, but not autonomous regions within Russia itself. Yeltsin sent hundreds of Interior Ministry troops to Grozny to enforce a state of emergency. They were surrounded at the airport by armed Chechens and sent home in buses.

Chechnya thus gained *de facto* independence, with General Dudayev as its leader. Moscow attempted but failed to regain control in a vicious 1994–96 war that left the centre of Grozny in ruins. In 1999, taking as a *casus belli* a number of deadly explosions at apartment blocks in Russia – which some observers maintain were set off by Russian *agents provocateurs* – President Vladimir Putin sent the Russian armed forces back to subjugate the Chechens once more. The Kremlin has declared victory, despite continuing sporadic violence, and Grozny is presently being rebuilt.

Georgia gained full independence with the break-up of the Soviet Union but internal rivalries tore the country apart. Zviad Gamsakhurdia was deposed in a bloody coup in 1992 which led to a three-year civil war, during which Rustaveli Avenue was laid waste. Inter-ethnic violence flared up again over South Ossetia and the autonomous region of Abkhazia, which declared themselves independent of Georgia. Of some 100,000 Ossetians living in Georgia proper, 60,000 were displaced and fled mostly to Russia, while 25,000 ethnic Georgians were expelled from South Ossetia and a quarter of a million from Abkhazia. Eduard Shevardnadze, the former Soviet Union Foreign Minister and a native Georgian, was elected president in 1995 and again in 2000, before being deposed in 2003 in the Rose Revolution. Under his successor, Mikheil Saakashvili, Georgia moved to align itself with the Western powers, and relations with a newly-assertive Russia deteriorated. The ethnic conflicts flared again and in August 2008 degenerated into outright war between Georgia and Russia, when Georgian forces sought to occupy South Ossetia.

Once again the Caucasus erupted in flames and a new cycle in its bloody history began.

Both Armenia and Azerbaijan gained independence by default when the Soviet Union collapsed in December 1991.

Nagorno-Karabakh declared itself an independent state aligned with Armenia and a full-scale war erupted between Azerbaijan and Armenia. Both sides used weapons and tanks bought from the disintegrating Soviet army and employed soldiers from Ukraine and Russia as mercenaries. Chechen fighters came to support Muslim Azerbaijan, but they could not turn the tide of battle. The Armenian side, fired by their sense of historical righteousness and a passionate love for their mountain pastures, gained the upper hand, taking control of fourteen per cent of what had been Azerbaijan territory. A ceasefire was brokered by Russia on 12 May 1994 which continues to this day, mediated by the Organisation for Security and Co-operation in Europe. The status of Karabakh has yet to be determined. Agdam is a ghost city and half of Agdam region is controlled by Armenian fighters, despite a UN Security Council Resolution demanding the unconditional withdrawal of occupying forces. There are an estimated 800,000 Azerbaijan refugees scattered about their own country, while 230,000 ethnic Armenians have been driven from Azerbaijan.

After Armenian independence, Levon Ter-Petrosyan was elected president and served from 1991 to 1998. Mutallibov became the first president of independent Azerbaijan but was forced into exile in 1992, and former Azerbaijani Communist Party boss Heydar Aliev assumed power in 1993 after a military insurrection. The Armenian border with Azerbaijan and Turkey remains closed. With two such hostile neighbours, Armenia has turned again to Moscow for security and Russian forces continue to occupy a military base in the north-western Armenian city of Gyumri and to control the borders with Iran and Turkey.

14

The KGB and Me

One day, just before I left Russia in mid-1991, I went to the regular press briefing in the Foreign Ministry press centre. There among a group of Russian journalists, I came face to face with Nikolai. We embraced like old friends and retired to the bar. "Are you still working for the KGB?" I asked after we gulped down a vodka. "Ho! Ho! You are a terrible man," he cried, giving me a thump on the shoulder.

My relationship with Nikolai went back more than ten years, to the first day I arrived in the Soviet Union, on assignment in April 1980, to report on the run-up to the Moscow Olympics. As I emerged from Moscow's Sheremetyevo Airport, I felt my arm grabbed by a round-faced man in his late thirties with short fair hair and a knee-length leather coat straining at its buttons. "My name is Nikolai," he announced. "I am from the Soviet Union of Journalists, I am here to help you." He told me he had been assigned to arrange interviews and translate for me during my stay. As we sped through Moscow in the back of an official-looking black Volga, he informed me that he had been a correspondent for the Soviet News Agency, TASS, in the United Arab Emirates for five years. This rang a bell. The previous month the former TASS reporter in Khartoum, Ilya Dzhirkvelov, had defected and told the London *Times* that all Russians working for the official Soviet news agency abroad were, in one way or another, agents of the *Komityet Gosudarstvyennoy Bezopasnosti*, the state security organ, known to Russians by its initials as the *Kay Gay Bay* and to us as the KGB. So I asked Nikolai straight out. "You are a KGB agent really, aren't you?" "Ho, ho," he cried, grinning and winking furiously. He put an arm round my shoulder and squeezed my knee with his other hand. "And what are you? MI6?"

Nikolai was nevertheless indispensable in penetrating the bureaucracy in Moscow, but he sometimes chided me if I questioned officials on sensitive issues, such as the oppression of religion or the Soviet occupation of Afghanistan. As we piled back into the car after one rather confrontational interview, Nikolai punched me on the shoulder. "You are an awful fellow," he said. To him I probably was. His culture demanded that news reporting should be harnessed in the interests of the state, while my definition of news was finding out what the state was up to.

My frustrations with Nikolai surfaced near the end of my month-long assignment. I had asked to see a collective farm and he arranged for me to visit a cotton plantation near Samarkand in Uzbekistan. We set out in a car bearing me, Nikolai, a local guide from the Intourist travel agency, a Samarkand journalist and a driver. We pulled up at the farm's roadside "Clubhouse" where a sumptuous lunch was laid out. A thin, obsequious man stood behind me filling my vodka glass to the brim, as the burly Uzbek farm director proposed numerous toasts to Soviet–Irish friendship. After lunch I asked to see the farm. "Let's go," said the manager. But I was merely taken a hundred metres up the road to a model worker's home with carpets on the walls and colour television, where I was required to eat more pilaf and drink more vodka toasts. I insisted again that I wanted to see the farm. We piled back into the Volga and drove to a scenic lookout in the hills. "Look," said Nikolai, pointing to the valley some kilometres away, "There is the farm down there." I learned subsequently that western journalists were routinely brought to the same "model farm" in Uzbekistan and given much the same treatment.

There was silence in the car as we drove back to Samarkand. I was fuming and hardly able to stay conscious after imbibing so much vodka. I had not been able to walk on the fields or see how the farm worked. We checked out of the hotel, went to the airport, boarded the plane for the four-hour journey back to Moscow and fell asleep. When we woke Nikolai was in a surly mood. "What's up?" I asked. He told me that he had been embarrassed when I asked someone rather loudly in the hotel lobby in Samarkand as we checked out, "Have you seen my KGB man?" "Oh, for God's sake, you *are* KGB," I replied. We got back on an even keel in the couple of days before Nikolai dropped me back at Sheremetyevo Airport for the flight home. "What will you do now?" I asked him. "I expect I'll have to look after some other difficult journalist from the capitalist west," he said.

Back in Dublin after that assignment, in a reversal of roles, I found myself helping a Soviet journalist in his reporting of Ireland. I would occasionally meet Dublin-based TASS correspondent Mikhail Smirnov for lunch, when he would ply me with questions about British–Irish relations and events in the North. Once we arranged to get together in Coffer's Restaurant in Dublin's Temple Bar. Meeting me at the entrance, he pointed to a Cortina that had pulled up with two men in leather jackets inside. "That's your Special Branch," he said. "They followed me all the way from Rathgar." I went over, tapped the window of the Cortina and said, "You can take a break. We will be in Coffer's for a couple of hours." The two plain-clothes men glared at me. After we ordered our steak and chips I said, half-joking, "Of course you are a spy. Everyone knows that." "Of course," he replied with a grin.

I related this incident on RTÉ when Pat Kenny interviewed me about working as a journalist in the Soviet Union, and asked if I was followed around there by the KGB. I said I wasn't, and that times had changed since the days when a *New York Times* correspondent strolling through Moscow famously bought two ice-creams and, without looking, handed one back to his shadow, who politely said, "Thanks." I pointed out, however, that the only resident Soviet journalist in Ireland was regularly followed and we both tut-tutted about that.

But the Special Branch was not being over-zealous. In 1990, Oleg Gordievsky, a KGB colonel who had defected to the United Kingdom, wrote a tell-all memoir, called *KGB: The Inside Story*, published by Hodder & Stoughton. I glanced through the list of Europe-based KGB officers in the appendix. There was an entry I half-expected to find: "Smirnov, Mikhail, acting KGB station chief, Ireland". So when I was next interviewed by Pat Kenny, I made a point of giving the Special Branch men credit for keeping an eye on Colonel Smirnov. From Gordievsky's disclosure, it was clear that my dining companion in Coffer's was in fact a graduate of special classes conducted in Moscow for UK and Ireland-bound KGB agents by the Cambridge spy Kim Philby.

Western journalists may not have been tailed going about their business in Gorbachev's Russia, though we all assumed that our apartments and offices were bugged. They had other ways of keeping an eye on us. After I had settled in Moscow I began to meet socially with my future wife Zhanna, then an assistant professor of English philology at the Krasnoyarsk Pedagogical Institute in Siberia, who was spending three years in Moscow studying for her doctorate in linguistics. Zhanna accompanied me to some dinner parties given by other correspondents and diplomats, including the *Daily Telegraph* correspondent Xan Smiley. Some of my western colleagues may have been wary of this Soviet citizen at their dinner tables, wondering if she was anything to do with the KGB. In fact it was Zhanna who was targeted by the security organs because of her association with us.

One morning in April 1988, she received a summons to present herself at the head office of her postgraduate course on the fifth floor of the Moscow Pedagogical Institute, near Kropotkinskaya metro station in central Moscow. Waiting for her was a neatly dressed young man in a leather jacket, who introduced himself as an official of the state security service. He asked her to accompany him to a nearby park. There on a bench he told her that his bosses at the KGB knew she was a friend of the *Irish Times* correspondent. The KGB was interested in finding out what was discussed at social events she attended with other foreign correspondents, some of whom, he warned, could very well have "other duties". He mentioned Xan Smiley by name. She said she would not spy on her dining companions. "Think it over," he said, and gave her a card with his telephone number.

The KGB had every reason to believe that Zhanna would co-operate. She was a model citizen. She had been a parliamentary deputy representing university students in the Krasnoyarsk Soviet and had succumbed to pressure as a teenager to join the Communist Party. First in her class at college, she was about to complete a doctorate which one day would guarantee a full professorship. But like tens of thousands of disillusioned party members, she was already thinking of resigning her membership and was affronted by the KGB assumption that she would work with them. The next day she told me what had happened as we walked along a busy street with lots of traffic noise around. No one would dream of having such a sensitive conversation indoors.

We didn't quite know how to react. I resisted the idea of writing anything in *The Irish Times*. The KGB was capable of making serious trouble for Zhanna and her family in retaliation. Eventually I went to the Irish embassy, situated on a quiet little street called Grokholsky Pereulok, and invited diplomat Judith Devlin – today a senior lecturer in the School of History at University College Dublin – for a walk in the embassy garden, where I told her what had happened. "I don't want you to do

anything," I said. "I just want you to have this on record if
something goes wrong."

Ten days later Zhanna was summoned once more to meet the
young KGB officer at the Pedagogical Institute. He took her out
to the same bench. This time he presented her with an internal
KGB book on foreign residents who had been caught spying and
asked her again to do what they wanted. Once more she refused
and I went to the Irish embassy to make a second report to Judith
in the garden.

After another two weeks, the pressure was stepped up.
Zhanna was summoned to meet the KGB agent at the National,
a grand hotel where Lenin once had an office and which was a
favourite watering-hole for state security officials. He was
accompanied by a more senior KGB official. Years later she
recalled that he bore a striking resemblance in looks and
demeanour to Vladimir Putin, then a KGB major, but the future
Russian president was officially stationed in East Germany at the
time. The two men ordered a sumptuous lunch, inviting Zhanna
to do the same. In those days of shortages, this would have been
quite a treat for most Russians. She refused even to take a drink
of water, insulted at the implication that they thought they could
buy her co-operation. The two played good cop–bad cop, with
the Putin-type playing the latter role. He expressed irritation at
Zhanna's stubbornness and warned her, "There are many enemies
who would like to harm the Soviet Union. As a good Soviet citizen,
you should be aware of that." He asked, somewhat contemptuously,
"Are you going to marry him?" She snapped, "Do you want me to
propose for you?" He leaned across the table. "Listen! Don't you
know we can make sure you don't get your PhD?" In those days
such a threat had to be taken seriously. Zhanna's doctorate could
be refused and her temporary Moscow residency permit
withdrawn, forcing her to return to Siberia without her degree.
They then tried another approach. They proposed that she
introduce a KGB officer to the *Irish Times* correspondent as "a

friend from Krasnoyarsk" who would prove helpful and fix up interviews (and perhaps become my controller). What could be the harm in doing that? She said she wouldn't and got up and left.

Shortly afterwards Zhanna delivered her dissertation at the Moscow Pedagogical Institute. The KGB threat did not materialise and she was awarded her doctorate. When she returned to Krasnoyarsk to teach for a year, a local KGB man came to interview her at her mother's apartment, having been sent the file from Moscow. The agent seemed less concerned about following up the case than with getting some lessons in English. The KGB threats ended in June 1989. That was when I married Zhanna in Moscow, and adopted her daughter Julia from her previous marriage. Before that she had resigned from the Communist Party and the KGB had given up on her. *Glasnost* had advanced to the point where there was more interesting information about the state of affairs in Russia to be gleaned from *avant-garde* Moscow journals than from the gossip around a correspondent's dinner table.

By this stage the KGB itself was coming under intense popular pressure. As discontent and dissidence became widespread in the declining years of the Soviet Union, the state security organs were overwhelmed. People who had suffered became emboldened.

On 30 October 1990, the Day of the Political Prisoner, thousands of people heaped bouquets of carnations and roses on a memorial stone they erected that day to the victims of totalitarianism outside the grim six-storey Lubyanka in Dzerzhinsky Square in Moscow, which served as KGB headquarters. The memorial was placed beside the brooding black statue of Felix Dzerzhinsky, who had founded the secret police in 1917 "to liquidate counter-revolution and sabotage". Many middle-aged and elderly women with memories of the "midnight knock" held up photographs of husbands or parents who had disappeared into the Lubyanka, never to be seen again. With tears in her eyes, fifty-four-year-old Yelena Bergavinova told me how her father Sergei Bergavinov, a senior official in the Soviet Communist Party, had been shot on Stalin's orders in December 1937, and her mother exiled to Siberia, where she died. "I had nowhere to bring flowers to," she said, "until now."

In August 1991, after the abortive coup, the fifteen-ton bronze monument to Dzerzhinsky was pulled down by a crowd with the help of a crane and consigned to the graveyard of fallen Soviet memorials at the Central House of Artists. On 21 December 1995, President Boris Yeltsin signed a decree disbanding the KGB, which was then reformed as the *Federalnaya Sluzhba Bezopasnosti*, or FSB, the state security agency of the Russian Federation. The FSB continues to use as its headquarters the Lubyanka – where a bust of Dzerzhinsky once more takes pride of place, put there on a pedestal in 2005 on the orders of Boris Yeltsin's successor as Russian president, former KGB officer Vladimir Putin.

15

An Irritated City

Though I left Moscow to take up my new post in Washington in 1991, I continued to make occasional trips to Russia, and in particular Siberia and the city of Krasnoyarsk, in the post-Soviet years. Zhanna's father Stanislav had moved the family there from Grozny in 1969. He had served five years in prison in the Caucasus for selling a car at a profit, a normal business transaction anywhere else in the world, but under Soviet communism a crime of *speculatsia*. When he finished his term, he chose to start a new life in Siberia. By reputation Siberia was just as forbidding to people living in other parts of Russia as it was to westerners, with its associations with cold and prison camps. But it had several attractions. The Soviet government offered inducements to new arrivals in the form of higher salaries. It was a place where people could lead a decent, if hard, life. Zhanna's father got work as a shoe designer, and her mother Marietta Suvorova became head of personnel in the regional shoe factory. They were soon well established and her father was able to build a roomy dacha outside town where the family could grow fruit and vegetables in Siberia's short, hot summers.

Krasnoyarsk, capital of a Siberian region more than thirty times the size of Ireland, was a closed city in Soviet times. It wasn't until October 1989, four months after we married, that I was given permission to visit Zhanna's family. However, my "minder" at the Soviet Foreign Ministry, Yuri Sapunov, insisted that my trip be classified as a *commandirovka*, or work-related journey. Paradoxically at that moment he could get special permission for me to go there as an accredited foreign correspondent, but not as a private individual.

I arrived after a five-hour flight from Moscow, the first westerner since the Second World War to be freely admitted to the city straddling the mighty Yenisei River. No one told me officially why Krasnoyarsk had been closed but it was easy to guess. It was at the heart of the USSR's military industrial complex and during the war whole armaments factories had been moved there from western Russia and Ukraine to escape destruction by the Germans. Just outside the city there was a radar station which the Americans complained violated the 1972 US–Soviet Anti-Ballistic Missile Treaty. And in the forest nearby there were missile silos with nuclear-tipped rockets aimed at targets in the United States. Moreover, Krasnoyarsk was at the apex of the "gulag archipelago", as the writer Alexander Solzhenitsyn described the system of communist-era labour camps and prisons in Siberia. As Zhanna's cousin Ararat drove us through town on my first day, he pointed out corrugated iron compounds and concrete walls topped with barbed wire, where armed guards were silhouetted in open watch towers. There were so many prisons in Krasnoyarsk, he joked, that it was better to live across the road from a prison than to live across the road from your home.

Since I was officially on a *commandirovka*, I had to follow a schedule of interviews and meetings with Krasnoyarsk state enterprises and institutions organised by the Soviet Foreign Ministry. One was with the House of Journalists, where I found myself answering, rather than asking, questions from a dozen local writers. They showed great interest in what I thought of *glasnost* and *perestroika* and what was going on in Moscow and the republics, and even greater interest in what I earned as a correspondent. A neatly dressed young man, the only one who did not introduce himself, asked the most questions and took the most notes. One of the journalists whispered to me as I left that he was from the KGB, and he was more interested in keeping an eye on them than on me.

After years of industrial and commercial stagnation, Krasnoyarsk was badly run down. Stores were poorly stocked in common with all Russian provincial cities at the time. Metal slogans rusted on the roofs of the crumbling old buildings on the main thoroughfare, Peace Avenue. The suburban apartment blocks were in poor condition, with filthy ground-floor entrance halls. The clanking cage-lifts with wooden door-flaps often did not work. The apartments themselves were spotlessly clean and well fitted out, with central heating and hot water.

The most modern and well-kept building in town was the grandiose Lenin Museum, which dominated a riverside square on the site of an Orthodox cathedral torn down after the Revolution. A large stone bust of former Soviet leader Konstantin Chernenko, whose death in 1985 had paved the way for Gorbachev's election as General Secretary of the Soviet Communist Party, stood in a corner of the square. Chernenko, who came from a village in a distant part of Krasnoyarsk region, had been discredited under *glasnost* as a neo-Stalinist, and earlier in 1989 a zealous reformer had thrown ship's paint over the bust. It had been removed for cleaning, prompting speculation that the Krasnoyarsk party leaders would consign it to the dustbin of history. But it had been returned, scrubbed clean, a visible triumph for stagnation, guarded by a Soviet militiaman.

Decades of repression had resulted in widespread political apathy in Siberia. But taking their cue from events on the streets of Moscow, small pro-reform groups started to gather in a pedestrian precinct to conduct open discussion about industrial pollution, which they believed caused a high number of cancer cases and miscarriages. They gave vent to their anger about a secret town thirty kilometres outside Krasnoyarsk called Ploschadka 27 or Site No. 27, where a cavern for spent nuclear fuel was being carved out beneath the pure waters of the Yenisei. Such bureaucratic irresponsibility resulted from the total lack of accountability that characterised Soviet governance everywhere.

When Mikhail Gorbachev came to the city in September 1988 to conduct a televised dialogue with people on Peace Avenue, he was taken aback by the virulence of the criticisms he heard about shortages in state stores and high charges in new co-operative ventures. Gorbachev had sought to release some entrepreneurial energy in the Soviet Union by allowing individuals to run small businesses, and some 900 cooperatives had been set up by enterprising locals, but they had met with resistance from ideologically rigid officials and from ordinary people who asked why they should pay higher prices for goods acquired from the state. After Gorbachev's visit, the city authorities lost some of their arrogance. They removed Chernenko's stone head in October 1990 and work was terminated at Ploschadka 27.

The mood of the Krasnoyarsk people in the last years of communism was described by the popular Siberian author Viktor Astafiev as "irritated". Over tea in his book-lined apartment on the fringes of the city, he explained that one of the reasons people were not rising up in revolt over the chronic state shortages was because of the abundance and beauty of the *taiga*, the coniferous forests that stretched to the horizon in every direction. Siberians thought little of spending a weekend hunting deer and bears, or collecting bilberries, cranberries, wild strawberries and whortleberries. "One day in the *taiga* is worth a season in Crimea," said the sixty-six-year-old author. (One of my most pleasant early memories of Siberia is of a picnic beneath tall Scots pines deep in the forest on a warm June day, with fresh lamb roasted over a wood fire and served with roasted aubergines and tomatoes.) The fact that most Siberian city-dwellers owned wooden *dachas* in the country also mitigated against hunger, explained Astafiev. They spent summer holidays and weekends growing fruit and vegetables, and making jams, compotes and other preserves for the winter, when snow covers the ground for seven months.

Each time we returned to Krasnoyarsk after the fall of the Soviet Union, Ararat Gukasian would meet us at the airport and drive us into town in his Lada. He was always laughing and telling anecdotes, and was the first to make a toast at a family gathering or to encourage others to do their party piece around the table. Ararat had arrived from Nagorno-Karabakh as a teenager to live with the Suvorov family. He served in the army, then studied law in university and joined the police force, eventually being promoted to the rank of major, attached to the homicide unit. He married a young Russian woman, Galina, and they lived in the apartment next door to Zhanna's parents on Railway Road.

We spent many hot summer days helping with the gardening at the family dacha in the village of Bulanovka, deep in an area of undulating woods and meadows about seventy kilometres north of Krasnoyarsk. It was so remote that the last ten kilometres of road was unpaved. An occasional car or motorbike with sidecar kicked up dust on the rutted village street, and sometimes a cow wandered between the weed-covered footpaths, but otherwise there were rarely any signs of life. The was no shop. However, the large garden at the dacha, one of dozens lining the edge of the forest, provided a daily feast of fresh fruit and vegetables, from blackcurrants, redcurrants, whitecurrants, strawberries, raspberries, gooseberries and plums to potatoes, lettuce, cabbage, cauliflower, cucumbers, onions, peas, beans, radishes, garlic and herbs; and in the greenhouses, tomatoes, peppers and even watermelons.

Just behind the dacha, a hundred metres into the forest, was a deep concrete silo where a nuclear missile was located. It was protected by seven perimeter fences, two of them electrified, and a ring of mines. Under a nuclear disarmament treaty with the

United States it was made redundant and in early 1994 a company of soldiers arrived and loaded the missile onto a specially built truck and towed it away. The electric fences were switched off and the minefield cleared, leaving only discarded signs stating, "Stop! Go back! Arms will be used without warning!" Children came to play in the dank underground passages of the silo, and gardeners took wire and fence posts when they needed them. We found marijuana plants growing around the site. An army officer returned one day and told the dacha owners to tape up their windows because they were going to blow up the silo. They managed to do so without causing any damage, leaving a big rubble-filled depression in the undergrowth.

We drove to Bulanovka with Ararat and Zhanna's father and her nephew Valyera Airiev, one winter day in 1999, when the snow was so deep that the garden gates of the dacha had almost disappeared under a waist-high drift with the texture of white sugar. We found that thieves had robbed the dacha and almost all the other summer homes in Bulanovka. They had broken a window at the back and taken away the television, refrigerator, kitchen table, chairs, dishes, cutlery, bedclothes and wall shelving. Fortunately they didn't locate the cellar, which was stacked with jars of fruit and sacks of potatoes and carrots. It was a disturbing discovery for the family, who had come to regard the village as a crime-free sanctuary, compared to the city where, like most residents, they lived in a mini fortress, with metal apartment doors and spy-holes.

That day we piled logs into the wood-burning stove until the brick walls warmed the dacha, and barbecued pork shashlik over a hole filled with hot coals in the frozen ground outside. After lighting another stove in the sauna, there was time for a steam bath and a rubdown with soft snow and one of those endless Russian discussions about the current state of affairs, and in particular the problem of crime in the region.

Krasnoyarsk has been associated with crime and prisons throughout its history. It was founded in 1628 by Cossack settlers and became a place of exile for Russians. Many were political outcasts, like the Decembrists in 1825, the Polish revolutionaries of 1831, and the Marxists of the 1890s, whose number included Vladimir Ilyich Lenin. But common law-breakers from Moscow were also despatched to Krasnoyarsk's prisons in such great numbers that, at the start of the twentieth century, almost a quarter of the inhabitants were classified as criminals. In the final years of the Soviet Union there was an average of one homicide a day, in a city of less than one million people.

This was not just a statistic to Zhanna. Her first husband, Victor, was beaten to death in the street in 1987 after an argument with two men, leaving her a widow with a six-year-old daughter, Julia. One of the alleged assailants was a hero of the Afghan war and the other the son of an important party official with good connections. The police were overwhelmed and under-resourced, and subject to political pressures. The public prosecutor never brought any charges against them.

As we sat around the stove, Ararat related how a criminal *mafia* had appeared near the end of the Gorbachev era and burned down the first co-operative restaurants for not paying protection money. Drugs had become a huge problem, associated with soldiers returning from Afghanistan. With the fall of communism, things had become worse. Many of the crime victims in Krasnoyarsk were *commersants*, business people who found themselves at the mercy of criminals prepared to use brutal methods to enforce the collection of debts or escape paying their own debts. "If you owe someone money it's easier to have them killed than to pay it back," said Ararat, who told me of one case where a *commersant* persuaded his partner to buy him out for 80,000 roubles, but his associate had him wiped out instead, for 6,000 roubles. Yura, an Aeroflot pilot and family friend, joked that the country was heading for an Italian solution – "either Sicily or Mussolini".

As some people in Krasnoyarsk grew richer and more vulnerable to crime, private protection agencies flourished, such as *Okhrana* (Security) or *Uragan* (Hurricane). They found many clients among the oligarchs who had built mansions among the wooden *izbas* on the edge of town. We drove one day along a snow-covered cul-de-sac in the Udatchny suburb to see the palatial redbrick home of Anatoly Bykov, director of the Krasnoyarsk aluminium plant, a huge complex of factory buildings set in the plains north of the city, that spewed toxic smoke from thirty-seven tall chimneys. Krasnoyarsk is rich in natural resources – gold, nickel, cobalt, copper, platinum, coal and timber – and sometimes violent struggles were waged over ownership of state assets privatised after the fall of communism. The house was surrounded by a high wall with spiked metal gates and a watchtower from which an armed man in silhouette observed us – a sentry of the new gulag for the rich. "Don't take a photograph," Ararat warned. Said to be the shadow master of Krasnoyarsk, Bykov had a private security fleet of sixteen cars, and swept through town in an armoured Mercedes with sirens screaming. He was eventually arrested and accused of the murder of a crime boss but the charges were dropped and he was released in 2002.

The police in Krasnoyarsk were demoralised by their inability to acquire the professionalism or equipment to cope with the crime wave. Even worse, Ararat said, they were not getting their salaries regularly. They had to accept gifts of cars and radio equipment from rich businessmen seeking their protection. The collapse of the economy in the final years of Boris Yeltsin's presidency left the government unable to pay state salaries. Payment sometimes came in kind. Zhanna's sister Larisa Airieva, then director of a music school, received a carton of socks one month in lieu of pay. Workers at the synthetic rubber plant who had been paid their wages in tyres stood at the side of the road outside, trying to sell them. The rouble's collapse in August 1999 brought more misery. Her mother Marietta had saved enough money in the Yenisei Bank to buy a small apartment but, becoming worried about the country's finances, decided to withdraw everything. The cashier had the money ready to give to her, but she hesitated to take it out and risk getting robbed, and was persuaded to wait until she found the property they wanted. Two days later all accounts were frozen. The savings were later made available, but at a tenth of their former value.

The old Soviet-era questions of "*Shto dyelat?*" and "*Kto vinovat?*" ("What to do?" and "Who is to blame?") still dominated conversations around Krasnoyarsk kitchen tables at the turn of the century. Few wanted to go back to the past, though a certain rose-tinted nostalgia existed for the Brezhnev days of relative stability and plenty. As always in Russia, there was an apt anecdote: "What came first, the chicken or the egg?" Answer: "Why, in former times there was everything." But in former times, obtaining "everything" meant standing in long, quarrelsome queues and sucking up to arrogant shop managers. "We all hate it that the most vulnerable suffer the most," Marietta said to me once, "but now I don't have to humiliate myself to buy cheese." Young people seemed most happy with the changes. They had quickly adapted to a new lifestyle. They cheered on the local rugby club, Krasniy Yar, planned foreign holidays, and studied to be lawyers and economists. They could watch MTV, the US music channel, which competed with the five Russian channels, and they dressed and wore their hair the way the performers did.

The commercial energy released with the fall of communism and the natural wealth of the region transformed Krasnoyarsk inside a decade into a modern European-type city, and the pace quickened after the economy stabilised under President Putin. The city fell in love with red brick. Even the concrete exterior of the biggest city-centre prison was faced with brick. The nineteenth-century buildings on Peace Avenue were renovated and coloured in light pastel shades of blue, yellow and brown. The shabby old Soviet-era stores gave way to delicatessens, boutiques, video stores, jewellers, cake shops, sushi bars and pet food kiosks. A Villeroy & Boch salon was opened near the restored Orthodox Cathedral of the Protection of the Virgin, which in Soviet times was a run-down museum. No longer "irritated", people laughed out loud in the streets. Glamorous women swept along freshly tiled pavements in ankle-length fur coats and wide-brimmed hats, and kids checked their emails on mobile phones.

The city, which flourished a century earlier as a centre for gold prospectors, merchants and speculators, witnessed almost overnight the return of the bourgeoisie and a revival of religion. On Easter Sunday, people took to greeting each other with the words "*Christos voskres*" – "Christ is risen" – and the reply, after three kisses on the cheek: "He is indeed risen."

But crime remained the scourge of the city. During my last conversation with Ararat, on the balcony of his apartment, one warm day in May, he told me that heroin and other drugs were becoming more prevalent as young men found themselves with money to spend. "The mafia have all the arms they want and they take thirty per cent protection from everybody, even the traders in the market," he said. Ararat, then forty-four, had just retired from the police after twenty years' service, and had gone into business with a Tajik partner importing fruit and vegetables, though he continued to act as a "consultant" to the police on serious crimes.

At 7.00 a.m. on 11 June 2003, Ararat stepped out of his apartment building to go to work. Two men got out of a parked white car and walked towards him. He tried to run but they shot him several times at close range and finished him off with knives. Zhanna's father Stanislav, who at age seventy-four still went every day to his leather workshop in the Pushkin Drama Theatre, emerged a few minutes later and found Ararat lying on the ground, as a few neighbours gathered around. The police arrived in great numbers shortly afterwards. Practically the first thing they did was search Ararat's eighth-floor apartment. They did not say what they were looking for, but there were rumours that

Ararat had a tape-recording that might incriminate someone. A local newspaper alleged that two members of the interior ministry were being investigated for the murder. Ararat was given a full-dress funeral, with uniformed police lined up all along the road outside the apartment block.

The family was not informed about what the police were looking for, or what the motive for the murder might have been, or who might have done it, or whether it was connected with Ararat's business or his police work. Nor were they ever told the outcome of any investigation, if there was one.

16

On Being a Pencil

The first thing I did after arriving in Washington in August 1991 as *Irish Times* staff correspondent was to apply for a "hard pass". One journalist from each major foreign newspaper was entitled to a solid, laminated, rectangular pass for admission to the White House. This coveted possession also allowed the bearer to cross lines manned by the Secret Service, the FBI and police forces anywhere in the United States. It once even got me back into the country after I had mislaid my passport on a trip to Canada. To get the hard pass, I had to submit to Secret Service vetting, which took some weeks and inevitably involved checking my file in the US embassy in Dublin. Apparently the decade-old "politically unreliable" note on my file did not make me a security risk, if it was ever there. In any event, I found the White House press corps to be much more politically unreliable than me, if one were to judge by the hostility of the questions about administration policies regularly directed to the press secretary. Many of the younger American journalists had come into the business inspired by the success of Bob Woodward and Carl Bernstein in forcing Richard Nixon out of office, and they dreamed of bringing down a president, so the atmosphere between the media and the White House was usually pretty strained.

The hard pass created a sense of privilege, enabling me to walk past the tourists peering between the railings on Pennsylvania Avenue and get cleared through the Secret Service kiosk. But the glamour soon wore off. The guards were loyal to the President and knew and often disliked journalists for their constant criticisms. We could not enter the White House proper but had to descend a narrow stone staircase, to a shabby basement annex that once housed a sauna and a dog kennel. The press room was little wider than a corridor, containing eight rows of six wooden tip-up seats like a miniature cinema with brass name-plates reserving most of them for the important American media. We foreigners had a difficult time finding a spare seat or putting a question during "feeding time", as the daily briefing was called, since the press secretary hardly ever looked beyond the front-row prima donnas. Space was severely restricted. Beyond a tangle of television cameras at the back of the briefing room were half a dozen small desks for the top news organisations and a couple of sound booths. There was no canteen, just a coffee machine that often didn't work. Everything was focused on the President's agenda, and everyone hung around waiting for briefings or to be shepherded like a pensioners' tour group behind a rope line to see the President shake hands with a foreign dignitary. A small rotating pool of reporters got a special early morning briefing in the White House press office, but there were no exclusives to be had for the likes of me in this caged existence and almost no access to the President and First Lady. Most foreign correspondents didn't bother attending regularly. Getting a question to the President or a call returned by a White House official was so unlikely, it was hardly worth trying.

The most practical, and the worst, advice I ever got about reporting America came from a British colleague whom I consulted on my arrival in the United States. "You get up at six in the morning, you read the *New York Times*, the *Washington Post* and the *Wall Street Journal* – and then you rewrite them," he told me. It was practical in this respect: these newspapers had huge reporting teams and access to the corridors of power, which a single European correspondent could not hope to match. But it was also the worst possible advice because, quite aside from the need to provide original, value-added material to justify the existence and expense of a foreign bureau, it was great fun reporting outside Washington's beltway. And nothing was more fun than following a presidential election, criss-crossing the vast United States, chronicling the greatest soap-opera of American politics, and occasionally joining the "boys on the bus", as reporters assigned to follow the campaigns were called in those politically incorrect days.

I had had my first taste of this a decade earlier, in 1980, when I came to the United States on assignment to report the closing weeks of the presidential election in which Republican Ronald Reagan was trying to unseat President Jimmy Carter. Accompanying the candidates around the United States, I found myself in the middle of a free-wheeling crowd of like-minded "hacks", who existed like soldiers on a battlefield, spending a lot of time waiting about and then engaging in short bursts of intense activity. And, like soldiers, we went where the generals went and deployed under their officers' commands. When they roped us like cattle into a bus or onto an open Chevy truck, we (well, not me personally) responded by baying like farmyard animals, and blowing kazoos and Donald Duck quackers. Bemused citizens waiting to glimpse their candidate might first hear in the distance a long-drawn out "Mooo!" as the travelling media were herded into the motorcade.

I was unofficially a "pencil", i.e. a reporter with a notebook. As one got onto the campaign bus, the cry would go up, "Pencils to the back!" The camera crews with their bulky equipment always had to sit in the front seats nearest the door, so they could get in and out easily. It was the same on the aircraft provided for the media, which often witnessed scenes of near-anarchy. Hardly anyone sat in their seats or strapped on safety belts as the plane taxied down the runway, and the pilot would take off as steeply as possible to allow the more free-spirited among us (again, not me personally) to surf down the aisle on trays, crashing into the back toilets to loud cheers. Plastic chickens, spiders and bats were strung from the overhead lockers, along with balloons and party colours. Flight time was party time. Laptops hadn't been invented, so nobody worked. The air hostesses joined in the fun, strolling down the aisles throwing cans of beer for us to catch, or calling out "Drugs? Anyone want drugs?" as they dispensed aspirin and cough medicine.

When I took a trip on the plane of independent presidential candidate John Anderson, whose very honesty and decency ensured that he would fail, the correspondents once piped him down the aircraft steps with their whistles and kazoos to the tune of "Hail to the Chief", a sympathy gesture to which Anderson responded with a rare grin and a mock salute. Even on Ronald Reagan's plane, where only pool reporters were allowed, there was sometimes fun and games. Nancy Reagan dispensed cheap candies after "wheels up", and at 30,000 feet she had a playful habit of rolling an orange down the aisle like a bowling ball – a tradition kept up by Hillary Clinton in her unsuccessful bid for the Democratic nomination in 2008.

There was, nevertheless, little love lost between the reporters and the candidates. Many star correspondents spent months travelling from city to city on the candidates' planes at enormous expense – usually one and a half times the first-class fare – without ever getting to speak to the person whose every move and action they were paid to observe. Neither Ronald Reagan nor Jimmy Carter were given to cosy chats at the back of the zoo planes. It became something of a game to get a snatched comment from the candidate as everyone milled around at a campaign stop. "Can you say anything to Irish-American voters about your policy towards Ireland?" I asked Reagan as he walked to the bus after a visit to a hog farm. "No, I can't," he replied with a warding-off gesture, to make it clear he couldn't answer any question. The members of the Reagan press core heard his stump speech so many times that they could, and did, mouth it along with him. I was able to do the same myself after travelling with Reagan as a "pencil" on a 300-kilometre "Victory '80 Bus Tour" through Illinois, with stops at Peoria, Normal, Eureka College, Bloomington, Lincoln, McClean, Springfield, Pawnee and Butler, at every one of which he would repeat such lines as: "We used to talk about two cars in every garage; well, we've got that now: they're both Japanese and they're out of gas."

American reporters tried to avoid the lesser campaigns because they rarely made news and that part of their reporting career was likely to be swallowed up into nothingness. One writer assigned to a no-hope candidate tried to phone a story to his office and was put on hold so long that he fell asleep and was still on hold when he woke up six hours later. In this respect foreign correspondents had an advantage over their American colleagues. We could pick and choose campaigns to follow and obtain a better picture of what was happening across the political spectrum. For American writers, getting on the winner's bus was the big prize, leading to fame and book contracts, but predicting early on who would be the winner was a difficult business. The candidates were not party leaders, but individuals who emerged, often from relative obscurity, to identify with one party or the other, and then try to accumulate enough money and hangers-on to conduct a primary campaign and convince Americans they were fit to be the country's chief executive for four years. They often made up policy as they went along, and they were judged by their one-liners as much as by their policies.

It was a one-line riposte that helped Ronald Reagan defeat Jimmy Carter that year. I went to Cleveland, Ohio, for the single televised debate between the two candidates, held a week before voting day, and tried to imagine myself as a regular American figuring out whom to vote for. Carter had been trying to frighten voters by depicting Reagan as a Cold Warrior who could not be trusted on foreign policy. But Reagan projected a folksy image, lacing his replies with dollops of off-by-heart campaign speeches, delivered with the skill of the experienced Hollywood actor that he was. Jimmy Carter, I reckoned, won the debate on the strength of his intellectual argument, but he picked on Reagan all evening, and when he accused his adversary of being ill-informed on health care, Reagan replied with a sigh, "There you go again!" The line, played over and over on the television news, became the message. Already blamed for inflation, petrol queues and the hostage crisis in Tehran, Carter came across as preachy, and Reagan as someone unfairly put upon. The old ham actor employed a similar technique when debating with Walter Mondale four years later. Challenged about his age – he was then seventy-four – Reagan replied that he would never for political purposes take advantage of his opponent's youth and inexperience.

As Jimmy Carter struggled to retain the White House, I left the boys on the bus and flew to Iowa, where he had famously jump-started his presidential campaign. In the hamlet of Irish Settlement in Madison County, John Connor, a tall, quiet-spoken farmer whom I had met when he had greeted Pope John Paul II a year earlier, told me he had voted for Carter in 1976 but could not stomach the thought of voting for him again because of his bungling ineptitude on the economy. I found similar dissatisfaction with one-time Carter voters among Jewish retirees in Florida, blue-collar workers in Michigan and company executives in Ohio. It was no surprise to me that Reagan won the 1980 election, and by a huge majority. Deceived by pre-election opinion polls showing the two contenders almost level in the closing stages, a number of pundits who stayed inside the beltway were still calling it for Carter right to the end.

The conventional wisdom in 1991 was that the presidential election the following year would be a rather boring affair, as

George H.W. Bush, who had become president after two terms as Reagan's vice president, would win simply by showing up. Early in the year his approval rating had soared to eighty-eight per cent after the successful US-led military campaign to evict Saddam Hussein's invading forces from Kuwait. The Democratic Party was in disarray and its big names – Al Gore, Dick Gephardt, Sam Nunn and Jay Rockefeller – were refusing to run against a seemingly invincible president. The Governor of Arkansas, William Jefferson Clinton, was considered a long shot when he announced in September that he would seek the Democratic nomination.

When the campaign started I flew to Iowa and went with John Connor to the district Democratic caucus, held in the front room of Joyce Kooker's farmhouse, one of 2,189 similar meetings that made up the Iowa caucus on 10 February 1992. This was real grass-roots politics. Eighteen neighbours, lounging in a circle of sofas, armchairs and kitchen chairs, took a cursory look at leaflets for Bill Clinton and other Democratic runners, Paul Tsongas and Bob Kerrey, chatted a bit over tea and cookies, and then voted *en masse* for Iowa senator Tom Harkin, an old-fashioned "Grapes-of-Wrath" Democrat, who had no chance of the nomination, but who was a local favourite. Here, however, I picked up some interesting information. I was disabused of any notion that Bush had retained his popular post-Gulf War support. John Connor bitterly regretted deserting his Democratic roots in the three previous presidential elections to vote Republican. Many farmers had had to sell parcels of land to stay in business, as prices for milk, cattle and hogs had fallen steadily under Reagan and Bush, he said. A true-blue Republican neighbour, Richard Hanrahan, took a break from hauling corn silage the next day to tell me he too would not vote for Bush. "You can't raise corn and beans and make money any more," he complained.

I moved on to New Hampshire for the first Republican and Democratic primary elections a week later. A conservative journalist, Patrick Buchanan, had challenged the President for the Republican nomination, and was giving out false lips at rallies to mock the pledge made by Bush in his 1988 campaign – "Read my lips, no new taxes" – which he had spectacularly broken. Sitting presidents do not usually campaign in primaries, but sensing danger, Bush hastily called an election rally in the gymnasium of Pinkerton Academy in the town of Derry, New Hampshire, three days before voting. This rally would be a test of his popularity. The first person I interviewed there, Bob Boilard, turned out to be a sailing companion of Bush from neighbouring Maine, and the second, Emile Roy, was the President's holiday barber. It was rent-a-crowd. Despite the presence of Arnold Schwarzenegger and his out-of-state friends, George Bush still couldn't quite fill the gym. It was evident he was not going to be a "shoo-in" for a second term.

The Democratic candidate was also struggling. Just before the Democratic primary in New Hampshire, *The Star*, a ninety-five-cent scandal sheet, splashed a story about singer Gennifer Flowers, under the headline "My 12-year Affair with Bill Clinton". This enabled the campaign reporters, who knew about Flowers but had been constrained by her previous denials from writing anything, to come down from their high moral ground and run with the story. Criticism of American journalists by historians for failing to report on President John F. Kennedy's affairs – which had threatened national security – had created a climate in which the new generation of reporters felt less of an obligation to ignore the private lives of politicians. They were raring to go.

Bill and Hillary Clinton in turn used the media for damage control. They offered themselves to CBS for a special *60 Minutes* interview, shot against a tableau arranged by Hillary of a log fire with brass fireguard, to convey a warm family setting. "You're looking at two people who love each other," said Bill Clinton, when asked about his marriage "arrangement". The public reaction was positive. The press backed away from the story, slightly ashamed of its muck-raking, and reluctant to play a part in bringing down an energetic and intelligent Democratic candidate of high-minded ambition. At the Democratic Governors' dinner in Washington's Shoreham Hotel a week after the CBS interview, hundreds of shrieking women in sequins and hearty men in tuxedos gave the Clintons a tumultuous welcome as they arrived hand-in-hand. "Most of the money is going for Clinton now," House Speaker Tom Foley told me as he tucked into his veal chop. On 18 February, Clinton came second in the New Hampshire primary, called himself the come-back kid – a phrase that his wife would use sixteen years later in the same primary – and went on to do sufficiently well to secure the nomination.

The American media also gave Clinton an easy ride over one of the most cynical acts of his campaign. He returned to Arkansas in January 1992 so that he could supervise the execution of Ricky Ray Rector, a cop-killer whose botched effort at suicide had left him so brain-damaged he saved the dessert of his last meal for after his execution. If Clinton, who espoused "liberal" ideals, had any doubts about his role in the state killing of a mentally deficient person – banned ten years later by the US Supreme Court as "cruel and unusual punishment" – he didn't entertain them at a time when he needed the "red-neck" vote.

I was always opposed to capital punishment and once forced myself to attend an execution in the United States so I could report on what it meant in practice. I chose the execution of a person who had committed awful crimes, to lessen any feeling of sympathy I might have had. It was scheduled to take place at dawn inside Florida State Prison, not far from Jacksonville. The judicial killing by electricity of thirty-three-year-old Michael Durocher, who had brutally murdered his girlfriend, her five-year-old daughter, his six-year-old son, a flat-mate and a man he robbed, was carried out shortly after he had consumed a breakfast of five pounds of jumbo shrimp, batter fried, with melted butter and ketchup, a pint of chocolate ice cream and a two-litre bottle of Coke. Two prison officers strapped him to a three-legged chair by arms, chest and waist, clamped a leather chin strap over his mouth and tied a black mask over his head. A prison officer rolled up the prisoner's right trouser leg and bound an electrode and sponge below the knee. At 7.06 a.m. a hidden executioner, who would receive a fee of $150, pulled a switch. A large puff of smoke rose from Durocher's knee. A person literally fries in the electric chair, and in post-electrocution autopsies the liver can be too hot to touch by hand. His clenched right fist snapped inward, the thumb sticking out. One witness leaned forward with an intake of breath; otherwise none of us in the observation booth made a sound. Two doctors in white coats fussed around Durocher with stethoscopes. It was six more minutes before they were able to pronounce him dead.

I didn't smoke cigarettes at the time but outside the prison I took a cigarette from one of the local reporters. I found myself shaking. We talked about Durocher. "He's a sweetheart" spat out the reporter, who fully approved of what he had just seen. Another joined us to wisecrack that executions were "a way of life" in Florida. I came away from the experience sickened by what I had seen and more convinced than ever that capital punishment brutalised the state itself and everyone associated with it.

George Bush had a miserable time trying to stay presidential and above the fray as Clinton surged ahead in the 1992 election. On a trip to Japan he caught a stomach bug and threw up over the trousers of the unfortunate Japanese Prime Minister, Kiichi Miyazawa, at a state dinner. It was one of those cruel incidents that define a politician in the United States. The media made it a metaphor for a failed presidency. The US economy slipped into recession, and both blue-collar and white-collar workers experienced falling living standards. Bush secured the Republican nomination again, but fell back in the polls as the number of jobless rose. By the time of the Republican Convention in Houston in August, his camp was using the fear factor that Carter had employed so unsuccessfully in 1980, trying to frighten voters at the prospect of giving the presidency, as Bush's key strategist Mary Matalin put it, to a "philandering, pot-smoking draft-dodger". The convention is remembered, however, for Pat Buchanan's intolerant and xenophobic opening night speech about culture wars in the United States, which alienated moderate Republican voters.

The Democratic convention in New York's Madison Square Gardens, on the other hand, was a Broadway spectacular, designed to redefine the philandering candidate, sometimes called "Slick Willie", as a family man with the vision to change America. No one listened to the speeches. Wandering around the floor during debates, I encountered a man ringing a bell, another with a false nose and a third cradling a baby. Men in baggy shorts and ten-gallon hats argued and joked with women in business suits. Other delegates wandered round gossiping, waving placards and looking for celebrities like Oliver Stone. Hillary Clinton was repackaged too. She transformed herself from an assertive lawyer, which wasn't going down well with focus groups, into a wide-eyed mother figure, eager to talk about child-rearing and making cookies.

After the Democratic convention, Clinton and his running mate Al Gore and their wives Hillary and Tipper set out across the country in a caravan of silver luxury buses with smoked windows, to address rallies in Pennsylvania, West Virginia, Ohio and Kentucky. Democrats were haunted by the memory of 1988 when Michael Dukakis went home after the convention and lost a seventeen-point lead. Clinton was not going to make the same mistake.

In September, in the closing stages of the campaign, I joined the "boys on the train", as President Bush tried to win back popular support by travelling from Ohio to Michigan on a seventeen-carriage train, called the "Spirit of America". Bush was hoping to emulate President Harry Truman's famous train journey in 1948, which helped him defeat the hot favourite, Thomas Dewey, with a substantial voter swing in the last two weeks. As Bush's train chugged past trailer parks and frame houses, we leafed through a Truman biography, which told how every single journalist on the Truman train had wrongly forecast that he would be beaten, despite huge, enthusiastic crowds at each stop. This time, however, the crowds were thin. There was ritual cheering and applause, but many spectators kept their arms folded. One man in a field near Toledo dropped his trousers and mooned his President as the train passed. At most stops a man dressed as a chicken appeared, taunting Bush for his refusal to agree a date for a debate with his Democratic challenger. "There he is, the chicken, . . . from Oxford, England," cried an exasperated Bush at Bowling Green, hoping to remind voters of Clinton's stay at Oxford during the Vietnam War draft. A number of times, exploiting a vein of redneck provincialism, he referred to Clinton's "Oxford cronies" and to his opponent as an "Oxford debater". The word "Oxford" was designed to taint Clinton, a Rhodes scholar, as elite and foreign. Bush went on to deride Clinton for "seeking foreign policy advice from the rock group U2", a reference to a radio interview Clinton had given to Bono.

One of the defining events of the closing stages of the 1992 election was a report in the *New York Times* that Bush appeared "amazed" upon seeing a demonstration of a supermarket scanner. It was a bit unfair. The writer exaggerated a pool report, but it got widespread coverage and enhanced the perception of the President as out of touch with working Americans.

Another incident portrayed his photogenic Vice-President, Dan Quayle, as rather dim. Quayle told a child in a classroom at Trenton, New Jersey, that potato should be spelt "potatoe". The US media had a field day. "It was a defining moment of the worst kind imaginable," Quayle would admit after the election. "Politicians live and die by the symbolic soundbite."

He should know. I went one hot mid-October morning to a Quayle rally at Auburn University in Alabama. Arriving two hours early, I saw Republican Party officials produce from a large cardboard box dozens of hand-written posters of various sizes, made to look as if they had been scrawled by enthusiastic fans in a garage, and pass them out to students arriving for the rally in a corner of the university baseball stadium. This was pretty routine stuff for all candidates in American elections. Television crews arrived and were escorted onto a platform facing the podium, with the students on risers behind waving the placards. No other camera angles were allowed. A band blasted out "Where's that Tiger?" as the Vice-President appeared, jumping onto the podium and making a pistol with his thumb and finger as if greeting a top supporter – he always did this in front of cameras, noted the *New Republic*, even if it was only to the backside of a Secret Service agent. "Do you want a president who is going to raise taxes?" he called out. "No!" they shouted back. And after a couple more exchanges like that, the Vice-President and his wife tossed Frisbees into the crowd and were gone, heading back to Air Force Two in their reinforced black limousine. On television that evening the national news showed Quayle, shirt sleeves rolled up, against a tableau of cheering supporters, as he delivered what looked like the high point of a lengthy political speech.

Both campaigns positioned their candidates in front of cheering supporters, the difference being that Bill Clinton was getting genuine, enthusiastic, Truman-like crowds at every stop. He worked a rope line at a college in Billings, Montana, signing homework books for teenagers too young to vote, as daylight turned into darkness and long after the cameras had gone. This meant long delays in the schedule of his final plane-hopping swing from Little Rock, Arkansas, to Pueblo, Colorado; Cheyenne, Wyoming; Billings, Montana; Seattle, Washington; Eugene, Oregon;

and Orange County, California. The press plane always took off after the candidate's plane and arrived before it, to allow the camera crews (and the pencils) to record the candidate's departure and arrival. (This practice was called the death watch: if the plane crashed on take-off or landing, the networks didn't want to miss it.) As always we found it almost impossible to get near the candidate. At one stop I saw a colleague from a British Sunday newspaper, desperate for an original story, push his way towards Clinton and call out, "What did you learn at Oxford?" The candidate replied, "I learned a lot," before being swallowed up in the crowd. I could only admire my colleague's genius for turning a sow's ear into a silk purse. His subsequent report began, "Pausing in his hectic campaign to discuss with me his days at Oxford University, Bill Clinton . . ."

The anarchy on the press plane terrified newcomers who hitched a lift between touchdowns. The Governor of New Mexico's personal bodyguard, a well-groomed Hispanic-American in white Stetson with a .45 inside his neat suit, squeezed into the seat beside me in Pueblo. "Unbelievable," he muttered, as the aisle surfers skidded past us on trays and the hostesses cheered.

That election, which Bill Clinton won with forty-three per cent of the popular vote against thirty-seven per cent for Bush and nineteen per cent for independent Ross Perot, was probably the last hurrah of the "pencils". Future presidential elections would be dominated by twenty-four-hour cable news channels and the internet, which would make everyone a political analyst, without ever getting on a bus.

17

Dining for Ireland

Ireland has one unique advantage over other countries in its relations with the United States. The taoiseach is guaranteed access to the White House on one day a year, St Patrick's Day, to present a bowl of shamrock to the United States president. Before Bill Clinton, American presidents considered this a pleasant but inconsequential formality, requiring only a green tie and a few words about the contribution the Irish had made to the United States, always including of course how Irish architect James Hoban had designed the White House. Otherwise they largely adhered to the long-established Cold War convention, that Northern Ireland was an internal problem for the United Kingdom – with which the US had a "special relationship" – and was therefore none of America's business. On George H.W. Bush's last St Patrick's Day in office in 1992, the Taoiseach, Albert Reynolds, did not bother coming to Washington, sending the Minister for Foreign Affairs, David Andrews, in his place. No Dublin-based political correspondent thought it worth their while to make the journey either. The Irish Ambassador, Dermot Gallagher, suggested that I turn up in a good suit so he could slip me into the White House as a member of the official delegation. I recall seeing the Secretary of State, James Baker, hanging around as I posed with the President for a picture by the unlit Oval Office fireplace, wondering if he had nothing better to do with his time.

Bill Clinton changed all that. During his 1992 presidential election campaign he told a group of Irish-American activists that in the aftermath of the Cold War a new "governing rationale" was needed for US engagement in Northern Ireland, and he made a number of promises, including a visa for Gerry Adams and the appointment of a peace envoy for Northern Ireland. The prospect of real presidential engagement on Ireland encouraged Albert Reynolds to come to Washington for Clinton's first St Patrick's Day event in the White House in 1993, accompanied by several Irish political correspondents. Clinton marked the occasion by announcing the appointment of Jean Kennedy Smith as ambassador to Ireland, and he promised to lend his support when needed to any peace initiatives. Reynolds told a jubilant John Hume in Washington's Phoenix Park Hotel afterwards that what had happened was "beyond my wildest dreams". The President held a news conference that day inside the White House for Irish journalists, another first, and attended the annual dinner of the Ireland Fund, where he sang "When Irish Eyes Are Smiling" along with a distinguished gathering of Irish Americans and with Phil Coulter on the piano.

After that I began to get my calls returned by the White House and interview requests taken seriously. In early December 1993, the President agreed to answer a series of written questions from me on aspects of his policy on Northern Ireland and the evolving peace process. Written answers were more important than oral responses because they represented considered administration policy. I was told I would get the answers on 17 December. The day came and went. White House communications director Mark Gearan told me there was some issue with the wording. The draft responses, prepared by officials, had, I learned later, been shown to the Irish embassy for comment. Clinton's new "governing rationale" meant that the playing field was now level, if not tilted towards the Irish. Subtle changes suggested by Irish diplomat Michael Collins, who knew that Reynolds was exploring initiatives to encourage an IRA ceasefire, were incorporated after three days of textual exchanges. A draft reply stating that Gerry Adams could not get a US visa waiver because of immigration laws regarding terrorist activity was amended to read, "We will, of course, keep the issue under review as the developing situation warrants, especially in light of events flowing from the December 15th Joint Declaration by Prime Minister Reynolds and Prime Minister Major." This meant that for the first time the visa issue was linked to political developments. Shortly after we published this response, the Irish-American lobby organised a snap conference on Northern Ireland in New York and at short notice invited all the Northern Ireland party leaders, including Adams, who promptly applied for a visa waiver.

The visa waiver application became a hot potato for the White House. The British government, the CIA, the FBI, the Justice Department and the Democratic House Speaker, Tom Foley, all opposed granting it, while a group of important senators led by Ted Kennedy, Chris Dodd and George Mitchell, as well as Jean Kennedy Smith in Ireland, John Hume and (ever so quietly) the Irish government, voiced their support on the grounds that it would show the IRA there were political dividends to be earned if it gave up the use of violence. Few Washington-based reporters followed what was going on. Most of the British correspondents regarded news relating to Northern Ireland as a distraction from the greater issues burning up the wires between London and Washington, and the regular White House reporters were preoccupied with their domestic issues, so I found that I was often alone in making the calls from day to day. Thus I was able to establish, at about eleven o'clock on Sunday, 30 January 1994, that the President had, just minutes before, signed off on a historic decision to lift the decades-old ban and allow Adams to visit New York for the conference. This was a great scoop. Even the British government did not know yet of the decision, which it would inevitably regard as a betrayal of the special relationship. The problem for me was that I also knew the President would make a formal announcement later in the afternoon, which meant that every newspaper, not just *The Irish Times*, would have the story the next morning.

In the news business, information is a commodity, sometimes to be exchanged among colleagues in the profession. I called Susan Cornwell, White House correspondent for Reuters and a friend from Moscow days, and told her about the President's decision. Susan, one of the few American reporters who followed events regarding Northern Ireland, had to confirm the story herself before putting it out on the wires, which she did by using a classic ploy. She telephoned the Justice Department, where, as she anticipated, she got a "no comment". Then she called the White House and told Nancy Soderberg, staff director of the National Security Council (NSC), that she had been talking to the Justice Department and that she knew a decision had been taken to give Adams a visa waiver. Both assertions were, strictly speaking, true. "They shouldn't have told you," Soderberg replied, inadvertently giving Susan the confirmation she needed. Reuters put the story out early that afternoon. Incredibly, the White House had still not got around to informing the British Ambassador, Sir Robin Renwick, who had been warning the administration daily that a visa to Adams would be seen in Britain as rewarding terrorism. Hearing it from the media added insult to British injury. So, inadvertently, I had worsened a rift between Washington and London.

Months later when I interviewed Soderberg for a book I was writing about Clinton's involvement in Ireland, she recalled with some annoyance that there had been a "leak" from the Justice Department about the visa decision. British diplomat Jonathan

Powell, who lobbied hard against the visa, complained in his book *Great Hatred, Little Room*, published by Bodley Head in 2008, that the White House "didn't tell us what their decision had been until it was on the wires" and that British Prime Minister John Major was furious and had instructed the embassy to cease co-operation with the NSC. Powell had opposed the visa vigorously, as he was paid to do, he recalled, but in retrospect Clinton was "clearly right in the decision he made". One might also conclude in retrospect that the furious British opposition also helped the peace process since it allowed Gerry Adams not only to show the IRA that politics could achieve more than the bomb but that it could also give them a big victory over the British at their own game.

The following Saint Patrick's Day President Clinton threw a splendid party in the White House for Albert Reynolds and the Irish visitors, which included an even bigger media contingent. Normally only pool reporters were invited to such events, and they would be corralled behind a golden rope in a corner to observe the great and the good for a few minutes, before being escorted out. But the White House threw the event open to all the Irish reporters covering the Taoiseach's visit, and we found ourselves mingling with Hollywood celebrities like Paul Newman and Richard Harris, as well as top administration officials and heavyweight senators and congressmen. Chuck Feeney, the philanthropist whose biography I would later write, was there with Niall O'Dowd's group of Irish-American peace-makers. This was unprecedented access for all of us to Washington's power elite. We were given the run of the second floor of the White House and wandered in and out of drawing-rooms, looking out at the magnificent views over the Washington Mall and sampling the buffet of Blarney cheese, Irish coffee cake and green chocolate bowler hats filled with ice-cream.

Information and contacts have always been the life-blood of Washington, and dinner parties the mechanism to bring together politicians, journalists, diplomats and government officials. No embassy could match the British for their insider guest list, which regularly included secretaries of state and military brass, but at Irish embassy dinners I now found myself sitting beside "power" guests like FBI Director Louis Freeh and Ben Bradley of the *Washington Post*. Out in the suburb of Chevy Chase, a Dublin-born hostess, Stella O'Leary, and her partner Tom Halton, had important figures like Education Secretary Dick O'Reilly to their dinner parties. Another frequent guest was former US Senator Eugene McCarthy, who could always be depended upon to recite reams of W.B. Yeats, or his own poetry, before the evening was out. McCarthy had a prodigious memory and a mischievous sense of humour. He told us how once, when he was invited to the Yeats Summer School in Sligo, he reckoned there would be recitals after hours, so "I decided to memorise something most of them wouldn't have done, and when they got done with 'Easter 1916' and 'The Second Coming', I'd say, well now, anybody here know 'The Wanderings of Oisin'?"

When the first visa waiver for Gerry Adams yielded the dividend of an IRA ceasefire on 29 August 1994, the Sinn Féin leader was granted permission to return to the United States and this time to visit Washington. Adams was still a political "untouchable" as far as the British and Irish governments were concerned. The White House lifted an order banning official contacts with Sinn Féin, but in response to a personal plea from John Major, pointing out that the IRA had not declared its ceasefire permanent, Clinton agreed that the White House would not engage with Adams on this occasion. I had never met Adams and, with the approval of my editor Conor Brady, I invited him to a private dinner in our house in Bethesda, to which I could attract some Washington movers and shakers. Nancy Soderberg accepted an invitation, though she had to get Clinton's personal clearance for what would be an "off-campus" encounter with the Sinn Féin leader. Dean Curran, Deputy Assistant Secretary of State, also got special clearance. The other guests included Democratic Senator Chris Dodd and the *Washington Post's* Pulitzer Prize-winning columnist Mary McGrory, whose reporting dated back to the Eisenhower era and who was very sceptical about the peace process and Sinn Féin.

Word of the event leaked – this was Washington after all – and it became a story in the British media because a White House official would be attending and this could be seen as a breach of Clinton's promise. It was a novel experience to find myself on the other side, creating rather than reporting news, though this was never my intention. Peter Hitchens, then correspondent of the *Daily Express* and a good friend who had a deep abhorrence for Sinn Féin, had fun writing a story about how he would be checking next morning under his car, to make sure the visitors to his neighbourhood hadn't left a "peace-making device" there. Ben Macintyre in *The Times* speculated that "any hope that Mr O'Clery's guests could quietly enjoy grilling Mr Adams over grilled turbot has now been dashed, since the dinner party venue is likely to be besieged by reporters". The *Irish Echo* speculated, tongue in cheek, that the menu would be Anglo-Irish stew, Codology, Paisley pudding and "leak" soup. *The Guardian's* Martin Walker seemed a bit put out when asked during an interview on National Public Radio if he had been invited (he hadn't), but he claimed that he had made it clear (not to me) that he did not wish to be invited into Adams's company, and rather churlishly he wondered aloud if we would be serving "kneecap soup".

We weren't besieged by reporters after all because, just before the event, Vice-President Al Gore agreed to take a telephone call from Adams, so the off-campus meeting between the Sinn Féin leader and Soderberg became moot. I sat Adams between Mary McGrory, who decided she didn't like him, and Nancy Soderberg of the White House, who decided she did, which counted more.

Loyalist politicians soon began making the transatlantic crossing after loyalist paramilitary groups also declared a ceasefire, on 13

October 1994. Gusty Spence, David Ervine and Billy Hutchinson of the Progressive Unionist Party, which had ties to the UVF, and Joe English, Gary McMichael and Davy Adams of the Ulster Democratic Party, which was close to the UDA, were hosted on a trip to the United States by Bill Flynn's Mutual of America company in New York. Ed Kenny, a vice-president in Mutual, who had just resigned from a twenty-five-year career in the FBI, was delegated to escort them to Washington. He quipped to me, "Six weeks earlier I probably could have been surveilling these guys." They were able to meet congressional aides on Capitol Hill but diplomatic and social Washington was still closed to loyalist paramilitary representatives – so I invited them also to our house, along with some British colleagues, including Hitchens, who declined to shake their hands, saying, "I have a no-handshake policy on Northern Ireland". Earlier the *Express* man had refused an invitation to shake hands with Gerry Adams on a television programme because of his support for political violence. The following year the loyalists came back for a party at the house during an investment conference for Northern Ireland, held in Washington at the initiative of President Clinton. Dermot Gallagher and his wife Maeve came along, as did several senior members of RTÉ and a number of visiting Irish journalists. Michael Keane, editor of the *Sunday Press*, had occasion to remember that day well. He got a call from Dublin to say that the *Irish Press* Group had closed and he was out of a job. Joe English borrowed my daughter Julia's guitar and, to the astonishment of the guests, strummed a republican favourite, "The Fields of Athenry", following which Billy Hutchinson announced – joking of course – "We've been watching who joined in. Now we've identified who the republicans are."

Eventually everyone became *persona grata* in the US capital and the Clintons' St Patrick's Day party turned into one of the glittering occasions of the Washington social calendar. In an effort to encourage the peace process, the White House also opened its doors to all Irish political representatives who came to Washington. No other country's politicians enjoyed such privileged access. The hard pass came into its own and Irish policy came up regularly at "feeding time" in the White House press room and at the President's press conferences. Even when Clinton held a press conference in Hong Kong during a visit to China, I was brought up to the front row by his press secretary, Mike McCurry, so that he could take a pre-arranged question from me about Drumcree. It was a unique time in the relationship between a small European country and the most powerful nation in the world.

When George W. Bush became President in 2001, his domestic, foreign and socialising priorities were different. No longer would Northern Ireland politicians blithely stroll up to the West Wing of the White House and gain automatic access to officials of the National Security Council or to the President himself. The White House parties were downgraded to modest receptions. But by then it didn't matter very much. The Washington involvement in the peace process had served its purpose.

Coincidentally, under the new administration, the hard pass for overseas journalists was no longer given out, unless the reporter guaranteed to attend briefings every day, which most foreign correspondents would consider a waste of time, especially since they are now televised live.

18

The Bishop Casey Affair

In February 1992 a man called Arthur Pennell telephoned the
Irish Times newsdesk in Dublin to make a startling allegation –
that Bishop Eamon Casey of Galway was the father of a teenage
boy whom he and his partner Annie Murphy were raising in the
United States. The duty news editor, John Armstrong, passed the
information on to me in Washington. I drove to the address he
had given in Ridgefield, Connecticut and rang the bell of their
apartment.

I didn't relish the assignment. I was not in any way protective
of the flamboyant sixty-five-year-old Bishop, though I admired
him as a co-founder of the homeless charity, Shelter, and for his
work for the Irish in Britain, and I regarded him as the most
progressive of the conservative Irish bishops, well known for his
criticisms of apartheid and of US policies in Central America. I
feared I might be wasting my time, just as the presidential
primaries were getting really interesting. Even if true, there were
good reasons for *The Irish Times* to be apprehensive about
accusing an Irish Catholic bishop of fathering a secret love child,
given its origins as a Protestant paper. Getting it wrong could
bring the wrath of the Catholic establishment down on our
heads, discredit the paper, and bankrupt us if the Bishop took a

successful libel action. Moreover, the paper might simply decide not to publish what was a private matter between two adults. These were the days before the Church was embroiled in sex scandals and we had no real idea of the extent of sex abuse and cover-up in the Irish priesthood. Many Irish people saw the members of the Catholic hierarchy as the country's moral guardians and knelt and kissed the rings of bishops as a matter of course. This was dangerous territory.

Edinburgh-born Arthur Pennell greeted me in his pronounced Scottish accent and took me upstairs to their flat. Annie and her son Peter were there. She was a slim woman of forty-three, attractive, composed, but full of anger and nervous energy. Peter was a good-looking, strapping eighteen-year-old with a strong resemblance to Bishop Casey. From his confident demeanour, it was obvious he was a key figure in the drama, despite his youth. He was determined the truth should be told, he said, and this was that Bishop Casey was his father. After a preliminary chat, Annie suddenly turned to Peter and said, "Take down your trousers." He obliged. He pulled up his shirt tail to display on his thigh a large birthmark. "You will find that Eamon Casey has the same birthmark," she said. She proceeded to tell me, without any embarrassment, that the affair had happened when Casey was Bishop of Kerry and she had been sent to Ireland by her father to recover from a messy relationship. He was then forty-six and she was twenty-four. She described how she had given birth to Peter in a hospital in Dublin, where the nuns tried to force her to give him up for adoption. Bishop Casey had since then paid her substantial sums of money for Peter's maintenance and education. For fifteen years regular payments, lately of $275 a month, had come to her via a solicitor in County Kerry or from a Polish woman in Rochester, New York, who sent personal cheques, and sometimes from a lawyer in New York.

Whatever right to privacy the Bishop might have had, the payments raised questions of public interest. Casey had no known personal wealth, which indicated that the money could have been misappropriated from diocesan funds or provided from a Catholic Church slush fund to hush up scandals.

Pennell seemed resentful of the Bishop's pre-eminence in their lives and of Annie Murphy's obsession with him. He said he had known the Bishop was Peter's father since the start of his relationship with Annie, whom he had met at a session of Alcoholics Anonymous. He first saw the Bishop on US television one day in the mid-1980s, when Peter was barely a teenager. Casey was shown criticising President Ronald Reagan over his Central America policies. Pennell recalled that he shouted to Annie, "Hey! Let Peter see his father!" After that they discussed confronting the Bishop to get him to acknowledge his son.

In May 1988, Pennell did confront the Bishop, at the door of his residence in Galway. He didn't beat around the bush, he said. "I'm Arthur from Connecticut. I've been with Annie for many years and I'm bringing up your son. What are you prepared to do about it?" Casey invited him in. He refused, said Pennells, to admit that Peter was his son, explaining, "It could have been Paddy the porter, or a hotelier, or her ex-husband." Annie said later that she did not have a relationship with anyone else in Ireland and the reference to "Paddy the porter" was a joke – he was a porter in the Burlington Hotel in Dublin where she had worked. In Pennell's account of the meeting, the Bishop also threatened to resign right away if Pennell made public any story about him being the father. Murphy explained that, after this, she decided to sue the Bishop "for his brutal abuse of me". An action she took for damage to her health when the baby was born – she had had a clot in her leg – led to legal negotiations that concluded on 25 July 1990, when she received two cheques of $90,000 and $8,000 in a private settlement of her claim on the Bishop. Her lawyer, Peter McKay, received $25,000 for legal fees. The transaction was handled on the Bishop's side by a lawyer-priest from Brooklyn, Monsignor James Kelly, who did not charge for his services. Bishop Casey came to New York to sign the necessary papers.

Peter told me he managed to see his father privately after the signing. "It was a five-minute conversation basically pertaining to how my studies were, how my Mom was, and how he prayed for me three times a day. Basically it was short, concise and swift and he was out of the door." He added witheringly: "He didn't look at me while we were talking." The Bishop treated him as "a small clerical error in his life". That was one reason why he wanted the facts published.

The last time Annie had seen the Bishop before going to *The Irish Times* was on 21 August 1991. They had arranged to meet in the Hotel Grand Hyatt in New York to discuss Peter's college fees and her request for help in selling a small house she had bought in Ireland. She got a friend and Peter to make a video secretly of the two sitting together in the lobby as evidence of their liaison.

"Why make it public now?" I asked. "I feel that Eamon is a hooligan," she said. "He thinks it's a game. And I like a game, too. But this is my son and I can't play that game, so I feel the gig's up." How could he have prevented this happening? "All he ever had to do was just call occasionally, and say, 'How is Peter doing?', and heartfelt, as if he meant it." He could have been "Uncle Eamon", so "Peter could have some kind of identity and maybe . . . he could have seen him in the summer or just had the doors open, and not treat him as something to be mortally ashamed of and to brush under the rug."

Annie gave me copies of letters from the Bishop, one on notepaper headed "Mount St Mary's, Galway", dated 23 November 1976, which said: "I hope the situation for Peter and yourself has improved since you wrote. I will put the other matter in hand immediately, not because of your threat, but because I can quite appreciate your difficulties. It will take a little time to get it organised but it will be with you well before

Christmas. God bless and keep you both, Annie." It was signed "Eamon".

I must have made a good impression. Annie would later describe me, in her book *Forbidden Fruit*, co-authored with Peter De Rosa and published by Little, Brown, as "a tall handsome man with friendly eyes [who] struck us instantly as not only very professional but someone we could trust". I did promise to follow up the story as far as I could go, while warning her that publication of any scandal touching the Catholic Church in Ireland would require handling with great care and attention to detail and that, even if true, the paper might not publish. She said they had chosen *The Irish Times* to tell their story because people would believe it if it appeared there. They had tried to interest a local US television station a month earlier, but it had not taken the matter up, she said, out of fear that the IRA would come after them.

I reported back to Conor Brady that the story rang true, and sent him a copy of my taped conversation with Annie Murphy so he could get a sense of her. He set up – and swore to secrecy – a newsroom team consisting of chief news editor Eugene McEldowney, news editor John Armstrong, religious affairs correspondent Andy Pollak, and a libel lawyer. The editorial team looked at the story from all angles. What if the Bishop of Galway was not the father, as he had intimated to Arthur Pennell in Galway, and that he had been blackmailed into paying maintenance? What if he had been paying the money on behalf of someone else? Casey had never admitted paternity in writing to anyone – neither to Murphy nor to his lawyers. There was another consideration. Annie Murphy's intermediaries were in negotiations about further maintenance with the Bishop, and might be using the threat of exposure in *The Irish Times* as leverage. If both parties reached a settlement and Annie then denied what she had told us, what would we do?

Bishop Casey in fact had started sending money again to help meet Peter's college expenses. He had authorised two cheques, drawn on a Home Savings Bank in Brooklyn by Father Kelly, for $6,500 and $3,350 towards Peter's college tuition. I asked Annie to request that her lawyer, Peter McKay, co-operate in locating other documents. We were principally interested in the origin of the large sums of money paid out earlier by the Bishop. But she rang me to say her lawyer did not wish to co-operate with the press. McKay confirmed this to me in a rather abrupt telephone conversation.

In March 1992, as *The Irish Times* was meticulously following the money trail, Annie telephoned me to say that McKay, Pennell, her son Peter and Father Kelly were all involved in new negotiations for a final settlement. This would be to the tune of $125,000 to $150,000 for Peter's education. Part of the deal would be no publicity. However, she said, she was not involved and wanted to play straight with me. "You know me. I'll go to the end" to make the story public, she said.

These were the first signs of divisions within the family over how to handle the situation. A few days later Arthur telephoned to say that by contacting McKay I had stirred up a "hornet's nest". McKay had entered negotiations with Father Kelly, who was now offering $150,000 in the name of the Bishop for Peter's college education. The problem was, Pennell said, it had been made clear to them that any story in the papers would kill the goose that had laid the golden egg. They wanted to accept the money and not now have the story published. "Eamon is going to give us that – fifty per cent right away, the whole lot by the end of the year," he said. Also, Bishop Casey now wanted to see Peter. Pennell said he didn't like to see Peter "jerked around" by a "newspaper out to make money". I reminded him rather sharply that he had approached us with the information and it would be our decision whether to publish or not. Pennell said that, in that event, he wanted to see the story first (something we would never allow) or we should wait until the end of the year. "I don't want to be in the position of taking the money and then next day saying, 'Publish'," he said.

He then announced rather dramatically that someone had been trying to kill Peter. "We have a police matter on our hands," he said. Their car had been tampered with five times "by professionals" who had loosened the wheel nuts. Pennell had contacted the police but they had "pooh-poohed" the whole thing. "It has come to the point," he said, "where I'm not interested in anything except $150,000 for Peter. If I have to, I will get a gun to do what I will have to do." "Are you threatening me?" I asked. "No! No! No!" he said emphatically. He meant he would get whomever was out to get Peter. I later contacted the police for confirmation of the reported threat. They said they had received a complaint from Pennell but they were not taking it seriously. In several telephone conversations, both Pennell and Murphy repeated the allegations that their car was being interfered with and that someone was trying to get them or Peter. They suspected "agents of the Vatican". Annie said that a woman with a child called at their apartment asking to use the telephone and that, after she had left, a tape with a recorded conversation between Arthur and Father Kelly had gone missing.

Bishop Casey, meanwhile, had been left in no doubt about how fraught the situation was becoming for him. When he rang the Connecticut apartment just before the final negotiations got under way, Peter answered the phone. Casey asked for Annie. She grabbed the receiver in a fury. There followed "a terrible fight between Eamon [and me] and I mean brutal," she told me over the telephone. "All the seventeen years of anger just blew in his face. I said, 'You keep calling and not even saying, "Hello, Peter, how are you?"' I told him that I didn't care what happened to him and that I had put the video up on him and that he was set up and 'you've had your chances, no more chances', and I said I'd be just as apt to come up there at Easter and 'pull your damn hat off'." Shortly afterwards she rang Mount St Mary's, Galway. "I got his secretary on the line," she said, "and I said that Eamon had had a son, and that . . . 'you'd all better get used to a shock'." He didn't ring back, she said. "I think he was in shock because I had told the secretary."

On 23 April Arthur Pennell telephoned me again. They had had no further contact from Father Kelly, he said, but they didn't know why. The deal had obviously fallen through, either because the Bishop could not raise the money or he had decided it was hopeless and that in any event he couldn't do anything at this stage to stop publication.

I agreed with Conor Brady that the time had now come to go to Brooklyn to ask Father Kelly, as Casey's lawyer, to convey to the Bishop a request for an interview about the origin of the money. Father Kelly was the parish priest of the mostly Hispanic Parish of Saint Bridget. It was a tough neighbourhood. I had to step around used syringes to approach the door of the presbytery of his church on Linden Street. A down-to-earth community priest, fluent in Italian and Spanish, Kelly had studied law to fight cases in court for his parishioners. He seemed to find the whole affair very distasteful. His attitude, when I telephoned to arrange a meeting, was "What took you so long?" He told me that the Bishop was on holiday in Malta and went into another room to call him there. Shortly afterwards he emerged to tell me that Casey had agreed to an interview and would explain about the money. He said he would shortly leave Malta, pay a brief visit to Rome, and return to Ireland on 5 May. He would meet me at noon that day in the Skylon Hotel near Dublin Airport. He only asked for one thing, that we delay publication until after he had performed confirmations in Galway on 7 May.

I flew from Washington to Dublin to conduct the interview along with Andy Pollak. We booked a room in the Skylon and waited in the lobby. And waited. The Bishop never turned up. We returned to the office and made calls. No one knew where he was.

The next day Conor Brady summoned his team for a conference in Jurys Hotel. He knew the time had come to publish, but he was apprehensive. We looked at all the angles. He asked us, "Are we being set up?" "No," I replied. "Write the story," he said. I produced a lengthy article detailing Annie Murphy's claims and the payments she had received and the failure of the Bishop to meet us and answer questions about the money. The story was scaled back by the ever-cautious editor, to say simply that Bishop Casey had paid money to a woman in Connecticut who had a child. As we were going to press, the Vatican issued a statement that Casey had resigned as Bishop of Galway.

Only then did I realise what the detour to Rome had really been about. The Bishop had confessed everything at the Vatican. He had been instructed to return to Ireland, pack up and leave the country, without talking to anyone from *The Irish Times*.

The story caused a sensation. The editor's decision to hold back information on the first day paid dividends, as we were able to dole out more and more of the details as the rival newspapers tried to catch up. A few days later the Bishop announced in a statement that he was Peter Murphy's father and admitted that the money had been taken from diocesan funds – and replaced that week by "several donors".

It transpired later that Casey left Ireland unnoticed on an Aer Lingus flight to New York and stayed for six months in a contemplative monastery before going to Ecuador to work as a missionary priest for six-and-a-half years. Just over a year after he resigned as Bishop of Galway, he travelled to Connecticut and quietly made his peace with Peter, who was then a student at the University of Connecticut.

After Annie published her book about the affair, she left the Connecticut apartment and went to start a new life elsewhere. Before doing so, she said she was splitting up with Pennell.

Two years later Bishop Casey called Dublin newspaper editors from Ecuador. He told each of them that he had been alerted to the fact that the *Sunday Independent* was advertising an exclusive interview with him in its next edition. He wanted to say that he had not given an interview to the newspaper. "You owe Conor O'Clery an interview," Brady told him. "Why don't you talk to him?" "I tell you what," replied the Bishop, "I was in the food court of Union Station in Washington waiting to catch a train, and he was sitting two tables away, and he didn't recognise me." He paused, then, recalled Brady, he added with a laugh: "Mind you, I was wearing a false beard at the time!"

In 1998 Bishop Casey became a hospital chaplain in the Arundel and Brighton diocese in England. He returned to live in Ireland, at Shanaglish, near Gort in County Galway, in 2006. In an interview with Tralee historian and broadcaster Maurice O'Keefe after his return, he said he had left Ireland when he did because he wanted "to get out before the media descended on me". Annie Murphy told the *Daily Mail* that Casey had developed a good relationship with Peter and that she regretted writing her kiss-and-tell memoir and hoped he would have a happy retirement.

The Casey scandal came at a time when many Irish people were beginning to question the dictates of the Catholic Church about their personal lives, especially on moral issues like abortion, divorce and contraception. The downfall of the popular Bishop marked the beginning of a profound change in attitudes towards the supposedly celibate Catholic clergy, and undoubtedly helped accelerate a fall-off in church attendance which continued through the 1990s. It undermined the authority of the twenty-eight bishops who made up the Catholic Hierarchy. Worse revelations followed about the corruption of young boys by paedophile priests, which further diminished the role of the Catholic Church in an increasingly secular and well-off Ireland. The mishandling of abusive priests brought about the resignation of two other Irish bishops, eight American bishops and Cardinal Bernard Law of Boston. Bishop Casey's actions came to be regarded in retrospect in a more sympathetic light. The disclosure in 2006 that a seventy-three-year-old priest in Galway had had a child created little comment and the local bishop defended the couple's right to personal privacy.

19

Shaking Hands with the Devil

I travelled from Washington to Buenos Aires in mid-March 1995 to cover a three-nation state visit by Irish President Mary Robinson to Argentina, Chile and Brazil. I looked forward to the trip. I had come to admire the President. As an articulate, well-groomed lawyer, she portrayed Ireland as an enlightened and modern country. American politicians and academics swooned over her. My reports on her earlier visits to the United States were effusive. In *The Irish Times* of 19 May 1993, under the heading, "President returns from US trip with enhanced status", I wrote that she had reinforced her stature as a European stateswoman. When she spoke at Harvard on 11 March 1994, in a debate sponsored by my newspaper, the headline read: "Rapt audience for President's speech on UN: Some have mentioned Mrs Robinson as a possible successor to UN Secretary General Boutros Boutros Ghali". I wrote that she brought to the occasion "a moral integrity unsurpassed among international political figures and heads of state".

Right from the first day of the Latin American trip, however, things started to go wrong. The first item on the agenda was expected to be a visit by the President to an impoverished parish in Moreno, outside Buenos Aires, served by Dominican nuns. The invitation to visit Barrio José had been extended many weeks earlier and the venue had been checked out by an Irish official. Sister Joan O'Shanahan, originally from Tullamore, County Offaly, told me that locals had made Irish flags and kids had rehearsed a welcome routine. Father Tom O'Donnell of the Palatine Order said they had set aside a sum equivalent to €2,000 from their scarce resources to provide refreshments for the presidential party. Sister Veronica Rafferty of Derry said they believed they had got the green light for the visit in a phone call from Áras an Uachtaráin in February.

But when the President arrived in Buenos Aires, it became clear that there would be no side-trip to Barrio José. The nuns and their charges were acutely disappointed. However, learning that Mrs Robinson would lay a wreath at a memorial in central Buenos Aires to Admiral William Brown, an Irish immigrant who founded the Argentinian navy, some of the nuns and about twenty people from the barrio set out by bus to greet her at the memorial. Delayed by rain and mud, they arrived thirty minutes after the President had performed the ceremony and returned to her suite in the five-star Alvear Palace Hotel. I had lingered at the site to interview people, and called the hotel to tell the President's special adviser, Bride Rosney, what had happened. She asked me to direct the bus to the Alvear Palace, where Robinson greeted them amid emotional scenes. One Argentinian woman, in tears, told her, "Thank you, and thank Ireland for the Dominicans."

Bride Rosney blamed the government of President Carlos Menem of Argentina for the debacle. She said that the visit to the barrio was "not appropriate from the Argentine point of view". It would focus on poverty at a sensitive time politically since Menem was facing a presidential election. The headline on my story read: "Argentine politics splits President and the poor". Eileen Whelan of RTÉ, the only other Irish reporter on the trip, filed a similar report for television and radio news.

More embarrassments followed. Some 350 representatives of the 300,000 to 400,000-strong Irish Argentinian community, most of whose ancestors came from the Longford-Westmeath area, were invited to meet Mrs Robinson at a reception in the Alvear Palace Hotel. However, many ordinary Irish Argentinians were disappointed that they were not given a chance of seeing the first Irish president to visit their country and several called the local Irish-community radio station afterwards to complain. Such an opportunity had been provided on her trip to Australia in 1992 when Mrs Robinson greeted a large crowd in an open park in Sydney, and where, according to a contemporary *Irish Times* report by Brian Donaghy, the President "charmed the socks off" the Irish community. A prominent Argentinian of Irish origin told me that the failure to provide an open event in Buenos Aires left many bruised feelings. "It's the first time in history that an Irish president came here and the grassroots Irish Argentinians didn't even get a look-in," he said. Usually aggressive with reporters, Bride Rosney found herself on the defensive. "It's a pity people will feel they were cut out because it would always be her top priority to meet with as many representatives as possible," she said.

The critical reports in *The Irish Times* and on RTÉ created tension between the official party and the two reporters, and also between the President's inner circle and the accompanying officials from the Department of Foreign Affairs, which tended to suffer the wrath of the presidential party in such situations. I recall squeezing into a hotel lift with several members of the President's entourage and feeling the icy chill of disapproval as we ascended in silence.

I was having my own problems with communications to Dublin. When the President visited an 8,000-acre ranch owned by an Irish Argentinian, I filed my report by telephone to a copytaker in *The Irish Times*. The first sentence began, "A group of twenty mounted gauchos greeted the President, Mrs

Robinson, when she arrived at the Duggan ranch in the Argentine pampas country yesterday." Owing to what we call a "communications error", the early, or country, edition of *The Irish Times* told readers mistakenly that "A group of twenty *thousand* gauchos" greeted the President. It was corrected in time for the city edition. A night editor at our rival daily, the *Irish Independent*, which had not sent a reporter to Argentina, "lifted" the early edition story from *The Irish Times*, and splashed the account of "twenty thousand gauchos" on the front page of their city edition.

The next stop on the President's tour was Santiago, capital of Chile, where President Eduardo Frei hosted a state dinner in her honour in the presidential palace on 27 March. Frei was only the second democratically elected president of Chile since the military regime led by General Augusto Pinochet had stepped down in 1990. Pinochet, who brutally repressed dissent as leader of a military junta for seventeen years, remained head of the Chilean armed forces and in this capacity turned up in the line of dignitaries to greet the Irish visitors. At the request of Mrs Robinson's party, Chilean security officials ordered me, Eileen Whelan, RTÉ cameraman John Coughlan, and soundman Jim Hall to leave the reception room, so that there would be no record of her encounter with the seventy-nine-year-old former dictator.

Allowed in later, Eileen Whelan and I chatted with Pinochet, an avuncular figure with rotund belly and a little white military moustache, and kitted out in white ceremonial jacket with five gold stars. He told us that Mrs Robinson had shaken his hand (as did we). We confirmed this with Bride Rosney, who emphasised how the President, shocked to discover Pinochet was there, had put on her "Harry Whelehan" face when offering her hand – a reference to the disapproval she evidently showed when required to appoint former attorney general, Harry Whelehan, as president of the High Court, after he had mishandled an attempt to extradite a paedophile priest to Northern Ireland where he faced criminal charges. The *Irish Times* headline reflected Bride's spin: "President accords Pinochet only a frigid handshake". Nevertheless, the Irish President, a champion of human rights, had shaken hands, however stiffly, with someone synonymous with the brutal suppression of human rights, and had made sure it was done out of sight of the media.

In Chile, the President did visit a poor community outside Santiago served by Irish nuns, but the headline on my report, "President finally makes contact with the poor of Latin America", did little to improve media relations with the official party. The three-nation trip ended in Brazil where, in keeping with the bad luck dogging the tour, there was a leak in the ceiling of the President's hotel room, and invitations to a reception hosted by Mrs Robinson were sent out in European rather than Brazilian Portuguese, which was offensive to Brazilians.

The President returned to Ireland to face what she described in her authorised biography as "a feeding frenzy of criticism". She blamed the Department of Foreign Affairs for leaving her "unprotected". She was exposed to a sharp editorial in *The Irish Times*, in which Conor Brady suggested that the President's three-nation trip was designed to secure international support for the post of United Nations secretary-general when it became vacant in two years and this was why she had allowed host governments to dictate the schedule. The South American tour, he wrote, had been characterised by rather transparent attempts at buck-passing, and some people saw "a growing tendency to hauteur and stiffness" in the President. This was strong stuff, coming from the newspaper that had championed Mary Robinson during her election and since.

Olivia O'Leary and Helen Burke, co-authors of *Mary Robinson: The Authorised Biography*, published by Hodder & Stoughton, noted that the President's toughest critics, Independent Newspapers, made hay with the missteps in South America. But for whatever reason, "Mary and Bride allowed the media coverage of the visit to get out of control". In South America "she was exposed to the cold gaze of *Irish Times* veteran correspondent Conor O'Clery [who] set a cracking pace followed smartly by Eileen Whelan and her crew".

The trip, they concluded, marked a nadir not just in her relationship with the press, but with the Department of Foreign Affairs. There was considerable resentment in the Department at being blamed by Áras an Uachtaráin for what went wrong, since Bride Rosney had the final say in what stayed on the President's schedule and what came off. The demands of three state visits in one week had placed an intolerable strain on the skeleton staff of Foreign Affairs personnel in South America, where there was only one Irish embassy, that in Buenos Aires. Stung by the finger-pointing, a senior official at the Department of Foreign Affairs was asked to compile an internal report on the visit and the media coverage for the Tánaiste and Minister for Foreign Affairs, Dick Spring. Geraldine Kennedy, then political correspondent of *The Irish Times*, wrote that she had learned that the report criticised the two journalists accompanying the President for highlighting what went wrong rather than what went right. *The Irish Times* in fact published three stories about the controversies, amounting to fewer than 2,000 words, and nine straightforward, uncritical accounts of the tour, totalling over 5,000 words, plus a 1,000-word interview with Mrs Robinson herself.

Mary Robinson did get a United Nations post when she left the presidency just before the expiry of her seven-year term. In September 1997 she was appointed UN High Commissioner for Human Rights, a major honour for a small country. In this capacity her office announced a year later that she would travel to Tibet during an official visit to China, starting on 7 September 1998. She would be accompanied by one reporter, Charlie Bird of RTÉ, who was making a documentary on her. I was then

Beijing correspondent of *The Irish Times*, and I applied for, and got, permission from the Chinese Foreign Ministry to accompany the High Commissioner. But when Mrs Robinson made it clear to the Beijing authorities that she did not want an Irish-only press entourage – no other foreign correspondents had been given permission to travel to Tibet to cover her trip – the initial permission I got from the Chinese was withdrawn.

Again Mrs Robinson got a bad press. The General Secretary of the International Federation of Journalists in Brussels, Aidan White, described as "bizarre" that the UN's leading campaigner for human rights "should have a hand in blocking a distinguished journalist from accessing a region which has been shrouded in secrecy and where abuse of human rights has been routine". In a scathing Irishman's Diary in *The Irish Times*, Kevin Myers wrote, "Quite right. Ban the bastard . . . Wouldn't want to be a representative of mere Paddies, now, would we?" *The Irish Times* accused Mrs Robinson of vetoing its reporter. She denied that this was the case, but accepted that the matter could have been handled differently. Asked on RTÉ if I saw a connection between the reporting of the South America trip and the Tibet affair, as some commentators suggested, I replied that I couldn't imagine this to be the case.

The point was rather overlooked in the controversy that it was the Chinese authorities who manipulated the press coverage. *The New York Times*, the *Guardian* and other world media organisations were barred from covering the first-ever visit of a UN Commissioner of Human Rights to Tibet, not by Mary Robinson, but by the Chinese government. There would have been no media controversy surrounding her trip if there had been freedom of movement for Beijing-based correspondents throughout China.

Charlie Bird was somewhat embarrassed by the contretemps. He called me from Lhasa on both days of the Tibet trip so that some account of the High Commissioner's visit could appear in the paper of record.

The next time I encountered Mary Robinson was at a press conference in Jakarta, in September 1999, at the height of the crisis over human rights abuses in East Timor. It was a packed affair, with up to one hundred members of the world's media jostling for position. After it ended she made her way through a mêlée of camera crews and reporters to come up to me, and made a point of shaking my hand. "I'm glad to see you here," she said. "I'm glad to see you here, too," I replied.

In Tiananmen Square, Beijing, in May 1989 during student demonstrations for democracy

Durty Nellies, Beijing's first Irish pub

Showing a visitor the Great Wall of China, September 1998

Beijing market, after snowfall, 1998

Pro-democracy Chinese students on their way to Tiananmen Square, Beijing, before the crackdown on 4 June 1989

British embassy in Beijing, after the assault by nationalist demonstrators, May 1999

Anti-NATO demonstrators in Beijing in May 1999, after the US bombing of the Chinese embassy in Belgrade

Ping Cuo Jie Bo, Tibetan vice mayor of Lhasa: "Make sure you get the bust of Mao in the picture."

Former Tibetan serf, Thaje, in his Lhasa shop

With Mongolian herder, Byambasuren, during the devastating zud of 1999-2000

Wan Azizah, leader of Malaysian pro-reform party: "Tell me all the gossip about Charles Haughey!"

Civil rights activist, Tian Chua, being detained during pro-reform demonstrations in Kuala Lumpur in 1999

A defiant Kuala Lumpur protestor faces water cannon using green dye, after the imprisonment of Malaysian politician, Anwar Ibrahim, in 1999

Indonesian soldiers fraternise with anti-Suharto rioters, 14 May 1988

Indonesian soldiers ham it up for *The Irish Times* after the fall of Suharto, in Jakarta, May 1998

Irish Minister for Foreign Affairs David Andrews greets voters during the referendum on East Timor independence, August 1999

East Timor independence figure, Manuel Carrascalão, who told the 1999 meeting between David Andrews and Bishop Belo that his son was being murdered nearby

All that was left of Bishop Belo's church in Dili, after the attack by pro-Indonesian militia, September 1999

Hotel Turismo in Dili, after liberation by Australian-led force in September 1999

20

Civil War without the Rifles

In the autumn of 1995, Canada was convulsed by a constitutional crisis over separatist demands in Quebec, the French-speaking province where about a quarter of Canada's thirty-two million people live. Flying to Montreal from Washington one cold October morning that year, I wondered if the United States' northern neighbour was about to suffer the fate of the Soviet Union and break apart.

To native English speakers, Quebec has the feel and sense of a "foreign" place. Montreal is the second-largest French-speaking city in the world. The old city of Quebec, perched on a rock above the Saint Lawrence River, where narrow streets of slate-roofed granite houses cluster beneath the grand Château Frontenac hotel and where restaurants specialise in *moules marinière*, is more like a town in the French Alps than one in North America. People follow French as avidly as US politics, read French language newspapers, and tune into both French Canadian television and TV channels from France. Many have never been to the United States. Away from the tourist areas one rarely hears English spoken. Vehicle licence plates carry the slogan *Je me souviens* (I remember) from the 1883 coat of arms of Quebec's Parliament Building façade, though no one can remember what is meant to be remembered.

Quebec is a French-speaking island in an Anglophone sea, clinging tenaciously to a language that is mocked by Canada's neighbour to the south and laughed at as old-fashioned by sophisticates in France. It has stringent laws to protect the language, which are tolerated, even encouraged, by the federal government in Ottawa. Unlike the Baltic republics of the Soviet Union, where the language of the "mother country", Russia, was forced upon the citizens, Quebec has a legal charter, upheld by the Canadian Supreme Court, that declares French to be the official language of its government and law, as well as the normal and everyday language of work, instruction, communication, commerce and business. All children attending public schools have to do so in French. Commercial premises are required to include French instructions with all products and to display signs with greater visibility in French, though Chinese restaurants are an exception. The law is enforced by the *Office québécois de la langue française* (Quebec Office of the French Language) which can impose substantial fines for non-compliance, and is widely derided by critics in Canada's English-language media as the language police.

In the early 1990s Canada's ten provinces tried but failed to agree constitutional changes designed to make Quebec "distinct", so as to diminish separatist tendencies. In 1995 the people of the French-speaking province got a chance to put the matter to a vote and decide whether to carve out a separate place for themselves in North America. A referendum was set for 30 October on the proposition that Quebec should become "sovereign". Most people, in Quebec and beyond, saw it as a vote to break up Canada, because Quebec was, inconveniently, wedged between five of the country's English-speaking provinces to the west and four to the east.

The prospect of Quebec going it alone was so real that on 25 October the Canadian Prime Minister Jean Chrétien, himself a French Canadian, made an emergency broadcast to Quebec's

7.3 million people, urging a "No" vote. I went to listen to it in Le Sacrilege, a dimly lit bar in the old city of Quebec. The thumping rock music was turned down and the roar of conversation faded as the gaunt face of Chrétien appeared on the screen, looking grave.

"The end of Canada would be nothing less than the end of a dream, the end of a country that has made us the envy of the world," said Chrétien, in French. "Do you really think that you and your family would have a better quality of life and a brighter future in a separate Quebec?"

"Yes!" called a tall man in a leather jacket as the white-haired barman gave a mock salute towards the television. "Too late, too late," cried a woman waving a cigarette, as the Prime Minister went on to promise that Quebec would be treated as a "distinct society", without saying if he had actual constitutional change in mind. *"Vendu! Vendu!"* *("Sell-out.")* a man called out from the crowded bar room.

US President Bill Clinton's face appeared on the television screen as the news came on. I heard him say that he could not understand why a country that was a model to the world was contemplating a split. By then the rock music had been turned back up and hardly anyone was listening. Five years earlier, as the Soviet Union was falling apart, President George H.W. Bush had also warned in a speech in Kiev of the terrible consequences of Ukrainian nationalism. No one had listened to him then either. Ukraine had simply gone ahead and declared independence, set up its own armed forces, and established a new currency, customs and passports.

However, Quebec's idea of separating itself from a democracy with the most desirable lifestyle in the world (according to a 1992 UN report) was very different from that of the captive countries like Ukraine which sought to escape from a failed totalitarian union. Quebec's nationalist leaders wanted to keep the same postal system and have the same Canadian dollars and Canadian passports. The proposed Sovereignty Bill they signed stated: "We wish to formulate along with the people of Canada, our historic partner, new relations that will allow us to maintain our economic ties and to redefine our political exchanges." Sovereignty, it declared, meant that Quebec would pass its own laws, levy all its taxes and conclude its treaties. But everyone could claim both Quebec and Canadian citizenship. Quebec would apply for UN membership but would continue to participate in Canadian trade and defence alliances. All Canadian laws would remain in effect until amended by a Quebec assembly; all federal pensions and allowances would continue; and Canadian Supreme Court judges could become members of a Quebec Supreme Court.

The "sovereigntists" were in fact not proposing complete independence; they were seeking authority to renegotiate the federal link as "a new economic and political partnership", with full separation only if a satisfactory outcome was not reached within a year. Someone described it as "divorce with bedroom rights".

"The questions of army, passports, currency, these are all secondary," said Michel Noël, a heavy-set farmer with thick eyebrows who was organising the "Yes" vote on the 200-square-kilometre Ile d'Orleans in the Saint Lawrence River, north of Quebec city, and who spoke only French. Sitting in the kitchen of his maple-floor farmhouse overlooking the river, I asked, courtesy of a volunteer translator from the "Yes" campaign, if he was voting on economic grounds. The farmer spoke without pause for ten minutes, making points by banging his finger on the kitchen table so hard that the coffee cups rattled, at the end of which my amateur "translator" said simply, "He agrees." I did, however, manage to ascertain that Noël believed Quebec agriculture had suffered from unfair, subsidised competition from other provinces, and that he wanted Quebec to negotiate its own farm prices and control immigration – i.e. prevent an influx of English-speakers. He would be happy to continue using Canadian money whatever happened, though if they got a new currency, he would like Queen Elizabeth to be replaced on the dollar bills by someone like the Quebec poet Félix Leclerc.

The sympathies of most of his neighbours were evident from the blue and white Quebec flags with the *fleur de lis* fluttering in the cold breeze by the roadside. There were "*Oui*" signs everywhere, some formed by heavy shading of the first three letters of the word "Quebec" to pick out "Oui". An occasional Canadian flag identified "No" voters. The issue was bitterly contested among these neighbours. Some people on opposite sides did not talk to each other. "The debate is very emotional, especially for the older people who have been active all their lives," said thirty-year-old Dominique who worked in the Pantoute bookshop in Quebec. "For them, it's now or never."

People of Michel Noël's generation were old enough to remember when French President Charles de Gaulle in 1967 lent his prestige to the fledgling Quebec independence movement, with his cry of "*Vive le Québec libre!*" from the balcony of the Montreal City Hotel, stirring old resentments at the loss of Quebec to Britain in 1763. Quebec nationalism was more violent then. During the 1960s the left-wing Front de libération du Québec (FLQ) exploded more than 200 bombs. Its campaign culminated in the "October Crisis" of 1970, when FLQ cells murdered the British Trade Commissioner, James Richard Cross, and a Liberal cabinet member, Pierre Laporte. Such was the public revulsion that the physical force movement came to an abrupt end. The first sovereignty referendum was held in 1980 when sixty per cent of Quebec province voted "No". The Parti Québécois, which won power in 1994, was now giving the nationalists a second chance.

The "No" vote was strong in some regions of Quebec, such as the Eastern Townships, a rich agricultural area east of Montreal where the sense of being "Canadian first and Québécois second" has always been strong. Blue and red *"Non"* signs vastly outnumbered *"Oui"* slogans on the telegraph poles of Waterloo, a village of 4,000 people, of whom twenty per cent were English-speaking. In the Jac-Mi travel agency on the main street, Denise Comeau Herbert, a French Canadian, had placed a single Canadian flag on the filing cabinet to display her federal sympathies. "I travel a lot," said Madame Herbert, who sat on the town's eight-member council. "Every time I come back I realise we have a great country in Canada. Our bellies are full. I'm not missing anything in life." She feared that the "Yes" campaign was really separatist. "People are frightened," she said. "They fear an explosion. They want to stay Canadian. I am getting my son, Louis Philippe, to apply for a Canadian passport before Monday, just in case. They say we will keep the same currency, but when Slovakia split with the Czech Republic in 1993 they promised to keep the same money but the currency broke up. They want to negotiate separation, but if you divorce, you decide the conditions first. You don't decide afterwards who pays the mortgage."

Madame Herbert organised a trip by thirty-four residents, led by the mayor, Bernard Provencher, to the city of Waterloo in the state of Ontario, to twin the communities and reinforce their mutual Canadian identity. They were overwhelmed with hospitality there and plied with turkey dinner, schnapps and German sausages. There was a display of Irish dancing, and a twinning ceremony in English and French. "They were so truly concerned about Quebec staying in Canada," said Provencher.

What the Waterloo residents witnessed in Ontario was the stirring of a remarkable outpouring of affection by English-speaking Canadians for the French Canadians, with the aim of getting them to stay in Canada. Up to then the "No" campaign had been dominated by economic arguments, but the rest of Canada (known in the media as the "ROC") had woken up to the profound implications of what a radio caller termed "a civil war without the rifles". They were coming to realise that the 128-

year-old federation could not endure if a quarter of its citizens left and the remainder of Canada was riven in two. More than half of ROC Canadians said in a poll that the message they would send Quebec was "We love you". A week before polling, 5,000 people in Toronto carried slogans to a rally with placards saying the same thing. In Alberta a farmer ploughed a three-kilometre message in a canola field: "*C'est Mieux Ensemble*" ("It's better together").

All this was a good sign for a future partnership between a sovereign Quebec and Canada, said the charismatic Bloc Québécois leader, Lucien Bouchard, answering a reporter in English. But later, speaking in French, he said scathingly, "Oh! Their hearts are beating for us now. They go: Boom! Boom! Boom! But it is too late!" It seemed indeed that he was right. In an opinion poll in the *Montreal Gazette*, on the Friday before the referendum, forty-six per cent of Quebecers said they were for sovereignty and only forty per cent against.

But it wasn't too late. That same day tens of thousands of people from all over Canada converged on the centre of Montreal for a "Stand Up For Canada" rally in the Place du Canada. Young people with red Canadian maple leaves painted on their faces filled the square and clung to trees. They climbed scaffolding around the monument to Sir John Alexander Macdonald, the nineteenth-century founder of the Canadian federation. For hours the vast crowd roared, applauded and sounded klaxon horns in an exuberant display of support for keeping the country united. Thousands waved Canadian and Quebec flags together to show their support for keeping the French-speaking province in the Canadian Federation.

Many demonstrators had travelled all night to be at the rally. Lisa Nelson, Suzanne Turmel and Carol Bellefleur said they had journeyed eleven hours without eating in a convoy of thirty buses from New Brunswick, to show they cared that Quebec should stay part of Canada. "I came here because I love Canada with all my heart," said landscape gardener Brendan Young, who had driven seven hours from Ontario with a huge Quebec flag and was driving straight back. "I've taken French immersion classes, I respect the Quebecers so much. Just don't leave."

The "Yes" campaigners were furious at the help given by federal organisations to swell the rally. Air Canada and Canadian Air both reduced fares by up to ninety per cent for people attending the demonstration. English-speaking schools in Montreal closed for the day to allow teachers and students to go to Place du Canada. "It's our country. We love Canada, we were born here, we want to die here," said a teenage girl with a maple leaf painted on her cheek, surrounded by excited classmates from Pierrefonds Comprehensive High School.

The love-bombing worked, just. In the referendum vote, 50.6 per cent of people in Quebec province voted "No" to the proposition: "Do you agree that Quebec should become sovereign after having made a formal offer to Canada for a new economic and political partnership within the scope of the bill respecting the future of Quebec and of the agreement signed on June 12, 1995?" It was a defeat of only 50,000 from almost five million votes. The Quebec cause was lost again and Canada staggered back from the brink.

The failure of the constitutional approach left many ultra-nationalists embittered, but there was no hint of a resort to political violence as in the 1960s – though in 2001 a die-hard member of the FLQ, Rhéal Mathieu, fire-bombed three Second Cup coffee shops in Montreal, which had the desired effect of forcing Canada's largest specialty coffee retailer to change some of its signs to read Les Cafés Second Cup. Mathieu served ten months in jail.

Nine years after the failed referendum, the fortunes of the Quebec nationalists rebounded, mainly because of a ruling Liberal Party scandal, which caused a furore throughout Canada and offended Quebecers in particular. It involved the allocation of millions of federal dollars to ensure that the Canadian flag flew all across Quebec to discourage separatism, much of which ended up instead in Liberal Party coffers. The scandal developed into a full-blown political crisis, forcing the Liberal Prime Minister, Paul Martin, to call an election in July 2004. As Canadians went to the polls, it was nearly certain that neither the Liberal Party, which had governed Canada for eleven years, nor the Conservative Party would be able to form a majority government in the 308-seat parliament. In such circumstances Gilles Duceppe, the leader of the Bloc Québécois, the federal party that promoted Quebec sovereignty, planned to emulate Charles Stewart Parnell – the Irish Party leader who secured promises of Home Rule in return for underpinning the Liberal Party in the British House of Commons – and wrest promises of greater self-government from the centre by supporting one of the country's two mainstream parties. He told me that he envisaged the two Canadas relating to each other like two countries in the European Union.

But the Canadian Liberal Party unexpectedly got just enough seats to form a government, and once again Quebec nationalism was set back by the narrowest of margins. The Bloc Québécois vote declined at the next general election in 2006, when it lost both the popular vote and a number of seats in the federal parliament and a Conservative government came to office. However, the debate on the status of Quebec remained unresolved, and the federal government continued to seek ways to recognise and absorb Quebec's heritage within the federal structure. On 27 November 2006, the House of Commons in Ottawa approved a motion, moved by Conservative Prime Minister Stephen Harper, "that the Québécois form a nation within a united Canada". The resolution was widely seen as an attempt to boost the Conservative Party's standing in Quebec. Meanwhile, Canada continued to operate a constitutional system that cynics say works well in practice but could never work in theory.

21

Arresting Experiences

While based in the United States I decided to take an intensive course in Spanish, as I occasionally had to visit South and Central America and other Spanish-speaking regions, such as my local supermarket. Naturally, as soon as I completed it, I was posted to China.

For some months after setting up the *Irish Times* bureau in Beijing in the autumn of 1996, I attended Mandarin language classes. I got to a modest level of colloquial fluency but I could never quite master the written characters, and resigned myself to working through an official interpreter, an earnest young man supplied by the Chinese Foreign Ministry.

My only previous visit to China had been in the summer of 1989, at the height of the Tiananmen Square student demonstrations for democratic reform. I had travelled with the press corps from Moscow to cover a summit meeting between Mikhail Gorbachev and Chinese leader Deng Xiaoping. During the summit, hundreds of thousands of Beijing people poured onto the broad avenues, chanting, "We support the students". As they passed the Jianguo Hotel where I was staying, a thirty-member orchestra in evening-dress played in the lobby "It's Now or Never". It turned out to be never. After the summit, Deng

Xiaoping ordered in the tanks and hundreds of protesters were killed. The government cracked down on dissent, banned the foreign press and resumed full control of the domestic media.

Western reporters were soon allowed back and one evening shortly after I arrived to take up full-time residence in Beijing, several of us gathered in the Jianguo to reconstitute the temporarily disbanded Foreign Correspondents' Club of China. The club had been founded a century earlier, and one of its members, George Ernest Morrison, Peking correspondent of *The Times*, was reported killed in the siege of foreign legations during the Boxer Rebellion. He survived to read his own obituary in his newspaper. I got membership card No. 8 in the revived club, considered a number of good fortune in China.

The main role of correspondents in China at this time was to record the economic and social transformations sweeping the vast country. Where the Soviet Union's evolution from communism to capitalism was marked by openness, democracy and chaos, China's communist leadership chose the path of continued authoritarianism, combined with free-wheeling capitalism. In 1992 Deng Xiaoping, seeking to introduce competitiveness into a stagnant command economy, electrified the country with his proclamation, "To get rich is glorious." His message was that people could make as much money as they liked, so long as they did not challenge the system. Anyone who did could be harassed and locked up. They must especially not commemorate, publish or say anything about the victims of the bloodshed in Tiananmen Square, as that could imply that the government had committed a crime and thereby undermine its legitimacy. Only the Beijing taxi-drivers in their little Xiali saloons retained a cheerful disdain of all authority, and it is from them I learned some of the subversive anecdotes that betrayed the real feelings beneath the surface of Chinese life, such as the story of the newspaper photograph of Li Peng, the Chairman of the National People's Congress, who was widely blamed for the crackdown, posing with pigs at a farm, with the caption: "Li Peng is the second from the right." The masses, however, accepted this Faustian bargain. A generation of Chinese was "spooked" by the Tiananmen Square massacre and young people channelled their energies into making money and turning China into a consumer paradise.

The process had barely got under way when I arrived. An internal paper prepared by the Irish embassy in June 1994 recommended that anyone coming to live in Beijing should stock up with life's necessities at Musgrave's Cash & Carry in Ballymun. It listed – important things first – Irish whiskey, Cork Dry Gin, Baileys Irish Cream and Irish Mist. It warned of a shortage of J-cloths, Brillo pads, wax polish, washing-machine powder, dish-washing liquid, baby foods, milk formulae and disposable nappies. It advised diplomats to bring adequate stocks of thyme, tarragon, sage, oregano, Italian seasoning and basil, which told as much about embassy cuisine as it did about Chinese shortages.

The list rapidly became redundant as supermarkets, five-star hotels, computer shops, ATMs and designer stores were opened across Beijing. The first Irish pub, Durty Nellies, threw open its doors in 1998, allowing Chinese customers to contemplate portraits of Michael Collins and Oscar Wilde over a pint of Guinness. Almost overnight, it seemed, everyone acquired a mobile phone. Expensive cars appeared on the streets. A Chinese businessman sitting next to me at an Irish embassy dinner turned out to be Beijing's Ferrari dealer – when I asked his connection with Ireland, he told me he had a horse running at the Curragh. The skyline from my city-centre apartment window soon changed from old Beijing to Manhattan. High-rise office blocks replaced centuries-old courtyards and narrow laneways.

I soon came across more people who had taken Deng's advice to heart and unleashed their money-making talents, such as Li Anli, a former Air China stewardess who made so much from her trading company in Shanghai that she was able to buy her own corporate aircraft, an event reported in the official media as a "glorious" piece of news, and investor Rong Yiren, a scion of the richest family in China before the Communists came to power in 1949, who came to be revered as the country's most famous "red capitalist". Most of the new rich started up with cash from families and friends rather than loans from China's banks, which devoted most of their assets to bank-rolling failing state enterprises. By 1999, a dozen of the fifty richest Chinese had been appointed to the 3,000-member National People's Congress, the unelected legislature that formalised the policies of the Chinese Communist Party. For these capitalists it was a case of "if you can't beat them, join them", but the Party was also happy to co-opt them into the charade that passed for national political debate in China.

The entrepreneurial energy unleashed by Deng Xiaoping brought about a speedy transformation of a country where life had changed little in the previous 4,000 years. China's social pyramid had survived almost intact over the centuries, as had the unique legalist tradition of governance inherited from Qin Shi Huang, the country's founding emperor. Only in China could one interview a bureaucrat charged with civil service reforms who recalled how officials of the Han dynasty (206 BC–AD 220) dealt with the problems of nepotism, as my friend Jasper Becker of the *South China Morning Post* pointed out in his book *The Chinese*, published by John Murray. The catastrophic failure by Mao to engineer the most egalitarian society in history had given way to acceptance of one of the most unequal. The Chinese peasantry, who still constituted a billion people in the late 1990s remained subject to the imposition of crushing taxes. Urban elites lived as well as their western counterparts, but half the population could not read or write, and a third existed below the poverty line. At least there was enough rice to feed the population, a basic requirement for government legitimacy. This had not been the case in living memory. On a trip up the Yangtze with Jasper

Becker in 1999, we found old people who could recall – and took part in – acts of cannibalism during the Great Famine of forty years previously.

After China began to open up to the world, the central government decided to make Shanghai a great financial powerhouse. The first step was to open a stock exchange. This was located in the former Astor House Hotel, a building in Renaissance Revival style whose pre-Revolution guests included Charlie Chaplin and Bertrand Russell and which happened to have a suitably sized ballroom to use as a trading floor. "Most of the investment comes from big Chinese enterprises but millions of ordinary Chinese have bought shares," explained official Li Qian one morning in 1997, as we watched dozens of young men and women in red waistcoats logging share transactions on computer screens. Like punters in a betting shop, investors crowded around a big manually operated board showing fluctuating prices. One of them, called Lu Hu Yun, told me he had left Shanghai to work in a restaurant in Australia but returned when friends told him he could make better money on the exchange. "I play the market full time now," he said, tipping back his baseball cap. "I buy cheap shares and I've doubled my money." The millions raised by new companies floating shares on the exchange helped power the growth of a dazzling new financial city in Pudong New Area, just across the Yangtze River, where today the Shanghai Stock Exchange occupies a futuristic glass-and-metal building and ranks as the fifth largest in the world.

Buying and selling shares is a legal way to satisfy the Chinese passion for gambling. Betting on games of chance is forbidden, even at horse races. Beijing race track, where I went to see some Irish-bred horses in action one afternoon, had a banner across the finishing line that declared, "Resolutely Enforce the Central Committee's Strict Injunction against Gambling". Despite this, "guessing" the winner for a return on money was allowed: racegoers could buy "prediction vouchers" in what was called a "horse-racing intelligence contest" and collect cash rewards as high as twenty-to-one at "redemption counters". Whatever it was called, I ended up with a pocket full of beaten dockets.

The Chinese writer and poet Ding Jing Tang was eleven years old when he first arrived in Shanghai in 1931 from northern China. "I felt I was abroad in a foreign country," he recalled as we sipped green tea in the Shanghai Literature and Art Publishing House. "There were many beautiful houses and rich people. It had a Paris flavour." Shanghai was then occupied by the European powers and British, Italian, French, German, Japanese and American troops patrolled the streets. Local Chinese could not enter the big fashion and jewellery stores on the Bund, the grand waterfront lined with edifices built in art deco and various European styles. The poet remembered the famous Cathay Hotel, now restored as the Peace Hotel, as "a prestigious place for foreigners such as arms dealers and opium merchants". After the Second World War the American and British forces controlled the city and "they were very rude to the Chinese people," said Ding, who had secretly become a communist in 1938, "but with Liberation in 1949 we got rid of all our foreign rulers". The poet was banished to the countryside for his foreign connections when China was convulsed by the Cultural Revolution of 1966–76. Red Guards roamed the streets destroying everything western. "They even stopped women and made them take off their high heels," he recalled.

By the mid-1990s Shanghai again had big department stores selling American and European fashion, perfumery and jewellery. Has it become a foreign city once more? I asked Ding. "No, I don't think I am living abroad this time," he said, his face crinkling as he laughed. "I think Chinese people should be open to the world but on the basis of equality. When young I always dreamed of a proper country where people can make friends with foreign people equally. This dream has come true." I came across many Chinese people who felt like that, and who took great pride in the material advances being made. For the first time in a history of national humiliations under European and American powers, they could feel confident enough to embrace and imitate western ways, in fashion and the arts, as a matter of choice.

As in pre-revolutionary days, wealthy patrons emerged to play a big role in reviving Shanghai's arts scene. Bonko Chan, a flamboyant businessman in his thirties, was responsible for introducing Shanghai to *Aida*, *La Traviata* and other operas. Shanghai sought to re-establish itself not just as China's financial capital but as its pre-eminent cultural centre. In 1997, when The Chieftains came to Shanghai, the only suitable venue for their performance was a small auditorium in the Portman Shangri-La Hotel. (At least this was an advance on their first tour in 1983 when they were put up in a shabby government hotel and assigned an official interpreter who was so humourless, Paddy Moloney recalled, they nicknamed her "Doris Karloff".) By the year 2000 I was able to attend a baroque music concert given by the German Das Neue Orchestra in the French-designed Shanghai Grand Theatre, a shimmering white edifice with three auditoriums, in another of which a full orchestral performance was being given.

Beijing competed with Shanghai in cultural events and in 1999 allowed the staging of a lavish production of the once-banned Puccini opera *Turandot* in the Forbidden City. It was the biggest and most extravagant western cultural event to take place up to then in modern China, marred only by loud giggles from the audience at the appearance of the amply proportioned western diva playing the role of the enchanting young Princess Turandot.

The opening up of the Chinese economy in the 1990s could be monitored by chronicling the arrival of western conveniences such as ATMs and American fast-food chains. A seminal moment came in February 1999 when Ikea opened its first Beijing store. Its glass doors led from a dusty, chaotic street into a world of space and minimalism, a pristine universe of monocultural, bourgeoisie consumerism. It contained the same brightly coloured sofas, gate-leg tables, foldaway beds, and white-wood picture frames as any Ikea store in Europe. It was an instant hit. "It has become the place to spend an afternoon," said the store manager, Gordon Gustavsson. "Instead of going to the park they come here and walk around inspecting everything, sitting on the sofas, chatting, drinking tea, eating biscuits. Afterwards it's like a tornado went through the store."

I knew everything had changed, changed utterly, when the first Starbucks coffee shop opened, near my office. It soon became a common room for western journalists, where we could exchange news over a roast espresso about the latest economic miracle, or the latest internet site to be blocked, or the latest correspondent to be detained and given a hard time by officials of the *Gong'ánjú*, otherwise known as the Public Security Bureau.

Almost every foreign correspondent in China is detained or harassed at some time. The authorities strictly controlled the Chinese media, stifling debate on sensitive political and social issues, and they also seemed determined to manipulate us as much as possible, not simply because our sometimes critical reports might give China a bad image abroad, but because they might filter back to people in China. I found myself temporarily locked up one April afternoon in 2000, when I went to see a retired professor of philosophy, Ding Ziling, at her ground floor apartment on Beijing University campus. Mrs Ding was the mother of a seventeen-year-old student killed in the Tiananmen Square crackdown in 1989, and was under twenty-four-hour surveillance, because she had lobbied for an official apology for the killings and aid for bereaved families. That day she was expecting a visit from seventy-nine-year-old Lois Wheeler Snow, who had arrived from Switzerland and wanted to give Mrs Ding a small personal contribution. Mrs Snow was the widow of the celebrated American correspondent Edgar Snow, who reported from the communist side during the revolution, and whose book *Red Star Over China* is a classic account of the rise of Mao Zedong. When the grey-haired former professor saw that a few foreign journalists were outside, she emerged from the door to talk to us, but several plain-clothes men with little zipper handbags, who had been loitering nearby, ran over, formed a ring around her and shuffled her back inside. Then they turned their attention to me and my colleagues from CNN, National Public Radio and *Asahi Shimbun* of Japan. "Come with us," they commanded. We refused, because they would not show any badge of identity. They linked hands, corralled us in their middle and propelled us bodily to the university security bureau a few hundred metres away. There they confiscated our film and tapes, put us into separate cells and instructed us to write "confessions". I wrote, "I came here to see a meeting between two elderly women and did not break any law." They let us go after two and a half hours. The two elderly women never did get to meet.

I was given similar treatment in Fujian Province a few weeks later. I flew there from Beijing after the deaths of fifty-eight Fujian migrants in a container at Dover, as they were being smuggled into England. I hired a tourist guide as interpreter and took a taxi to the coastal town of Jinfeng, home of some of the Dover victims. As I interviewed a shopkeeper in a quiet street, the men with zipped purses arrived. A Pajero and a military-style jeep drew up outside and several Public Security Bureau officials crowded into the shop. My interpreter said something and got a slap in the face. We were ordered back into the taxi and taken in convoy fifteen kilometres to the county police headquarters in Changle. There I was marched down a corridor lined with interrogation rooms, inside which I glimpsed five other foreign correspondents, rounded up like myself. "You need permission from us to interview people," said my interrogator, lighting a cigarette with a Hell's Angels lighter. "Will you give me permission?" I asked. "No," he said. He smiled at his own wit. We were all eventually released and ordered back to Beijing.

When the Foreign Correspondents' Club gathered in a Thai restaurant one autumn evening in 1999 to discuss what to do about being followed, detained, interrogated and threatened, the authorities knew exactly where we were meeting – plain-clothes men openly tailed some of us to the venue. Top of the agenda that day was the harassment of reporters covering the banned Falun Gong movement. Falun Gong was founded in 1992 by Li Hongzhi, a martial arts master from Jilin province, who claimed that it cured sickness through respiratory and meditation techniques. Its adherents could be found in city parks seeking the *gong* or inner energy by performing *bao lun* (embracing the wheel) and *da zuo* (sitting in meditation). It had devotees in high places, including the Foreign Ministry and the People's Liberation Army. But some voices had been raised accusing Li Hongzhi, who lived in New York, of subjecting practitioners to a systematic form of mind control. In April 1999 several Falun Gong followers were beaten up by police when they protested in Tianjin about a critical article in an official newspaper. Some days later at least 15,000 members of Falun Gong gathered to protest outside the vast government compound in central Beijing known as *Zhongnanhai*. I am sure of this number because I had time to count them. From nine in the morning until ten in the evening the demonstrators sat cross-legged in long lines, six to eight deep, maintaining almost total silence. Some read little blue books of spiritual guidance. At one point, when the setting sun made a fleeting appearance, they turned towards it and applauded. "Did you see it?" a middle-aged man asked excitedly.

The emergence of a large cult-like organisation capable of staging the biggest demonstration against the government since 1989 was something the communist government could not tolerate. The state responded by doing what it knew best. Falun Gong was outlawed as a dangerous cult and vilified in the official media. Defiant practitioners were imprisoned and some were tortured and killed. Reporters who tried to interview members were threatened with expulsion.

At our meeting in the Thai restaurant we decided to respond by doing what *we* knew best – we wrote a letter. It was addressed to the Foreign Ministry and to the State Council. It stated: "In the past several days, a number of our FCC [Foreign Correspondents' Club] members have been subjected to blatant harassment by police and security agents, simply because they had covered activities of Falun Gong practitioners. Our members have been followed, detained, interrogated and threatened. Television reporters have had satellite transmissions interfered with, and video shipments delayed . . ." It went on in this vein. The letter had no perceptible effect.

The plain-clothes men with the task of maintaining order were themselves responsible for organising the most violent street protests in Beijing since Tiananmen Square. This came about after the 7 May 1999 bombing by NATO planes of the Chinese Embassy in Belgrade, which killed three Chinese journalists and outraged the Chinese public. This revived the historical antagonism towards the British and the Americans which now extended to all "long-nose" foreigners. (When I went in Beijing, as a fellow journalist, to sign a book of condolences for the reporters, Shao Yunhuan, Xu Xinghu and Zhu Ying, I was rudely told I was not welcome.) The day after the bombing, large groups of workers, students, doctors, journalists and artists descended on Beijing's embassy district in buses provided by the authorities. Security police directed them along the narrow, poplar-lined avenues around the British and American embassies. They carried a sea of placards with such slogans as "Revenge", "Smash America", "Fuck NATO" (a favourite), "Teeth to teeth, eye to eye", and "Blood for blood".

Mingling with the crowds, I saw men breaking up paving slabs and handing chunks of concrete to the students as they approached the embassies. Among them I recognised the thugs with zipped handbags from Beijing University. They encouraged the demonstrators to throw volley after volley of rocks, plastic bottles, eggs, paint bags and even old shoes (a huge insult) at the embassy buildings. This continued day and night, until every window was broken and the walls covered with paint stains. Opposite the British Embassy a cheer-leader sitting in the branches of a tree sounded a gong each time a window was hit. The government had evidently decided to channel nationalist emotions into a violent, but controlled, demonstration. For the western journalists it was history repeating itself. The foreign legations were being besieged and we were all George Ernest Morrison.

At the height of the protests, I made my way to the British Embassy, where people were chucking stones and paint bombs over the gates. All the tedious hours of Chinese language tuition paid off when demonstrators asked who I was. "*Wo shi I-ar-lan ren. I-ar-lan bu shi bey-ue,*" I said, over and over. "I am Irish. Ireland is not in NATO." I handed out my Chinese language business cards as evidence of my nationality. They left me alone, until a middle-aged worker with broken teeth and wearing a T-shirt rounded on me and began shouting unintelligibly. He ignored my "not in NATO" defence. People gathered tightly around. I recalled that a BBC reporter had been beaten up here earlier. "*Ting bu dong,*" I cried, "I don't understand." He screamed louder, spittle flying into my face. Then a man in the crowd said, in perfect English, "He is telling you to get out of the country, please, as you are all British lackeys." I pleaded with him, "Tell this nice gentleman that I am from Ireland, and we have been fighting the British for 800 years." He translated. The man looked at him, then at me, then he grinned and shouted, "Hurrah!" Everyone shouted, "Hurrah!" I backed away, smiling and bowing. The story got around, and got distorted: several months later a reporter from the *International Herald Tribune* asked me, over dinner in Taipei, if it was true what he had heard, that I took the opportunity of a lifetime to throw a stone at a British embassy. Perhaps he was winding me up, but I suspect not.

For two days the avenues outside the British and American embassies resounded to the crash and thud of rocks hitting glass and concrete, punctuated by yells of abuse. The windows of a two-storey Irish Embassy residence building adjoining the US compound were smashed. A rock flung into the Irish garden hit Guili, an Uighur-nationality childminder, leaving her bruised and terrified. Evan, the ten-year-old daughter of the Irish Ambassador, Joe Hayes and his wife Deirdre, was told by a young Chinese man outside the Friendship Store, "It is a good job you are not American, little girl . . . we will kill all Americans." A crowd attacked a Toyota Privia van driven by a HSBC bank executive from Dublin, Malachy McAlister, smashing the back window and tail lights. Anti-western sentiment had its limits, however. Student "rioters" took time out to rest in Pizza Hut and Dunkin' Donuts.

On the third day, the sound changed to the clunk of stones falling from the pockets of demonstrators onto the road. They were instructed to "decommission" their projectiles by a portly Public Security Bureau official, dressed in red sweatshirt and wearing dark glasses. Enough steam had been let off. The students went back to their universities and the American Ambassador, James Sasser, emerged from his desecrated building with bags under his eyes. He and his staff had survived the three-day siege on Marine Corps combat rations, along with Indian curries and chocolate doughnuts that Joe Hayes's wife Deirdre had passed over the wall from the Irish Embassy garden at the height of the assaults.

In those days Ireland was represented in China by three diplomats and support staff in Beijing and one trade official, who was actually based in Tokyo. China was fast becoming an important player in the global economy, yet Ireland devoted comparatively fewer diplomatic resources to China than other countries did. Finland had ten trade and diplomatic officials in China, Belgium eleven and the Netherlands twelve. New Zealand maintained a presence of ten diplomats and trade officials in Beijing, though it had an economy smaller than Ireland's. Alone in the European Union, Ireland had no representation of any kind in Shanghai, one of the world's biggest and fastest-growing cities. This was no longer good enough. There were so many Irish doing business in China and in other Asian countries at the end of the twentieth century that they formed a significant part of the Irish diaspora and in Beijing and other Asian cities the annual St Patrick's Day ball was the best-attended expatriate event of the season.

Moreover, at the time when I set up the *Irish Times* Beijing bureau in 1996, I found there had not been a single Irish ministerial visit in three years, compared to other European countries, which were averaging four or five a year, and consequently there were no reciprocal Chinese government visits to Ireland. This led to a rather curious diplomatic incident in April 1997. That year China threatened European countries with retaliation if they voted to censure it over breaches of human rights at the UN Human Rights Commission in Geneva. One common form of retaliation was the cancellation of a ministerial visit. Just before the vote, the Chinese Foreign Ministry called in the Irish Ambassador and told him that Dublin could expect a visit from Premier Zhu Rongji. This would be a major event in bilateral relations. But after Ireland voted to censure China on human rights, the Chinese Foreign Ministry said, "We're cancelling the visit, as a protest." It may have been a coincidence. But to me it looked as if they set the visit up just to knock it down and snub the Irish government.

The following year the European nations opted for dialogue rather than confrontation with China on human rights, and

Irish–Chinese relations were put back on track in September 1998 when Bertie Ahern arrived in Beijing on the first visit by a taoiseach to China. He was accompanied by Celia Larkin, whose presence caused something of a protocol issue for his Chinese hosts, but after some deliberation they decided to treat her officially as the Taoiseach's spouse and the couple were lodged in Dwelling No. 18 at the official Diaoyutai guest residence. Tiananmen Square was decked out with Chinese and Irish tricolours for the official welcome for the Irish party. As Ahern and Zhu Rongji walked along a red carpet towards a podium, a seventy-five piece brass band struck up a perfect rendering of "Amhrán na bhFiann" and field guns in the square banged out a nineteen-gun salute (only presidents get twenty-one). It was the first gun salute the Taoiseach had ever been given, and he commented afterwards with some delight that "it seemed to rattle the place". He then inspected a guard of honour of 150 heavily braided servicemen from the army, navy and air force, chosen not just because of their military precision but because they were all exactly the same height. Ms Larkin watched proudly from a podium standing beside Lao An, wife of the Chinese Premier. Next day Ahern met President Jiang Zemin, who concluded their meeting by listing the Nobel laureates won by Irish authors up to the poet Seamus Heaney and commented, "I would say that the Irish are a genius people for literature. Why, most of them seem to have won the Nobel Prize for Literature." Before leaving Beijing, Bertie and Celia dropped in for a pint in Durty Nellie's. In Shanghai the next day the Taoiseach's party and accompanying journalists were given a tour of the Bund on a harbour cruiser. During this cruise we all stayed on the deck too long and got a bit too much sun. Later, when I was conducting a formal interview with Ahern in his hotel suite, Celia Larkin came up behind me and rubbed some after-tan lotion on my scalp, which made concentration rather difficult.

On his return to Dublin the Taoiseach set up an Asia Strategy Group to recommend improvements in Ireland's presence in the region. Enterprise Ireland offices were opened, under Asia Director Michael Garvey, in Beijing, Shanghai and Hong Kong, and a consulate was established in Shanghai headed by Consul-General Geoffrey Keating. Ministerial visits became routine, if not always trouble-free. When Tánaiste Mary Harney arrived in Beijing in September 2000, her baggage was mislaid and she was left with only her travelling clothes. The embassy sent a car to fetch Gu Yuanhong, a Chinese tailor who has made clothes for diplomatic staff, from his home in a Beijing *hutong*. In four hours he ran up a black silk jacket and other accessories, just in time for Harney's first appointment with Chinese Vice Premier, Li Lanqing.

Despite the new policy on Asia, the Irish embassy in Beijing in 2008 was still a modest operation compared to other diplomatic missions, with an ambassador, a counsellor, a first and second secretary, and ancillary staff. The workload has increased considerably. With the Chinese economy growing fast, parents can send their one son or daughter abroad to study and return to take their place in a new, educated, high-tech society, and many have chosen Ireland. The 2006 Census revealed that there were 16,500 ethnic Chinese officially living in Ireland, though informal estimates put the figure at five times that.

The dialogue between European countries and China over human rights had little noticeable impact on the Chinese government. The suppression of dissidents and Falun Gong went on. Foreign correspondents continue today in China to be subject to "violence, destruction of journalistic materials, detention, harassment of sources and staff, interception of communications, denial of access to public areas, being questioned in an intimidating manner by authorities, being reprimanded officially, being followed, and being subjected to other obstacles not in keeping with international practices", according to the website of the Foreign Correspondents' Club of China in early 2008. The previous year it logged 180 violations of Chinese regulations, which state that foreign journalists could travel freely and interview anyone who consented.

In the run-up to the 2008 Olympics, China promised that foreign correspondents would be allowed to travel where they liked, but after anti-China protests in Tibet in March which spread to other ethnic Tibetan regions of China, reporters were prevented from travelling to the affected areas. Faced with worldwide criticism of their response to the unrest, the Chinese leadership called for a media war against the "biased" western press. The Foreign Correspondents' Club complained of death threats against foreign reporters and official statements demonising the western media.

By contrast, when a major earthquake occurred in Sichuan Province on 12 May 2008, killing over 70,000 people, the Chinese authorities put few restrictions on reporters who came from all over the world, and for the first time foreign aid teams were allowed in. This was a major policy change. Ten years earlier, when a big tremor shook Zhangbei, north of Beijing in May 1998 killing forty-seven people, I tried to drive there but was turned back by officials who blocked access to all foreigners. And in 1970, when an earthquake killed 16,000 people in the province of Yunan, the catastrophe was kept secret from the outside world. "A number of foreign correspondents have expressed appreciation for the access they have had to the disaster area, and to timely information about the calamity," said FCCC President Melinda Liu a week after the Sichuan earthquake. "This is a positive development, considering the challenging circumstances." But it didn't last. In the following two months the Correspondents' Club documented sixteen cases where the police temporarily detained or ejected reporters from areas where schools collapsed, including *Irish Times* correspondent Clifford Coonan, and it accused the Chinese government of not living up to its Olympics promise of complete reporting freedom.

22

Long Live Democracy

A fan turned lazily in the ceiling of the officers' mess in a British barracks in Hong Kong. Lieutenant Colonel Bijaykumar Rawat, the Sandhurst-educated commander of the 1st Battalion, the Royal Gurkha Rifles, sat in an armchair, reading a three-day-old copy of the *Sun*. Across the room, which was hung with ceremonial swords, and just beyond French windows leading onto a manicured lawn, his second-in-command, Major John White, a tall, charming, very British officer, asked a waiter to bring drinks for himself and the visiting *Irish Times* correspondent. I had come to the British army base that humid November afternoon in 1996 to write about advance plans for the handover of Hong Kong to China, due to take place on 30 June the following year.

As I sipped my gin and tonic I felt an overwhelming sense of *fin de siècle*. The scene was a façade, like a stage set on a film lot. The other rooms in the battalion headquarters were empty. On the floor of the adjoining bar room, waiting for collection and shipment to England, were the trophies of 150 years' service with the Crown: five rather moth-eaten mounted animal heads (three leopards, a tiger and a lion); a dozen glass-fronted cases of medals and ribbons; five statuettes; three silver cups; and a framed photograph of a Colonel D.R. d'A. Willis. Outside, the parade ground of what had been the main British military garrison in Hong Kong was deserted, most of the 5,000-strong Gurkha force having departed for England. The mess had been left furnished, explained Major White, only so that expatriate guests could attend a ceremonial Beating of the Retreat and a farewell cocktail party that weekend, and enjoy, for a few hours, the knowledge that the sun had not yet quite set on the last citadel of the British empire in the Far East.

Thus, more than half a year before the handover of Hong Kong to China, the British retreat was well under way. They still went through the motions of ownership. Later, on the Chinese border down the road, I came across Private Craig Munro, from Fife in Scotland, squinting through mounted binoculars to read car number plates in Shenzhen, the Chinese city a mile distant. The twenty-three-year-old Black Watch soldier spotted a white People's Armed Police van, and noted it dutifully in his "Guide to Logging Chinese Security Force Registration Plates". This type of intelligence gathering had been going on for a century. Now there were only ten British soldiers left along the thirty-two-kilometre border, peering into China from five concrete posts known as "Mackintosh Cathedrals". "This surveillance is pretty symbolic," said Chief Inspector Charles Parker of the Hong Kong police, as we drove along the barbed-wire fence, past banana and vegetable patches, the next day. "It's all they do. And they will be gone by six p.m. on 30 June."

The fifteenth-century walled village of Kat Ring Wai nearby was already celebrating the imminent end of British rule. The red Chinese communist flag with its five stars was flying on roadside posters, proclaiming, "Congratulations on Unification with China". The entrance to Kat Ring Wai, manned by old women with rheumy eyes in wicker hats, was through a pair of narrow antique gates, two metres high, formed by intertwined circles of cast iron. These had been stolen in 1899 by the then Governor of Hong Kong, Sir Henry Blake, and kept at his stately home, Myrtle Grove in

Youghal, County Cork, for a quarter of a century, before they were returned. Ironically, Hong Kong's new post-colonial symbol, a five-leaf hybrid orchid, was named after Blake – "this arch-colonial Irish vandal", as Hong Kong historian Arthur Hacker called him.

The lotus-like *Bauhinia Blakeana* had already replaced the British crown on the insignia of 46,000 police and civil defence officials in Hong Kong, and it had long since displaced Queen Elizabeth II from the colony's coinage. As Hong Kong adjusted to the new reality, the word "Royal" was dropped from the Royal Jockey Club, though the Royal Hong Kong Yacht Club, like its Dun Laoghaire equivalent, decided to keep it. The Save the Children Fund had ousted Queen Elizabeth as its patron in favour of Tung Chee-hwa, anointed by Beijing to take over as Hong Kong's chief executive after the departure of the last British Governor, Chris Patten.

Patten still lived in splendour in Government House, high above Victoria Harbour. In the final months he had been pressing hard for democratic reforms, leading Beijing to claim that he was conspiring to create a political entity they could not control and annoying the British Foreign Office, which favoured kow-towing to the Chinese government. For his part Patten viewed the Chinese leadership as vindictive, irrational and incompetent, and the Foreign Office mandarins as appeasers.

"What have you learned from the Chinese?" I asked the last Governor in his office in Government House, where a crucifix hung on the wall behind his desk. "Oh, I think that's simple," he replied. "If somebody tries to bully you and you roll over, they do it again. I wouldn't have been able to govern Hong Kong so well if I had simply rolled over."

As the date of the handover approached, members of the international media began arriving in Hong Kong in large numbers. Seeking a defining picture of the end of an era, Hubert van Es, the photographer whose picture of Americans filing onto a helicopter captured the end of the Vietnam War, took a photograph of Chris Patten's dogs, Whisky and Soda, having sex on the Governor's carpet. He sent a copy to Patten, who was so pleased he asked for two more. Many journalists congregated in the bar of the Foreign Correspondents' Club (FCC), a colonial-style mansion on Ice House Street, made famous in *The Honourable Schoolboy*, the novel in which John Le Carré described long afternoons when bored members threw knotted napkins at wine bottles. As the handover approached, the place became too crowded for napkin-tossing, with reporters standing three-deep round the big rectangular bar, pointing out historic fixtures through the tobacco haze, like eighty-five-year-old Clare Hollingworth of the *Daily Telegraph*, who had once scooped the world on Hitler's invasion of Poland.

The FCC members were uneasy about the future, despite Beijing's promise of "one country, two systems" for mainland China and Hong Kong. The club promoted human rights and press freedom and was co-sponsor with Amnesty International of its annual human rights awards. Hong Kong was an information hub for Asia, and *Time, Newsweek, The Wall Street Journal* and the *International Herald Tribune*, all vigorous critics of China, printed regional editions in the colony. They had decided to stay on after the handover, though Reuters moved to Singapore, unsure if Beijing would keep faith with its promise to maintain Hong Kong's freedoms for fifty years.

Many of the stories filed from the FCC reflected the pessimism about post-British Hong Kong expressed by the leader of the Democratic Party, Martin Lee. The intense, fifty-eight-year-old lawyer contemplated a future where the rule of law was undermined, the press muzzled, democracy stifled, corruption rife and himself possibly in prison. In his law office, where a model Statue of Liberty dominated an array of freedom awards, he warned me that the "pervasive" corruption in China would come to Hong Kong, unless Beijing allowed the rule of law to prevail. Some expatriates wished Martin Lee, and the British press, would stop giving the impression that the lights would go out in Hong Kong on 1 July. *Fortune* magazine had led the way in June 1995, warning that Hong Kong was "destined to become a global backwater". A group of Hong Kong business professionals called a meeting in a hotel, two months before the handover, to protest at such "garbage" from the world's media. British-born publicist Ted Thomas told the well-heeled British expatriates who turned up that negative reporting was "seriously and materially damaging business". Jonathan Fenby, editor of the *South China Morning Post*, accused British and American reporters of being "malevolent and contemptuous of reality". Edward Oliver Plunkett, a Dublin-born, retired colonial police officer, voiced his fear, however, that if they opposed China's rule they could find themselves with "a chain between our legs". Thomas tried to interrupt but the octogenarian Plunkett chided him, "You are a blighter! I haven't finished."

The task of formally handing Hong Kong back to the Chinese fell to Prince Charles. With two days to go, the heir to the British throne arrived on a chartered British Airways jumbo jet, and took up temporary residence on the royal yacht, *Britannia*, moored in Victoria Harbour. Baroness Thatcher and her husband, Sir Denis, were welcomed into the Mandarin Oriental Hotel by Irish manager Liam Lambert, along with an eclectic range of English figures, including comedian John Cleese, broadcaster Sir David Frost and former Prime Minister, Sir Edward Heath.

They all gathered, along with the former Ambassador to China, Sir Percy Craddock, and former Governor, Lord MacLehose, on the evening of 29 June, for one of the last great acts of the British empire – the lowering of the flag at sunset on the roof of Hong Kong's Government House. It was a time for a stiff upper lip, if only to hide the icy animosities on the British side. Patten had been attacked by Craddock for antagonising the Chinese and Lord MacLehose had dismissed Martin Lee, who was among the guests, as the leader of "a small minority who make a lot of noise". A piper played "The Skye Boat Song" as the standard was lowered, in a perfect sub-tropical sunset, by two officers dressed in white uniform. Patten looked up, tears in his eyes. Prince Charles furrowed his brow and did not even glance up at the descending Union Jack. A steward then ran out with champagne and a choked-up Governor toasted "The Queen", whose birthday it was.

Meanwhile, lesser British mortals were having a much rowdier time at the Last Night of the Proms at the Academy for Performing Arts. The hall was packed with people wearing pith helmets and red, white and blue feather boas. They waved British flags, and sang along to Elgar's "Pomp and Circumstance". The actor Desmond Carrington rendered Noël Coward's lines from "Mad Dogs and Englishmen": "In Hong Kong they strike a gong and fire off a Noon Day Gun/ To reprimand each inmate, who's in late." The Noon Day gun, a Hotchkiss three-pounder made in 1901, was fired each day in front of the Excelsior Hotel on Victoria Harbour. The gun commemorated the real power in Hong Kong, the merchant house of Jardine, and would keep firing after the handover. In the second half of the concert came the moment of truth. The audience stood to sing "For He's a Jolly Good Fellow" to Chris Patten who had arrived from the flag-lowering ceremony, but as they settled down, the Hong Kong Sinfonietta began to play the Chinese national anthem. Everyone shuffled to their feet, apart from three loyalists who decided to make their last stand – or sit – for the empire.

And then the rains came. Next afternoon, on the last day of British rule, the heavens opened and a tropical rain descended on Hong Kong. It drenched a British farewell ceremony by the waterfront, as the Prince of Wales delivered Queen Elizabeth's goodbye message. The downpour was so heavy that only snatches could be heard by the VIP guests huddled on the dock beside the royal yacht: "Hong Kong . . . one of the leading cities of the world . . . success story . . . Britain proud and privileged . . ." The rain eased enough to allow us to hear Patten tell the gathering: "No dependent territory has been left more prosperous, none with such a rich texture and fabric of civil society, professions, churches, newspapers, charities, civil servants of the highest probity and the most steadfast commitment to the public good." His successor did not hear this testimony. Tung Chee-hwa was at the airport, greeting the Chinese President, Jiang Zemin, and Prime Minister, Li Peng, who had flown in from Beijing.

The final act was conducted at midnight inside the Convention Centre, a new waterside edifice, shaped like Darth Vader's helmet. Arriving soaked, I had to stand for half an hour under a lavatory hand-dryer, with trousered legs held high, first this way, then that, to catch the hot air to dry my clothes. In the chilly, air-conditioned auditorium, rainwater leaked from the ceiling onto my notebook. A wind machine kept the Union Jack and the colonial Hong Kong flag flapping energetically on five-metre high poles as 4,000 people, including Seamus Brennan representing Ireland, watched British soldiers, in bearskin hats and red tunics, ceremoniously give way to Chinese soldiers attired in communist-chic uniforms. At the stroke of twelve, the Union Jack began its slow descent down the flagpole. Prince Charles, in blue suit and tie, again stared glumly ahead, declining to allow the royal eye to witness the end of royal hegemony. In contrast, Jiang Zemin gazed enraptured as the red Chinese flag was raised seconds later, accompanied by Hong Kong's *Bauhinia Blakeana*, to flutter proudly in the well-aimed airflow. Many in the audience broke into spontaneous applause, but the seventy-five British VIPs, including British Prime Minister, Tony Blair, sat motionless. Patten threw back his head in a gesture which said everything. It was all over. Outside Martin Lee addressed a band of protesters, ending with the cry, "Long live democracy!"

Prince Charles and Chris Patten, no longer governor of anything, retreated immediately to the royal yacht. At 1.50 p.m. the three-masted ship sailed out towards the South China Sea, to ragged bursts of "Rule Britannia" from rain-soaked expatriates draped in Union Jacks.

Then it really rained. As I positioned myself under a corrugated iron bus shelter, to await the arrival of the Chinese troops, sheets of water swept in from Victoria Harbour. It was a "black rain" descending at fifty millimetres an hour, possibly the heaviest rainfall in Hong Kong of the twentieth century. It delayed the arrival of the first, absolutely drenched, Chinese soldiers, standing to attention on the open backs of five military lorries as they were conveyed past the Mandarin Oriental, just before dawn, on their way to the Prince of Wales barracks in Central Hong Kong. A few tipsy party-goers in evening-dress, waiting for taxis, waved and laughed from doorways. I met a colleague under a golf umbrella, who told me gleefully that he had stayed in the Foreign Correspondents' Club during the handover, so he could boast that he started a pint in a British colony and finished it in China, without ever leaving his bar stool.

One hundred days after the handover, I returned to Hong Kong. Nothing much had changed. The Foreign Correspondents' Club had lapsed into its customary torpor. The Chinese army base was still called the Prince of Wales Barracks. No Chinese soldiers were on the streets. The Chinese flag flew over Government Buildings, but the mansion remained empty as Tung Chee-hwa elected not to live there because of the bad *feng shui*. Books and newspapers critical of China remained on sale. The big topic of debate was the fall-off in the number of tourists, the city's third-biggest money-spinner. An English executive said: "Whisper it softly, but what has Hong Kong got for the visitor now? When the British left it lost a unique selling point – tea and cucumber sandwiches, Queen Victoria, men in silly hats – all that stuff." In his law office, Martin Lee acknowledged that life went on much as before, and that protesters still demonstrated, and no one had been thrown into jail for dissent.

Today Hong Kong retains most of its freedoms, though universal suffrage has been put off until at least 2017. Beijing has control of defence and foreign affairs, but its "special administrative region" maintains its own legal system, police force, money, customs policy and immigration policy. In 2007 Hong Kong ranked first on the Index of Economic Freedom, with "minimal" corruption, and eighteenth in the Index of Press Freedom, three places ahead of the United Kingdom.

23

Second Act of the Trilogy

No one I talked to in Macau, the oldest and last European colony in the Far East, seemed worried about the fact that on 20 December 1999 it was destined to be handed back to China by Portugal, and become, like Hong Kong, a special administrative region of China for fifty years. There was nothing significant about the date chosen for the handover except that, after regaining Hong Kong from the British, the communist government in Beijing wanted to enter the new millennium with the red flag flying over all of China. Portugal was happy to oblige. For decades it had been trying to give back what was now a mainly Chinese-populated city of 425,000 people, of whom only 1,000 or so were ethnic Portuguese and another 10,000 of mixed Portuguese and Chinese blood, known as Macanese.

In reality, it was not the Portuguese who ran Macau, but a Hong Kong–Macau business syndicate called Sociedade de Turismo e Diversões de Macau, controlled by Hong Kong entrepreneur Stanley Ho, which had a monopoly on the casinos, and which part-owned Macau's new airport, oil terminal, port, bridges, golf course, and the red-and-white jetfoils which brought tourists every half hour from Hong Kong. It was the only private company in the world with its own colony, and its biggest single money-spinner was the opulent Lisboa hotel and casino in the heart of the city.

The biggest bets in the Lisboa were wagered in twenty-one VIP rooms, with names like Treasure Island and Golden Dragon, located in upstairs corridors lined with gilt-framed sofas. The expressions on the faces of the unsmiling Chinese high-rollers and their busty Russian escorts rarely changed. The only sign of emotion I saw, when wandering around one day in 1997, was a player crumpling a card in disgust. The grim atmosphere owed something to the enormity of the risks involved. This particular gambler was a typical mainland official – the white socks were a giveaway – and he had lost a pile of big, flat chips that could have represented the annual budget of a small Chinese city.

This was no place for me. I headed for the slot machines on the ground floor where I changed a few *patacas* into chips, and almost immediately found myself ahead by the price of a modest lunch. I cashed in my winnings, happy to become a member of a very small club of speculators who can say they made money in Macau's gambling dens, and went to explore the tiny Portuguese colony.

The centre of Macau still retained a southern European atmosphere. There were lots of terraced houses with balustraded balconies and washed ochre walls grouped around the main square, the Leal Senado. In the Camões Gardens, old men took their songbirds for walks past a bust of the sixteenth-century Portuguese epic poet, Luís de Camões. School children in convent uniforms filed along cobbled side streets past old baroque churches. Above the town soared the gaunt outer wall of the ruined St Paul's Cathedral, once the most magnificent Christian edifice in the Orient, now a metaphor for the hollow façade of Portuguese rule.

I checked into the Pousada de São Tiago, a hotel built into a steep hillside and entered by a tunnel cut through the rock. It had four-poster beds, alcoves with statues of Our Lady of Fatima, and a shaded terrace where one could linger over lunch of *caldo verde* and *feijodas*, washed down with glasses of Mateus Rose. Home-sick Europeans loved Macau for its Portuguese cuisine, especially the *chorizo* and *Vinho Verde* at Fernando's on Hac Sa Beach.

Next day, four *cavaleiros* on horseback and matadors on foot, dressed in glittering jackets, tight pants and pink leggings, appeared on Avenida Infante D'Henrique, calling on the populace of Macau to attend the *touradas*, the Portuguese bull-fighting competition which had just arrived in colonial Macau for the last time. A bamboo stadium had been erected beside the Lisboa and the ground covered with sand for the performance of the fighters and twenty-four bulls, flown in from Portugal.

Unlike the Spaniards, the Portuguese did not slaughter the bulls in public, but there was plenty of bloodshed. The first bull, its horns sheathed and the number 135 stamped on its side, was fought by a *cavaleiro* who skilfully jammed a *bandeirilha*, a gaily coloured, razor-sharp javelin, into the beast's shoulders, causing a broad stream of blood to run glistening down the bull's side. When the rider had simulated a kill, the bull was hauled away at the end of a rope, and spectators showered the bullfighter with flowers in silver foil wrapping. The fights went on all afternoon and the injured bulls were taken to an abattoir, killed by injection and cut up for select Macau restaurants. Europeans often lectured the Chinese about cruelty to animals, but several Chinese activists turned up to protest at this European practice. Agnes Liu Oi Na, demonstrating outside the stadium, told me indignantly: "They are teaching our children to mistreat animals as good entertainment."

That evening I went to the Canidrome, the only dog-racing stadium in the whole of Asia, situated off the Avenida General Castelo Branco. I placed a bet on a frisky-looking dog and it paid out at ten-to-one, making me a member of an even smaller Macau club, a winner at both the casino and the dog track. The marketing manager, Brian Murphy of Newry, County Down, later took me for seafood stew at Miss Macau, a restaurant so-called because the three daughters of the proprietor had each won the Miss Macau beauty contest: pictures of their crowned heads graced the wall, along with a ceramic image of Our Lady of Fatima. "I had to go and look up Macau on the map when I was offered a job here twelve years ago," said Murphy, who was convinced that China would honour its promise not to interfere in Macau's way of life.

Father Lancelot Rodrigues, who had come from Malaysia sixty-one years earlier, and who ran the Catholic Social Services office in Macau, was also confident that little would change after the Portuguese had left, even though the Chinese government did not tolerate Rome's authority over the Catholic Church on the mainland. Sitting in his office in shirt sleeves and braces, the seventy-three-year-old priest sipped an early-morning Scotch as he explained that a bigger problem was a shortage of local vocations. "We have sixty or seventy priests in Macau but most of them are old," he said. From his seat in a corner, eighty-two-year-old Glasgow-born Father Alex Smith, who had been a ball boy for Celtic Football Club in the 1930s, nodded in agreement, adding, "We have a seminary without seminarians."

The run-up to the handover went smoothly, not least because the Portuguese had already given Beijing almost everything it wanted. Six years earlier they had even crated and shipped to Portugal a statue of a nineteenth-century governor, João Ferreira do Amaral, because China said it was "too colonial". Moreover, unlike the British, the Portuguese had never humiliated the Chinese with gunboats, as they had gained Macau through treaties rather than by force after its merchant seamen had first set up a trading post in 1557. And unlike Hong Kong, Macau was open to mainland Chinese. In the year before the handover, twenty-three million people visited the city to gamble, shop or work, most by simply walking across from the adjacent Chinese city of Zhuhai. Where Hong Kong controlled its borders, Chinese immigration officials alone decided who could enter Macau. The Portuguese Governor, General Vasco Rocha Vieira, enjoyed good relations with the *de facto* Chinese consul in Macau, Wang Qiren, head of the Xinhua News Agency Bureau. If the local pro-Beijing newspaper, the *Macau Daily*, criticised the Portuguese, which happened about once a month, Wang Qiren was likely to drop into the pink and white governor's mansion to apologise.

I returned to Macau for the handover, and found a city *en fête*. The Portuguese threw a gala farewell party on the last day, at which Luís Represas, a Portuguese singer, rendered his official composition, "Macau, Missing You Feels Good". At 11.57 p.m. Portugal's red and green emblem was lowered for the last time. At the stroke of midnight, the red flag of the People's Republic of China was raised to flutter crisply in a blast of compressed air over the heads of 2,500 dignitaries, including a once-more enraptured President Jiang Zemin. The return of Macau was the second act of the trilogy of the country's reunification, said President Jiang in his celebratory speech. It was now time for Taiwan to complete the reunification of China, following the return of Hong Kong and Macau.

At noon next day the People's Liberation Army rolled into town in bright sunshine. Five hundred soldiers, standing in open army trucks, jerked their white-gloved hands back and forth in ritual greeting like wound-up toy soldiers. They were welcomed almost as liberators, and engulfed in a wave of warmth and affection. For once propaganda coincided with reality. It was a defining moment for the PLA, whose reputation had been badly tarnished when it crushed democracy in Beijing's Tiananmen Square in 1989.

And nothing much changed. The gambling in the Grand Lisboa continued, even during the handover night. In the Cathedral Church of Macau, a choir practised for Christmas celebrations. In public parks next day, school children sang carols at giant nativity cribs.

Tourists tumbled off the jetfoil from Hong Kong as usual. Over time the street signs remained in Portuguese and Chinese, and coffee and pastries continued to be served at the little cafés in the Leal Senado. The *pataca* remained the local currency, pegged to the Hong Kong dollar.

Under communist rule, Macau in fact transformed itself into the biggest gambling joint in the world, overtaking Las Vegas and Atlantic City in revenue. In 2001 the gaming industry was liberalised and the licences were distributed among Stanley Ho's new consortium, the Sociedade de Jogos de Macau, the Galaxy group from Hong Kong and the Sands corporation from Las Vegas. The Grand Lisboa has now been exceeded in opulence by the Venetian, built by Sands on Macau's second island, Taipa. It has 3,000 hotel rooms, designer stores and a gaming floor the size of a small town. The "one country, two systems" idea is working so well in Macau, and is so profitable for the Chinese administration, that it is unlikely that anything will change even when the grace period as a special administrative region of China expires in 2049. It has, however, lost much of the feel of a southern European town and now resembles more than ever a typical noisy, chaotic Chinese provincial city.

24

No Third Act

Chinese President Jiang Zemin's wish that, after the handovers of Hong Kong and Macau, the incorporation of Taiwan with the motherland would be the third act of a "trilogy of reunification", had particular relevance for the 80,000 people living on Kinmen island off the coast of China. At low tide, less than a kilometre of water separates Kinmen from the mainland, but no one ever ventures down to the landward shore, as the sands are heavily mined. "If a cow wanders onto the beach, it becomes instant roast beef," a resident warned me, laughing. Like other visitors to the sub-tropical island, I contented myself with peering through military binoculars at the enemy from inside a concrete bunker.

Kinmen, known in the West as Quemoy and on the mainland as Jinmen, hugs the coast of mainland China, but is administered by Taiwan, 280 kilometres across the sea to the east. No more than 150 square kilometres, it has two modest-sized towns, joined by tree-shaded roads, where blue trumpet flowers and four-season orchids grow in profusion. In summer farmers spread sorghum across the tarmacadam surfaces to let traffic separate the grain from the chaff. Golden plovers and other exotic birds flash among the cotton, rowan and fir trees dripping with Spanish moss, used everywhere by the Taiwanese army to hide tank movements.

After General Chiang Kai-shek retreated to Taiwan with the remnants of his defeated Nationalist Army in 1949, the narrow stretch of turquoise water between Kinmen and the mainland became the military front between the two sides. In the 1950s the communist and nationalist forces exchanged intermittent fire across the narrow straits, and in one forty-four-day period in the summer of 1958, China bombarded Kinmen with approximately 480,000 artillery shells. This prompted a show of force by the US 7th Fleet, which ensured that there would be no follow-up invasion.

The war fever cooled and for a time the protagonists resorted to firing metal canisters packed with propaganda leaflets at each other. Kinmen lobbed them across on Monday, Wednesday and Friday, and China on Tuesday, Thursday and Saturday, so that no one got hurt. This eventually gave way to propaganda being blasted across the water by gigantic loudspeakers, which were finally switched off in the late 1990s. As the threat of attack receded, Kinmen was transferred from military to civilian rule, and the troop presence reduced. The famous "831" military brothel (831 was its telephone number) was closed and replaced by karaoke bars. Shell canisters were no longer used for packing explosives but as door stops or for making knives, which are much sought after by chefs and connoisseurs.

However, Kinmen, along with two other offshore islands, Matsu and Wuchiu, remained cut off from its natural hinterland. Just across the water lies the Chinese city of Xiamen, where Kinmen people have many relatives, including the survivors and descendants of 4,700 islanders who, half a century earlier, found themselves on the wrong side of the narrow channel. Xiamen is only half an hour's boat ride away, but at the time of my visit in August 1999, any Kinmen inhabitant wishing to visit mainland relatives had to fly to Taipei, the capital of Taiwan, and from there take a flight south to Hong Kong, and then a further flight north to Xiamen, an expensive and tedious journey of over 1,500 kilometres. I was living in Beijing at the time and, to get to the little offshore island, I had to fly three hours from Beijing to Hong Kong, wait two days for a Taiwan visa, then take another airline to Taipei, and from there a domestic flight to Kinmen. There were no authorised air, sea, postage or even telephone links between China and Taiwan. The Iron Curtain in Europe had never imposed such barriers between peoples. In practice, however, on Kinmen the smuggling of goods and people across the narrow waterway at Kinmen had increased to the point where it was "out of control", according to the island's Mayor, Chen Shui-zai.

That summer, tensions had escalated sharply again between Beijing and Taipei. Taiwan was preparing for its first democratic elections, and candidates had sought popular support by championing the cause of Taiwan as a separate country. A comment by outgoing Taiwan President, Lee Teng-hui, a veteran of Chiang Kai-shek's Nationalist Party, that in future Taiwan would deal with Beijing only on a "special state-to-state relationship", had been taken by the Chinese government as a move by its "renegade province" towards formal independence. Military rumblings from the People's Republic of China grew steadily louder. Chinese warplanes flew up the Taiwan straits past Kinmen. Asian newspapers reported rumours that Beijing planned to seize the island by force. Many of Kinmen's residents were evacuated temporarily to Taiwan proper.

"We are naturally worried that China might attack and we are on the alert," said the Mayor, who appeared remarkably sanguine about threats published just that week, in China's *Liberation Army Daily*, that frontline soldiers deployed within sight of Kinmen had vowed to smash Lee's "evil splittist plot". Generally the scene was calm, he assured me in his office where he kept on display a cast of a large shell used by the US 7th Fleet to protect the island in a 1950s' artillery duel. "Farming goes on and the tourists are still coming."

The Mayor's serene attitude was undoubtedly affected by China's habit of indulging in bellicose rhetoric and then doing nothing. Kinmen airport terminal, on the Friday afternoon I arrived, was full of boy scouts and other seasonal visitors from Taiwan, intent on enjoying the unmined ocean-side beaches, viewing the beautiful relics of Ming and Ch'ing Dynasty architecture and savouring local delicacies such as typhoon spirals and fried sand bugs. They also engaged in some patriotic tourism, crowding into the war museum where rows of gable-sized oil paintings tell the story of a 1949 battle in which nationalist soldiers defeated an invading communist force that arrived on 270 fishing boats. The most prominent painting shows General Chiang Kai-shek inspecting victorious soldiers from a jeep, which is always coming towards the viewer, whether looked at from left or right. "It's an optical illusion, just like the Mona Lisa's eyes," said the military guide proudly. Some of the bomb-proof tunnels on the island had been opened to tourists, including a vast sea channel dug into a granite hill, which was designed to take a dozen freighters at a time and would make an ideal location for a James Bond movie.

Like most people on Kinmen, its civilian boss was unhappy with President Lee for provoking Beijing's fury. Four out of five inhabitants supported eventual reunification, he said, but "if Taiwan had a better relationship with China, then Kinmen would have a better future". The Mayor had a personal interest in a political solution. Taiwan allowed its citizens to go to China through third locations like Hong Kong and Macau, but this right did not extend to mayors, so Chen Shui-zai was the only islander unable to get permission even to make the long roundabout journey to see his relatives in Xiamen.

I returned to Taiwan, this time to the capital Taipei, in February the following year, as presidential elections were in full swing.

The hot favourite was Taipei Mayor, Chen Shui-bian, of the pro-independence Democratic Progressive Party, a native-born Taiwanese who resented rule by the remnants of the nationalist forces. Chen had taken several steps to break with the past, including the "Taiwanisation" of city street names. He renamed Chiang Kai-shek Road Kaitegalan Road, after the earliest inhabitants of Taipei and proclaimed a new national day to honour the victims of the 2-28 incident of 1947, so-called because on 28 February that year, nationalist troops began a crackdown that killed between 10,000 and 30,000 Taiwanese protesting against their occupation. The massacre had been a forbidden topic until the lifting of martial law in 1987.

On one thing all Taiwan's political parties were united, however. They would not submit, like Hong Kong and Macau, to Jiang Zemin's overtures to return to the "motherland" under the "one country, two systems" model, certainly not while China had an undemocratic government. The forty-nine-year-old mayor, dressed in immaculate grey suit and tie and wearing rimless spectacles, played down China's sabre-rattling. "We will not declare independence if China does not invade us," he told me in an interview in his Taipei office. Anyway, there was no need to make any declaration, as Taiwan was already "an independent country". He wanted co-operation and not war, and competition rather than a permanent struggle, so there was no need for Beijing to "get too hyped up or too tense".

Chen Shui-bian won the presidential election, in the process toppling the eighty-nine-year political dynasty of the Nationalist Party in all-China history. In his inaugural address, he promised "Four Noes and One Without". There would be no declaration of independence, no referendum on independence, no change of national title from Republic of China to Republic of Taiwan, and no inclusion of the doctrine of "state-to-state relations" in the Taiwan constitution. The one "without" referred to a promise not to abolish the National Unification Council, which had been set up as a sop to Beijing's overtures.

In his tenure in office, which lasted to 2008, President Chen did, however, abolish the National Unification Council and on 30 September 2007, his Democratic Progressive Party approved a resolution asserting separate identity from China and support for a new constitution establishing the political entity of Taiwan as a "normal country". However, China's power of veto as a member of the UN Security Council ensured that Taiwan could not hope to be admitted to the United Nations.

China continued a military build-up opposite Taiwan though it was constrained by the prospect that any attack, or the seizure of Kinmen, could provoke US military action, isolate Beijing internationally and bring about economic sanctions and a loss of investment. In March 2008, having had enough of Chen's brinksmanship with China and wanting to try something a little less stressful for a while, Taiwan voters overwhelmingly elected Nationalist Party candidate Ma Ying-jeou as president, choosing the prospect of economic growth over fears that closer ties to the mainland might lead to a loss of independence. Relations between Taipei and Beijing began to warm up. In May 2008 Chinese President Hu Jintao welcomed the chairman of the Chinese Nationalist Party, Poh-hsiung, to Beijing and invited him to the opening ceremony of the Olympic Games in August. He also agreed to a dialogue to ease travel restrictions and other barriers between China and Taiwan. On 3 July 2008, regular direct flights between Taiwan and China began in a show of reconciliation.

In Kinmen pragmatism had already enjoyed a small triumph over dogmatism. A regular ferry service from Kinmen to Xiamen opened in 2001, though for Kinmen and Xiamen citizens only. Residents can today travel back and forth for tourism and trade, and several boats each day make the trip, as well as tourist dragon boats of patriotic Chinese visitors, who look longingly at the island through binoculars, and say what a beautiful place it is and how they long for it to be in the arms of the motherland, where it belongs. "Maybe some day we'll build a bridge across," Mayor Chen Shui-zai told me, wistfully. "But it won't happen today or tomorrow."

25

The Country that Isn't

It wasn't just the faux-western Hard Yak Café, or the clichéd pictures of Clint Eastwood and James Dean on the restaurant walls, or the wretched cuisine, or the sound of rats in the ventilation ducts, that made me take a dislike to the Hotel Lhasa. It was the feeling of being watched. Journalists based in Beijing are rarely given permission to visit Tibet, and when they are, they are required to stay in the 468-room concrete pile owned by the government in the capital, Lhasa. I found burly Chinese plain-clothes men hanging around the entrance watching every move, when I was allowed to travel to Tibet and checked into the hotel in June 1998. I didn't realise it then, but it was a particularly tense time in Tibet. Just four weeks earlier, five Buddhist nuns and three monks had died from beatings and suicide after staging a protest in Drapchi prison, something that would not become public for several months.

The government in Beijing has always been extremely sensitive about reporting of the Himalayan territory, which it claims as a historic part of the "motherland". The exiled religious leader, the Dalai Lama, has headed a government-in-exile since Tibet was seized by China in 1951, and its bitter relations with Beijing have been marked by sporadic upheavals and disturbances, including a failed uprising in 1959 that was followed by a harsh

251

crackdown in which tens of thousands of Tibetans died. The Chinese government refers to supporters of the Dalai Lama as "splittists" and the Foreign Ministry in Beijing gave us black marks if we dared to refer to Tibet as a "country" in our reports. It is officially the Tibetan Autonomous Region of China.

Prior to 1951 Lhasa was a small Tibetan town of about 25,000 people, the capital of a theocratic nation closed to the outside world. A wave of state-driven investment and an influx of Han Chinese had since then transformed it into a modern Chinese city, especially the western section which is dominated by department stores, restaurants, karaoke bars and office blocks. I found that most street signs had large Chinese characters and only small Tibetan writing, and many billboards, including those advertising Kodak and Volkswagen, had no Tibetan translation at all. According to a Chinese government White Paper, all signage on government institutions, streets, roads and public facilities in the Tibetan Autonomous Region had to be in both Tibetan and Chinese scripts, with precedence given to the Tibet language. "No one has violated that policy," the Tibetan Vice Mayor, Ping Cuo Jie Bo, insisted to me in his office. I asked about the many notices I had seen in Chinese only. He was silent for a bit. "This phenomenon is because they are just aimed at tourists, the majority of whom are Chinese," he eventually replied.

The Vice Mayor, who insisted that my photograph of him include his porcelain bust of Chinese leader Mao Zedong, rejected any suggestion that Chinese settlers had created an alternate society that denied Tibetans equal social and economic status in their own land. Ping insisted that the vast majority of the city's population of 400,000 were still Tibetan, but acknowledged this did not take into account Chinese residents on temporary permits.

Immigrant Chinese on such permits, attracted by interest-free loans and higher salaries, clearly threatened to outnumber the locals in their own capital. A trader from Sichuan province, who arrived in Tibet to sell shoes seven years earlier and who was making "easy money", said he reckoned a third of the population of Lhasa was Chinese from Sichuan province alone. The immigrants didn't learn Tibetan because they didn't need to, especially if they were not staying permanently, he explained. A taxi-driver reckoned that his fellow Chinese made up seventy per cent of cab drivers in Lhasa. For a nominal sum, anyone could get a temporary residence permit and stay for years, he confided. "Even if you don't, the police will not fine you if you are caught, though if your attitude is not good, they will give you a slap."

Beneath the Potala Palace, the thirteen-storey marvel of Asian architecture towering over the city, a large tarmacadam space had been carved out from the old Tibetan town to resemble Tiananmen Square. Here Chinese stall-holders sold souvenirs in the warm June sunshine, Chinese youths played pool on open-air tables and Chinese children clambered over a life-size model of a People's Liberation Army warplane. The Tibetans who had previously lived in the square had been relocated to Xuexin "village", a newly built community of Tibetan-style houses behind the Potala. I was brought there to visit an elderly Tibetan, Thaje, who had photographs of Stalin, Lenin, Marx, Engels, Mao, Deng Xiaoping and Jiang Zemin in the living-room of his six-room house. "I used to be a serf working in the summer palace of the Dalai Lama," he said, "Then I had little money. Now I make enough." He sold cigarettes, mineral water and packets of instant noodles through a little window. When I asked him what he thought of the Dalai Lama, his wife interrupted hastily: "We can't say what is good and what is bad. Whoever treats Tibet well is good. Now, Tibet is under the Communist Party and that is good." Despite their proclaimed devotion to communism, Thaje and his family maintained a Buddhist prayer room, and the previous day he had taken part in the circumambulation round the Potala, spinning a prayer wheel with other pilgrims and burning heaps of dry grasses along the road to commemorate the birth and nirvana of the Buddha.

The Tibetan secretary of the 600-member Xuexin community, twenty-eight-year-old Chong Da, told me that, under Chinese family planning policy, urban Tibetan couples were restricted to two children. The committee set quotas and decided when women could conceive. She'd had a baby two years previously and would have to wait one or two more years before she could conceive again, she said. Any woman who became pregnant outside the permitted time would be persuaded to have an abortion. In rural areas, according to Vice Mayor Ping, "there are no specific restrictions – people can have ten children if they want".

I climbed up the steep steps of the Potala Palace and entered its gloomy interior of chapels, altars, Buddhas and religious relics, lit by low-voltage neon strips and oil lamps fuelled from slabs of yak butter. The heart of Tibetan Buddhism, Potala Palace in the old days was described by Heinrich Harrer, author of *Seven Years in Tibet*, as "miserably dark and uncomfortable as a dwelling place", from where the lonely young Dalai Lama used to watch the goings-on of his subjects through a telescope, before being forced into exile. Now it was more like a Buddhist theme park for tourists. A featureless Chinese tea-room occupied a central area where visitors were informed (in Chinese only) of President Jiang Zemin's advice on "maintaining the solidarity of nationalities and national ethnic cultures." The vast building, which once housed the Tibetan government and was home to 175 Tsedrung monks of high standing, had a population of only sixty-five monks, some of whom surreptitiously asked me for pictures of the Dalai Lama. I did not have any and was mindful that some of the monks were said to be spies. Displays of the Dalai Lama's image were forbidden in monasteries, as his "splittist deeds" had compromised his position as a religious leader, according to Vice Mayor Ping. Photographs of the Dalai Lama were also prohibited in private homes, but, he assured me, if the common people displayed such items the government would not punish them; rather "it will try to persuade them to dispose of the pictures".

Wandering around inside the Potala, I came across a room equipped with rows of metal-frame chairs. This was a classroom for patriotic education, I was told, to counter the monks' splittist tendencies. The "patriotic campaign" was explained to me by Jagra Losang-dainzin, deputy director of the Tibet Autonomous Region Committee of Nationality and Religious Affairs, and one of 304 living Buddhas identified in their infancy as reincarnations of the deity. In dark suit and polo-neck shirt and sporting a gold watch, he looked just like the pro-Beijing bureaucrat he had chosen to become. He had opted for secular life, he explained, and had married and fathered three children, forfeiting the right to wear robes. This pro-China Buddha maintained that there were 46,380 monks and nuns in Tibet and 1,787 monastic sites and that the Tibet Autonomous Region was taking "concrete measures to protect freedom of belief". Much money had been spent restoring places of worship destroyed in the Cultural Revolution. At the same time, some feudal practices had been banned and monastic orders could not admit anyone under eighteen. "Monks and nuns are citizens of China and every citizen has the obligation to love his motherland," the living Buddha insisted. The patriotic campaign involved five courses: the anti-separatist struggle; socialist democracy and law; ethnic and religion policy; safeguarding the unification of the motherland; and adapting religion to the socialist cause. At the end of the sessions, all monks had to pass an examination on these topics. The living Buddha acknowledged that some monks – a "limited number, very few" – had "failed", and been forced out of monasteries because of their "counter-revolutionary minds". He pooh-poohed reports that 200 monks were in prison. "Less than that," he said.

Evidently the patriotic campaign was meeting stiff resistance. The Tibet Autonomous Region Congress acknowledged that year that "the struggle against separatism is protracted, acute and complicated" and that "opposing separatism is the top political task facing us". It resolved to "crack down according to law on criminal elements splitting the motherland".

Two kilometres west of the Potala, in the old Tibetan quarter, pilgrims prostrated themselves every day in front of the Jokhang, the most revered religious structure in a nation defined by religion. The old streets were full of Tibetans shopping for sandals, yak hair, snuff, herbs, spices, medicines, hardware, felt hats, cloth for prayer flags, and dozens of other daily necessities, just as they had done for centuries. Here one afternoon I called on the seventy-year-old Tibetan author and teacher Tashi Tsering, an enigmatic figure at the interface between Tibetan nationalism and Chinese communism, at his home in a narrow street. A supporter of Chinese rule, he had no fewer than seven photographs of the Dalai Lama on his living-room wall. "Most people have his picture; they respect him," he told me, matter-of-factly.

As we drank beer on the balcony, he insisted on quizzing me about the origin and decline of the Irish language. Tsering, author of the only Tibetan-English-Chinese dictionary, was a passionate advocate of Tibetan, which was having to come to terms with the prevalence of Chinese, just as the Irish had to accept English as the language of advancement. "The Tibetan language defines the nation and I am very much concerned about its future," he said, in near-perfect English, as he swatted a fly from the little bar where his wife Sangyela sold barley-based local beer, known as *chang*. Among Tibetans themselves, he believed, there was a decline in the quality of the language, which has thirty-four consonants and four vowels and which evolved from Sanskrit. "Young intellectuals are very good at Chinese and English, but they are not very good at Tibetan any more." In college, physics, geography and mathematics could be done only through Chinese, he said, adjusting his large gold-rimmed glasses. "If there are five Tibetans and five Chinese in a room, the language is Chinese." He sighed as he refilled our glasses. "We Tibetans are so weak, we can't demand our own rights!"

He was not a "splittist", he said, though he had met the exiled Buddhist leader in the United States the previous year and respected his desire to do a deal with the Chinese one day. Born in a Tibetan village in 1929, Tsering came to Lhasa as a thirteen-year-old member of the Dalai Lama's personal song-and-dance troupe. As he relates in his autobiography, *The Struggle for Modern Tibet*, he advanced himself by becoming a *drombo*, a passive sex partner to a prominent monk, and eventually secured a job in the Potala Treasury. Disillusioned by the rule of conservative and corrupt monks, he became attracted to socialism. When the Chinese arrived in 1951, he was one of a number of young Tibetan radicals who welcomed the prospect of social change. He was impressed by the way the People's Liberation Army grew their own vegetables. "The most startling thing I saw was that they picked up human excrement from the street with long ladles and put it on their vegetable gardens," he said. "I had never seen such a thing!"

He left for India in 1957 to learn more about the world and was drawn into the orbit of expatriate Tibetan activists, but never shook off his conviction that, as he put it, "the Chinese invasion of Tibet provided a once-in-a-lifetime opportunity for Tibetans who did not know how to conduct a revolution by themselves." Tsering returned in 1964 and joined the Red Guards during the Cultural Revolution, but was soon afterwards denounced as an

American agent. He was publicly humiliated, tortured and imprisoned. "They fried me, boiled me and cooked me," he said, laughing. He spent six years in prison, and was only released and exonerated in 1978. He became a professor of English at Lhasa University and sold carpets and yak-wool sweaters from his home to visitors from overseas, and with the profits, and matching government money, he built the first-ever primary school in his native village. He had since set up thirty-six rural schools with over 4,000 pupils. "If it had not been for my naïveté and foolish optimism," he reflected, sipping his beer, "I would never have survived and accomplished what I have."

Back in Beijing I wrote up my report on Tibet, carefully avoiding the word "country". Shortly thereafter I was dressed down by a Foreign Ministry official who invited me to lunch to discuss my reporting. "You called Tibet a country," he snapped. "I did not," I replied. "You did!" He reached into his briefcase and produced a cutting from *The Irish Times*. There was the word "country", not written by me, but in a headline over my article, penned by a subeditor in Dublin: "Tibet, the country [that] still hasn't come to terms with its role inside Chinese borders". I explained how this had happened but couldn't convince him there wasn't an anti-China agenda on the Foreign Desk. Years later, on 12 April 2008, the Chinese Ambassador in Dublin, Liu Biwei, walked out of a Green Party conference when party leader and Minister for the Environment John Gormley referred in a speech to Tibet as a "country" that had been exploited and suppressed.

Occasional talks between representatives of the Dalai Lama and the Chinese government over the years produced no results, despite the Dalai Lama's willingness to accept that Tibet is part of China. A new series of anti-China protests began in Lhasa on 10 March 2008, the anniversary of an uprising against Chinese rule in 1959. Tibetan rioters ransacked and burned rows of

Chinese-owned stores. The official Chinese media stated that eighteen people were killed by the rioters. The Tibetan government in exile claimed that more than a hundred Tibetans were killed in the unrest, which spread to ethnic Tibetan areas of Qinghai, Gansu and Sichuan provinces. The claims were impossible to verify. As soon as the trouble started, China evicted all foreign reporters from the Hotel Lhasa and sent them back to Beijing.

26

Who Killed Zorig?

In October 1998 I flew from Beijing to Ulan Bator, capital of Mongolia, with my colleague James Pringle of the London *Times*. We checked into a hotel and that evening set out for a restaurant someone had recommended. Snowflakes drifted into the headlights of our Lada taxi as it made its way through streets deserted but for an occasional figure hurrying by in the darkness, wrapped in a *del*, the cloak worn by Mongolian horsemen. We got out in an unlit street and I pushed open the nondescript wooden door of the address we had been given.

"*Bonsoir, monsieur,*" said a beautiful Mongolian woman in the hallway. "*Vous avez une réservation?*" She led us into a packed, noisy Corsican restaurant, where foreign and Mongolian diners were tucking into *Bouchées à la Reine*, and drinking Patrimonio wines. The *Café de France* was, we learned, one of a number of sophisticated western ventures to open in the remote Mongolian capital since the communists were swept from power in 1990 and Mongolia embraced capitalism.

All was not well, however, in post-communist Mongolia. We had not come to the central Asian nation to enjoy the French cuisine, but to report on an unsolved murder: that of Mongolia's most revered citizen and prime minister-designate, Sanjaasuren

Zorig. His brutal killing two weeks earlier was as shocking to Mongolians as the assassination of President Kennedy was to Americans. Zorig had led huge pro-democracy rallies in 1990 that ended seven decades of communist rule as a satellite of Moscow. He had defused a potential Tiananmen Square-type bloodbath by persuading 10,000 pro-democracy protesters to sit down, rather than confront armed soldiers. He was known as the "Golden Magpie" of democracy, named after the first magpie that heralds spring.

Released from the constraints of Marxism-Leninism, Mongolia had overnight become one of the most pro-business countries in the world. The newly rich flashed past old Soviet-made trolley-buses in BMWs and hung out at the stock exchange, an ochre-coloured former cinema that boasted a computerised dealing system, designed with the help of Harvard University graduates. Economic and political reforms had given Ulan Bator a veneer of prosperity. There were over 500 nightclubs, bars and restaurants in a city of 650,000 people, half of whom still lived on the outskirts in felt-lined tents known as *gers*. In the biggest nightclub, the Top Ten Disco, hordes of teenagers danced, watched striptease and drank Genghis Khan beer until four in the morning. Genghis Khan, the thirteenth-century Mongolian master of the universe, had been rehabilitated as a national symbol of independence, and his name now appeared on everything from beer bottles to matchboxes. The new Mongolian elite could also patronise the Churchill Tea Shop which specialised in Cornish pasties, the Matisse Art Café with its impressionistic paintings, and a sushi restaurant called the Sakura Harvest.

The rush by Mongolian democrats to embrace western ways excited American free marketeers, who saw this landlocked country of steppes and desert, wedged between China and Russia, as the bright shining light of developing-world capitalism. A Mongolian translation of US House Speaker Newt Gingrich's 1994 *Contract with America*, an election manifesto for smaller government and personal responsibility, had become the biggest publication in modern Mongolia, with 350,000 copies distributed among the country's 2.4 million people. Young bright-eyed Americans in striped, button-down shirts had opened an office of the International Republican Institute in Ulan Bator, and helped the four parties in a Democratic Coalition to defeat the reformed communists of the Mongolian People's Revolutionary Party, the MPRP, in 1996.

The Democratic Coalition had launched a sweeping privatisation programme and introduced a bill for a thirty per cent flat tax. They were egged on by officials from the Soros Foundation, the International Monetary Fund, the Asia Foundation, the Asian Development Bank, USAID and the World Bank, who had descended on Mongolia to nurse and cajole it through shock therapy. Christian groups also jetted in to seek converts from the Buddhist population, though a Mongolian magazine editor told me gleefully that nomads had gladly accepted bibles from the smiling missionaries to use the pages for rolling cigarettes. (In time George W. Bush, Donald Rumsfeld and US Air Force General Richard B. Myers would come to thank the country for joining the "Coalition of the Willing" and supplying 173 soldiers to support the US war in Iraq.)

The fall of communism had a downside. One-third of Mongolia's gross national product had come from Soviet subsidies. Big state enterprises closed down after the Russians left. Thousands of workers were laid off, while many free marketeers enriched themselves through privatisation of state assets. The Democratic Coalition government squabbled and parliament descended into chaos. The new financial wizards squandered $100 million, most of the nation's reserves, in a few days of amateurish trading on the stock market. A steep drop in world prices for Mongolia's main exports – copper, gold and cashmere – plunged the state into recession. According to the World Bank, by the mid-1990s one-third of the population lived below the poverty line and one in four children was chronically malnourished.

This resulted in the phenomenon of Ulan Bator's street kids, who by day lived by stealing, picking pockets, polishing shoes and carrying rubbish, and at night slept in the humid, insect-infested city sewers, huddling close to pipes carrying hot water to apartment blocks, if not working as child prostitutes. One of the foreign agencies helping the young people was the Christina Noble Children's Foundation. Having herself once been a badly abused street child in the Liberties in Dublin, Christina told me the children were suffering from lice, syphilis and herpes. Her organisation provided a mobile clinic and health education programme and was creating a village on the edge of town for street children and orphans.

In the summer of 1998 the combination of hopes dashed, increasing poverty and growing inequality led to a new political crisis. The coalition government resigned, accused of merging a bankrupt state bank with a privately run bank to hide bad loans made to prominent Democrats. The leading member of the Democratic Coalition majority in parliament, Davaadorjiin Ganbold, was blocked from forming a new government by the ex-communist Mongolian President, Natsaigyin Bagabandi. There were weeks of stalemate. At last, on Friday, 2 October 1998, the parties agreed on Zorig as a suitable compromise to head a new reform-minded government as prime minister.

That evening, at 10.13, Zorig telephoned Bulgan, his wife of three years, to say that he had stayed behind in his parliament office to play chess with a friend – he was president of the Mongolian Chess Association – and he would be home in ten minutes. What happened next was described to us by a Zorig family friend, over beer in the Top Ten Disco. As the father of Mongolia's democracy was being driven home, someone rang the doorbell of their fourth-floor apartment. A man and a woman wearing masks and armed with a knife and an axe knocked his wife down and shouted: "Where's the money?" They took

US$300, two rings and, unaccountably, some soy sauce, bound and gagged Bulgan with adhesive tape and waited for Zorig to arrive. When he opened the door the intruders stabbed him eighteen times, thrice through the heart. Before fleeing, one shouted to his wife that Zorig was "only the first we've done with, and there will be others". The bloody murder was discovered twenty minutes later by a neighbour.

Next day a shocked population was told that their national icon was dead. Television and radio played solemn music. Despite the robbery of valuables, almost everyone in Ulan Bator was convinced it was a political assassination. "This killing is a very big, serious political crime, directed against the democratic process going on in Mongolia," Ganbold told us in his parliament office.

The question "Who killed Zorig?" became a national obsession. Everyone thought of Zorig as "Mr Clean", an incorruptible politician and a nice guy, which perhaps was his downfall. The American Ambassador, Alphonse La Porta, told us he believed the killer of Zorig was clearly "someone who didn't want him to become prime minister". A leading suspect was the Russian mafia, which had connections to the debt-ridden state copper mine, Erdenet, a joint venture with Russia, which democrats wanted to privatise. As a minister, Zorig was involved in the sacking of the head of Erdenet, a former communist, and his replacement by a manager loyal to the Democratic Coalition. Paradoxically the murder might have an anti-Russian motive. On the day of the assassination Zorig's mother had received an anonymous telephone call from someone who said "Russians must get out of the country". Zorig had Russian ancestry. Another rumour had it that the killers were criminals who believed Zorig had won a lot of money at the casino operated by a German-Malaysian joint venture in the Genghis Khan Hotel. An official there assured us Zorig "was not a serious gambler". It could also have been a gangster slaying connected with gambling. The casino had been shut down in August by the

Democratic Coalition, which gave exclusive gambling rights instead to a Macau-based company. The German partners suspected large bribes had been paid and that money-laundering would be its real business, and they claimed that Zorig had refused a $50,000 pay-off to get on board.

The murder remained unsolved. Eighteen months later when I returned to Mongolia, people stated as a fact, without evidence, that the two murderers themselves were dead, disposed of by the mastermind of one of Asia's worst political crimes, so that they would remain silent forever. A statue of Zorig had been erected at the junction of Peace Avenue and Chinggis Avenue, depicting him in collar and tie and spectacles, with a cigarette between his fingers and a bundle of documents under his arm. Every day fresh flowers were laid at its base. The reformers had meanwhile failed to form a government. The former communist elite had returned to power in a wave of nostalgia for the old Soviet days of subsidies, free education and socialised health care.

By then the Mongolians had more immediate worries. The country was experiencing the harshest *zud* – extreme weather conditions – in thirty years. Starting in the summer of 1999, they had a black *zud*, a white *zud* and an iron *zud* – a drought that left little grass, followed by record heavy snowfalls, and then a cold so severe that a layer of ice prevented cattle from grazing through the snow. The multiple *zud*, which affected thirteen of Mongolia's twenty-one provinces, was the greatest disaster that could befall the Mongolian herders.

Its effects could be seen in a drive by Land Rover across the yellow steppes, where the spring sunshine had burned away most of the winter snows. Everywhere, stacked in piles many metres high, were dead cows, horses, ponies, sheep, goats and camels, their rigid legs sticking out at awkward angles. Some had perished just the previous day, when a raging wind came tearing down from the north. Most had died in the previous two months and their bones had been picked clean or they had been skinned for wool or cashmere. Others were savaged by wild animals. "This winter is a holiday for wolves, with the livestock too weak to run," said Enkhe, who guided me and my companions, Rob Gifford of National Public Radio and Miro Cernetig of the Toronto *Globe and Mail*, through shallow valleys teeming with marmots and field mice which had appeared in plague numbers, contributing to a disastrous overgrazing of the already withered pastures. Hawks and golden eagles glided low overhead, feasting on the mice.

A brown cow had been kneeling in front of Byambasuren's *ger* about 250 kilometres south-west of Ulan Bator for two days, its eyes blank and its head almost touching the ground. "It can't get up," said Byambasuren, a herder with close-cropped hair and ruddy cheeks. "It will die any day now." When it did, the skinny animal would be dragged to an already high pile of carcasses. Before the first blizzards came in September, the family of seven adults and thirteen children had 600 head of livestock, enough to meet their needs. Now they had only 200 sheep and goats and a couple of cows, and these too might be doomed. Byambasuren had 100 lambs enclosed in a separate tent and the family was giving them precious milk, sugar and flour to keep them alive. "I am twenty-eight and I have never experienced anything like this," said his wife, also called Byambasuren. (They had only one name each, since the communists banned surnames in 1921 to end clan allegiance; with surnames popular again, most people chose Borjiin, the family name of Genghis Khan.) "The first big snow froze so hard that the livestock could not graze and we ran out of fodder. Many families around here have lost all their animals and now they just help each other find lost horses and cattle." She spoke philosophically about nature's cruelty. "It's not people that have died, it's animals," she said.

But their existence as a nomadic people was in danger. Losses occurred every winter in Mongolia but not on this scale. From 33.5 million livestock registered in 1999, seven million perished.

The *zud* demoralised the usually good-humoured nomads living on the fringe of the Gobi desert. Custom required that households supplied food to visitors and they were ashamed at having next to nothing. The stories they told were of epic tragedies. We heard of a boy who had driven one hundred horses 500 kilometres to the north for better grazing but could not keep them alive. He returned with only his riding horse. Rob Gifford was so moved by the plight of one nomadic family that he got us to contribute US$25 each to buy a new cow – which the woman said she would name after us.

The pressure on the steppes was increased by the fact that conditions in Ulan Bator had become so hard that many people had returned to a nomadic existence. The herdsmen, lovers of stories, drink and good horsemanship, lived a life unchanged since the days of Genghis Khan, roaming freely in a country three times the size of France. After the break-up of collective farms created under communism, they were allowed to own more livestock, and the number of animals in Mongolia quickly increased from 25 million to more than 30 million. "If you work hard and look after your animals you can get rich," said a horseman one hundred kilometres south of Ulan Bator, as he looked for a lost camel.

That was not the experience of Natsag and Altangerel, a retired police official and his wife, with nine daughters, whose *ger* was situated on a gentle grass slope rich in buttercups and wild strawberries just outside the capital. The couple invited us into their conical roofed tent, containing a couch, bed, sideboard and stools arranged around a metal stove. After sharing some snuff and drinking a bowl of fermented mare's milk, they spoke sadly about life after communism. They had small pensions and twenty sheep, thirty goats and ten cows, many more than before the reforms, but "life is getting worse and we just have enough to feed ourselves because flour and rice are so expensive and the money for goat hair is very little now," said Altangerel. "During the Soviet period it was better for workers. The poorest are more poor now and the young can't find jobs." They were as devastated as everyone else by the murder of Zorig, but as for the foreign officials who had poured into Mongolia after the 1990 counter-revolution, "they haven't done anything for us," she said.

The drought continued for the next decade, right up to the present day. The country exists in a state of permanent economic crisis, with the US and Russia vying for influence, and big foreign corporations competing to buy up mining rights cheaply. In April 2008 some 20,000 people demonstrated in Ulan Bator over rising food costs and inflation of fifteen per cent. The steppes are now reported to be overgrazed and desiccated by drought. For the first time in centuries, working hard and looking after one's animals may no longer be a way for Mongolia's nomads to even guarantee survival.

27

Black Eye for Democracy

In 1998, Malaysia was thrown into crisis by the arrest of Deputy Prime Minister Anwar Ibrahim on charges of sodomy and abuse of power. Anwar protested that he had been framed because he was about to expose corruption in high places, while his critics alleged that he was attempting a power grab and had to be removed from political life. After a court hearing in the capital, Kuala Lumpur, at which Anwar appeared with a black eye and a neck brace, the result of a police beating, I took a taxi to his spacious family bungalow in the leafy suburb of Bukit Damansara, to interview his wife, Wan Azizah Wan Ismail.

There were more than a dozen international journalists camped outside the locked gates of the bungalow when I arrived. I gave my business card to a guard at the gate and joined the waiting group. After a few minutes a man came out of the house and asked, "Which of you is from *The Irish Times*?" I put up my hand. "Come with me," he said, opening the gate to let me through. I remember the moment well, if only for the expression of disbelief on the face of a rather arrogant American TV journalist, to whom I had been introduced shortly before and who had greeted me with the condescending remark: "*The Irish Times?* My, you're a long way from home!" (As indeed was he.)

I was shown into a wood-panelled living-room, with teak floor and French windows, where a few lawyers and friends of the family reclined on armchairs beneath a slowly revolving fan. Wan Azizah rose from a divan to greet me. She was a composed, elegant Malay woman of forty-six years, wearing a long dress and veil. She described how hooded police came to the house and arrested Anwar under the Internal Security Act. Two of the children tried to help their father but, with the muzzle of a machine-gun at the neck of her fourteen-year-old son, they had to let him go.

I realised why I had got preference over my colleagues when she then said, with a smile, "Tell me all the gossip about Charles Haughey." Wan Azizah had spent six years at the Royal College of Surgeons in Dublin in the 1970s, training to be an eye doctor, and had followed Irish politics ever since. She produced her 1978 College of Surgeons yearbook, to show me her class pictures from Ireland. As a Malay and a pious Muslim, she always wore a coloured *tudung* headscarf in Dublin, leading some Irish people to think she was a nun. A classmate had written: "She is well known on the Dublin buses as the gentle Chinese nun who wouldn't cross herself going past churches." She laughed at the memory of being mistaken for a nun. "What did you do when that happened?" I asked. "It was easier just to reply, 'Bless you, my son,' rather than correct them," she replied with a laugh. It said a lot for Irish notions of the Orient in the 1970s that a Muslim Malay like Wan Azizah could be mistaken for either a nun or Chinese.

Wan Azizah had returned from Ireland in 1978 with a gold medal and had married the man she referred to simply as "Anwar". Anwar Ibrahim, then thirty-two, was a fiery Islamic politician who, as a student leader, was interned without trial for almost two years for leading protests against poverty. However, the young radical had surprised everyone by joining the political establishment and throwing in his lot with Prime Minister Mahathir bin Mohamad.

I had become a regular visitor to Malaysia, a former British colony that was emerging as one of the tiger economies of South-East Asia. Since taking office in 1981, Mahathir's government had turned the mostly Muslim country of 26 million people into a high-tech manufacturing and telecommunications hub. In the decade up to 1997, the economy had grown at over ten per cent a year. Mahathir was the leader of the United Malays National Organisation (UMNO), the largest political party in Malaysia, and a founding member of the Barisan Nasional coalition that had ruled Malaysia since independence in 1957 on a populist platform of moderate Islamic principles and affirmative action for the fifty per cent Malay population. Its inevitable election victories resulted from a form of managed democracy, under which the Supreme Court had limited independence, and the media toed the government line.

In forty years of independence, Malaysia had almost eradicated poverty. The streets of Kuala Lumpur were jammed with Malaysian-made Proton cars and dominated by the Petronas Twin Towers, the third-tallest buildings in the world. The city had world-class hotels and marble and glass shopping malls. In some western-style suburbs like Bangsar Baru, one could find Chinese teenagers in mini-skirts and long-haired Malay youths hanging around coffee shops and bookstores. There were poor areas in the suburbs, but little of the abject misery that characterised many Asian capitals.

Mahathir chose Anwar as his deputy and political heir in 1993, at which point Wan Azizah gave up her job as a hospital eye surgeon, and undertook a role considered more fitting for an establishment politician's spouse, assuming honorary posts, entertaining important international visitors and raising her six children, five girls and a boy.

Their relatively tranquil life among the Malaysian elite came to a sudden end in September 1998 when the relationship between Mahathir and Anwar abruptly deteriorated. Anwar had challenged

Mahathir's protectionist policies and threatened to expose the cronyism and corruption which had enriched a handful of Malays. His arrest provoked sporadic demonstrations in Kuala Lumpur, some of which turned violent.

During the Asia-Pacific Economic Summit in the city in November 1998, a ritual Saturday-night protest outside the mosque in Kampung Baru attracted a bigger crowd than usual. It was just ending when I heard a gunshot, about five metres from where I was standing. A middle-aged man had spotted a plain-clothes policeman and kicked him. A second police agent, seeing his comrade in trouble, pulled a .38 handgun from a holster strapped to his leg and fired one shot at the ground. A tall youth with a baseball cap shouted, "You see? Who causes the violence here? Not us. It's the police." The agents fled, chased by bottle-throwing demonstrators and followed by international TV crews, and forcing the motorcade of the US Secretary of State, Madeleine Albright, en route to the Renaissance Hotel nearby, to make an emergency detour. A water cannon appeared and pointed its nozzle towards the watching journalists, and an amplified voice instructed us to disperse, which we did.

Thanks to repressive British legislation inherited when Malaysia won its independence, Mahathir's government could employ a range of measures to cope with unrest. These were included in the Internal Security Act, which resembled the old draconian Northern Ireland Special Powers Act. It allowed detention for sixty days in solitary confinement and then for periods of two years without trial.

Wan Azizah sat defiantly through all seventy-eight days of Anwar's trial in Kuala Lumpur in the spring of 1999, asserting her belief in his innocence and fuming at the trumped-up charges against him, which included an act of sodomy in a building that had not been constructed at the time. The verdict came on a hot, mid-April afternoon. I was waiting with other media outside the courthouse – the trial was closed to foreign correspondents – and happened to be the journalist nearest the door when a turbaned Indian lawyer came out. He slipped me a piece of paper and disappeared back inside. On it was scrawled the words "Six Years". I showed it to my colleagues. Supporters of Anwar crowded around.

The word went out, "Six years! Six years!" Several hundred angry young men gathered on the street, shouting *"Reformasi"* [reform] and "Mahathir go!" They blocked a road bridge behind the courthouse. A red water cannon roared up, followed by several riot control vehicles. Tian Chua, a well-known civil rights activist, sat down in front of the truck, a symbol of defiance like the lone protester who faced a tank in China's Tiananmen Square in 1989, but he was lifted bodily by two policemen in red riot helmets and a jet of liquid from the water cannon struck him with full force in the stomach. The cannon then sprayed a cascade of water mixed with green dye and pepper gas onto the crowds. Behind the action, young men attacked a white car marked "TV3" and smashed the windscreen, shouting, "Mahathir propaganda". One of the demonstrators cried out: "Die Mahathir! Write that."

On 4 April 1999 Wan Azizah formed a new political party, *Parti Keadilan Rakyat* (People's Justice Party), with Tian Chua as vice-president, to give the hot-blooded young reformers a political channel for their anger. From his prison cell, Anwar suggested a sunflower as the symbol for the new party, but she thought it smacked too much of sunflower cooking oil and the kitchen. She approved instead two Islamic crescents facing each other to form the outline of an eye – the famous black eye, an eye for justice and an eye on Mahathir.

While free to organise the new party, Wan Azizah came under police surveillance and she warned me when I called again to her bungalow that her telephone was tapped. Former acquaintances in the governing elite now shunned her family, she said, and the media portrayed her as a troublemaker. To give a live question-and-answer interview on CNN, she had to fly to Hong Kong. Her father, Dr Wan Ismail, was required to resign as chairman of an education company.

When the People's Justice Party contested its first election the following May, I went campaigning with Wan Azizah, sitting in the front of her black-and-silver Mitsubishi Pajero as she waved at crowds from the back. "They will be wondering who is the white man in front," she said, making fun of a comment by Mahathir about "white leaders" who dared question the jailing of her husband. On the way to the rally site, she leaned forward and asked me, "Do you know why the harp is the symbol of Ireland?" "No, why?" I replied. "Because Irish people are always pulling strings," she said delightedly.

At dusk, as we approached Kampung Medan, a built-up district south of Kuala Lumpur, she switched on the interior light to wave to long lines of people moving along the roadside towards the rally site. As the Pajero slowed to a crawl, she called out "*Reformasi*" to dozens of grinning young men crowding around to peer inside. "*Reformasi*," they shouted back, waving fists in the warm night air. "They're actually disappointed; they really want to see my daughter," she said with a giggle. Her beautiful nineteen-year-old daughter, Izzah Nurul, was a favourite with the crowds at opposition rallies. Wan Azizah's elderly father, also sitting in the back, shared the joke. "What a tragedy for them," he said, waving cheerfully. "All they get to see is an old man on this side."

The eye symbol had created a huge industry in political memorabilia. Among the stalls selling spiky durian fruit and fast food at the rally site, dozens of vendors displayed T-shirts, badges, flags, books, stickers, CDs, tapes and even plastic wall clocks, all featuring Anwar's black eye.

Wan Azizah spoke with passion and eloquence to thousands of enthusiastic supporters at several such rallies during her campaign. She had asked Corazon Aquino, former president of the Philippines, for counsel on the art of public speaking and had been advised by her: "Always talk about what you know about . . . tell it like it is, from the heart." Many people compared the two women. If Aquino could become the country's leader in place of her husband, why not Wan Azizah? She was indisputably taking her place in Asian political history, along with other courageous women, such as Aquino in the Philippines, Sirimavo Bandaranaike in Sri Lanka, Benazir Bhutto in Pakistan, Aung San Suu Kyi in Burma, Sonya Gandhi in India and Megawati Sukarnoputri in Indonesia. But Malaysia had a Westminster-type electoral system, unlike the Philippines' presidential type of government, and the leader of the majority party in Malaysia was the person who became prime minister. Mahathir's UMNO had a majority of the ruling coalition's 192 seats in the 222-member parliament and was far and away the best-financed political grouping in the country. To have any hope of making an impact in elections, Wan Azizah's fledgling party had to make common cause with other minority parties, and in those difficult days, this seemed an unlikely prospect.

She was elected a member of parliament for Permatang Pauh, the seat formerly held by her husband, and her party returned four other candidates. She retained her seat in the 2004 elections but the cause of *reformasi* was in suspension while her husband remained locked up. Meanwhile the quota system, favouring the Muslim Malays over the minority Chinese and Indian populations, came under international criticism and the primacy of civil law over Islamic law was weakened by a series of court decisions.

Anwar was released from prison in 2004, and though banned temporarily from standing for parliament, he led an opposition coalition in March 2008 elections that brought together the People's Justice Party and Islamic and ethnic Chinese parties. It won five state governments and increased its parliamentary representation from 20 to 82 seats. The Barisan Nasional coalition clung onto power but lost its two-thirds majority for the first time since 1969. Thrown into turmoil, the ruling coalition was forced to loosen its tight controls over the media and Anwar's party won the right to publish its own newspaper. With Mahathir no longer a political force – he retired in 2003 after twenty-two years in office – the man he tried to destroy was stronger than before, thanks in no small part to his Irish-educated wife, and for the first time Malaysia seemed headed towards a two-party system that could end communal politics. Then on 16 July 2008 Anwar was arrested again on new sodomy charges, and history began repeating itself.

28

The Little Cold War

One hot afternoon, having crossed the border from Malaysia to Singapore, I found myself sipping a Singapore Sling in the Long Bar in Raffles Hotel, figuring out tomorrow's story . . . it's surely what a foreign correspondent always dreamed about, living an experience that once made the city state one of the most desirable journalistic stop-overs in the world. So why did it feel a bit phony? Well, for a start, the Long Bar, the haunt of legendary scribblers, which used to be just off the lobby and across from the (long-gone) UPI office, was now on the third floor of an annex, where it had been relocated when the hotel was refurbished in 1991. Also, the other customers – like myself I suppose – had dropped in only because having a Singapore Sling, a combination of dry gin with Bénédictine, cherry brandy, Cointreau, Grenadine, pineapple juice, squeezed lemon and a dash of Angostura bitters, in the Long Bar was as *de rigueur* for visiting tourists to the island nation at the southern tip of the Malay Peninsula as an Irish coffee to Americans in transit at Shannon Airport.

The Singapore Sling was invented by bartender Ngiam Tong Boon for the travelling members of the upper classes in the early part of the twentieth century. Many famous writers, including

Somerset Maugham, Joseph Conrad and Pablo Neruda, sampled it while staying in Singapore. Maugham is said to have worked all morning under a frangipani tree in the palm court, turning the bits of gossip he picked up at dinner parties into short stories. The poet Rudyard Kipling recommended travellers to "feed at Raffles" but the hotel publicity omitted to mention that he also advised them to "stay elsewhere". British colonials resident in Singapore reputedly gathered in the Raffles lounge to sing "There'll Always Be An England" as the city fell to the Japanese in 1942. More than 300 Japanese troops committed suicide with hand grenades in the lobbies after the liberation of Singapore. Few hotels can boast such a colourful and bloody history.

With its refurbishment Raffles became something of a theme hotel and its name is now attached to a chain of opulent Raffles hotels around the world trading on the name of Sir Stamford Raffles, the British administrator who established Singapore as a free port two centuries earlier. The Long Bar, with its overpriced gin slings, was but one of fifteen "food and beverage facilities" and seventy specialty shops in the hotel complex. In the shops one could buy Raffles memorabilia, including pith helmets, miniature Singapore Slings (the top seller) and fluffy tigers commemorating the last tiger in Singapore, which was shot when cornered beneath the elevated Bar & Billiard Room in 1902. There were also Raffles plates and cutlery that you could purchase if, as my guide book put it, "you can't afford to stay at Raffles and nick your own". I could afford to stay for one night and I didn't nick the crockery. I did make a gaffe, however, when calling to make the reservation. "Could I have a room for the night?" I asked. "We don't have rooms, sir," came the reply; "only suites."

Like all good hotels, however, the staff knew where to get things that one needed, and when I checked in one day in October 1998 a friendly Raffles telephone operator, who knew somebody who knew somebody, managed to acquire for me one of the hottest items in town. This was a book just published called *The Singapore Story*, written by Lee Kuan Yew, elder statesman and Prime Minister of Singapore for three decades until 1990. In two days all 35,000 copies of the 680-page book had been sold out. It was the reason I was in town.

The Singapore Story caused a sensation in Singapore and in neighbouring Malaysia, and provoked what one Malaysian newspaper called a "miniature diplomatic offensive" to break out on both sides. It contained Lee's account of how in 1963 he led Singapore into a merger with the Federation of Malaya, which was then renamed Malaysia, and out again two years later after a rather bitter constitutional divorce. He had supported federation because the British were leaving South-East Asia and he feared for the future of his small mainly Chinese entity – 554 square kilometres at low tide – in the midst of "a Malay archipelago of about 100 million people". But the federation was plagued by disputes over taxation and policing, and by ethnic Malay resentment over Lee's attempt to organise the large Chinese minority into a political force throughout Malaysia. Lee claimed that the Malay-dominated government in Kuala Lumpur did not want the Chinese to be represented by a vigorous leadership with a multi-racial approach. The Malays themselves were fearful of being overtaken in numbers by the enterprising Chinese. At the time of the merger, the total population was forty-three per cent Malay and forty-one per cent Chinese. Both sides began having second thoughts about union. At one stage Lee asked the Malaysian leader, Tunku Abdul Rahman, if Singapore could be linked to its neighbour like Northern Ireland or the Republic of Ireland to Britain, and got the reply: "Somewhere in between." In the end they settled for complete separation.

In his book Lee accused the dominant party in Kuala Lumpur, the United Malays National Organisation (UMNO), of provoking the split by stirring up trouble in Singapore. He singled out a deceased Malaysian politician, Syed Ja'afar Albar, as the "hatchet man of the UMNO leaders hostile to Singapore", and a "totally ruthless and unscrupulous rabble-rouser" who had instigated racial clashes in Singapore which left twenty-three people dead. Syed Ja'afar's son, Syed Hamid Albar, happened to be the current Defence Minister of Malaysia, and he took personal exception to this.

A cold war had existed between Malaysia and Singapore since the split and it heated up somewhat the day that Lee's memoirs were published. Malaysia closed its air space to Singapore's warplanes, citing noise pollution and violations. The Malaysian Defence Minister alleged that ships and planes from Singapore were violating Malaysian territory. Singapore denied this and claimed that when a British Navy Lynx helicopter had crashed in a South China Sea exercise, it took over four hours for Malaysia to give clearance for a Singapore rescue helicopter. Singapore, moreover, complained that Malaysian police, in plain clothes, visited the Singapore offices of the US business network CNBC, without prior clearance, to protest about an interview given to CNBC by Wan Azizah, the wife of imprisoned former Malaysian Deputy Prime Minister, Anwar Ibrahim. Malaysian ministers accused Singaporean newspapers (banned in Kuala Lumpur) of provocations and the Singaporean media claimed that nationalistic sentiments in Malaysia were being stirred up by Prime Minister Mahathir to distract the public from his own troubles. Things got so unpleasant that Singaporean athletes were booed at the Sixteenth Commonwealth Games in Kuala Lumpur.

The crisis, however, did not stop Singaporeans driving freely across the kilometre-long causeway between the two states to the border town of Johor Baharu in Malaysia to do some cheap shopping. Petrol was so inexpensive in Johor Baharu that, to protect sales in Singapore, customs officials checked car gauges at the border. If the tank was less than two-thirds full, a fine was imposed, so some Singapore drivers kept their gauges jammed at full.

There was perhaps a psychological need for Singaporeans to escape from their authoritarian environment once in a while and experience a more free and easy lifestyle. In Singapore all aspects of life were regulated. Taxis were fitted with devices that made tinkling noises like a music box when the driver exceeded the speed limit. The roads were electronically controlled. The importation and sale of chewing gum was banned. Smoking was prohibited almost everywhere. Vandalising a car merited a caning. Jaywalkers and people who dropped litter faced heavy fines. Someone said of Singapore that it was a fine country – there were fines for everything. The result was one of the cleanest and safest cities in the world, an air-conditioned island of concrete, glass and shopping centres with manicured lawns and parks.

Johor Baharu, by contrast, had chewing gum on the pavements and all the aromas of Asia, some of which arose from open roadside drains. It also had the same sort of attractions that brought Americans to Tijuana in Mexico. There were nightclubs and karaoke bars with hostesses and private rooms. In side streets, dusky maidens beckoned customers under signs saying "Men's Romance Parlours".

However, Johor Baharu, founded in 1855 by the Anglophile Sultan of Jahore, Abu Bakar, and Malaysia's third city, with a population of 300,000, also had modern hotels and resorts where Singaporeans, South Koreans and Japanese could enjoy a golfing weekend more cheaply than playing at home. It had scores of excellent seafood restaurants and dozens of pubs serviced by trucks with familiar-looking harp symbols, delivering the city's most popular drink – Malaysian-brewed Guinness.

The sultan's palace-museum just outside the town, containing two identical thrones, with the sultan's just a little higher than the sultana's, had been left intact by the invading Japanese forces in 1943. It also survived a postwar communist uprising against the British in Malaya, which was defeated by troops under the command of Sir Gerald Templar, who coined the phrase about "winning the hearts and minds" of the population. The Northern Ireland-born general once told rebellious villagers, "You're a lot of bastards," which the Chinese interpreter translated as "His Excellency informs you none of your fathers and mothers was married." Templar then said, "But you'll find I'm a bigger bastard," which his translator gave as, "His Excellency does admit, however, that his father was also not married to his mother."

The dispute between Malaysia and Singapore was, at its core, a racial conflict between a Malay country and a Chinese neighbour, the former with a large Chinese minority and the latter a sizeable Malay minority. Both countries sought to justify restrictions on freedom of speech on the grounds that they had to make sure that nothing was written or broadcast that could cause disharmony within their multi-racial, multi-religious societies.

In Singapore, in response to demands from opposition leaders for greater freedom of expression, the government established a Speakers' Corner in Hong Lim Park, beside a large police station. I went along on the day it opened in September 2000. The first speaker, opposition politician Tan Soo Phuan, found he could hardly be heard over the noise of traffic and that the rules forbade the use of a microphone or bull horn. Just as Singapore was a "managed democracy", so Speakers' Corner was a model of managed free speech. Orators could not say anything that contravened the Penal Code, the Maintenance of Religious Harmony Act or the Sedition Act, which allowed internment without trial. They could not comment on racial or religious matters. Speeches could not be televised. Before stepping up on the soap box, speakers had to register at the police station with documents to prove they were Singaporean, and where their names would be kept on record for five years.

While native residents at least had a place to air some grievances, people in Asia's most spectacularly successful city seemed by and large unconcerned about the restrictions demanded by their political culture. There were only a couple of dozen spectators standing around when citizen Lim Kian Heng took the stand to criticise the police for illegal parking. After listening for a while, I retreated to Raffles Hotel for another Singapore Sling. It might be the tourist thing to do, but it was an extraordinarily refreshing drink on a hot afternoon. But I didn't try to write up my story in the Long Bar. Too many ghosts of correspondents past would have been looking disdainfully over my shoulder.

29

The Day of Living Dangerously

The Year of Living Dangerously is a novel by Christopher Koch about foreign correspondents covering the overthrow of Indonesian President Sukharno in 1965. Some thirty-three years later, it was the turn of a new generation of reporters to record the overthrow of his successor, President Suharto. It wasn't quite as bloody – thousands rather than hundreds of thousands died – but it was another year of living dangerously, or to be more precise, one particular day of living dangerously, when the capital city, Jakarta, was plunged into anarchy and Suharto's fate was sealed. That day was Thursday, 14 May 1988.

The fuse was lit two days earlier, on a typical sultry afternoon, with thunder rumbling from heavy clouds. At the time I was sipping coffee with a couple of colleagues in a little suburban café in Jakarta, discussing the growing calls for *reformasi* (reform) with Goenawan Mohamad, a renowned poet and editor of the banned dissident magazine, *Tempo*. For months the call for *reformasi*, led by students, had been gathering momentum throughout the country of some 200 million people, and peaceful demonstrations in Jakarta universities were becoming a daily occurrence. I recall asking Goenawan what *reformasi* really meant. "It means dump Suharto," he replied.

Not long before, it would have been perilous to say such things openly, as criticism of Suharto was a violation of the criminal justice code. But the majority of Indonesian people seemed to be saying little else. The country had been crippled by an economic crisis sweeping the Asia-Pacific region since the middle of the previous year. Its currency, the *rupiah*, had plummeted in value, banks had collapsed and unemployment had soared. Two weeks earlier, the government had raised prices to meet conditions set by the International Monetary Fund (IMF) for a $40 billion bail-out of the Indonesian economy. Subsidies on fuel and cooking oil had been removed, in line with IMF requirements, and the price of kerosene, the cooking fuel used by the poor, and of staple foods had almost doubled overnight. This alone was making an explosion inevitable, Goenawan warned.

As dusk was approaching, our mobile phones started ringing. Riot police had opened fire on a student demonstration at Trisakti University, a private education establishment for the sons and daughters of the Indonesian elite. We excused ourselves and drove the few kilometres to the university, situated at a busy junction on the road to the international airport. We found the street outside jammed with military vehicles but gained entry through a back gate and made our way to the administration hall. Two shots rang out as we skirted a small quadrangle, and students who were cowering under a concrete overhang shouted in English to be careful, because there were police or army snipers on an overpass outside. As we entered the main hall, about one hundred students who had been sitting cross-legged rose to their feet and broke into applause, believing that the presence of foreign correspondents somehow lessened their danger. We found that staff had transformed a conference room into a first aid point. Blood-soaked swabs lay on a table and the odour of iodine mingled with the peppery smell of tear-gas. A hand-written list of casualties in the registrar's office recorded four students killed by bullets.

Student leaders related what had happened. When some of their number attempted to march to parliament in mid-afternoon to call for Suharto's resignation, they found the road blocked by four armoured cars. There had been a stand-off but when a heavy downpour began around four o'clock, most went back onto the campus. TV camera crews packed up and left. However, as the rain cleared, a plain-clothes intelligence man among the students was identified and beaten. The police spy escaped, but riot police began firing live ammunition from a footbridge. "They shot my friend in the back of the neck," said a student with a white headband. "I pulled him up and my hands were all bloody."

The next day classes were suspended at Trisakti. Professors mingled with students in black armbands. Onlookers crowded around a list of victims pinned up in a room beside a yellowing poster of Princess Diana and wrote comments on a long white cloth such as "I hate Suharto" and "Suharto must go". The matronly Megawati Sukarnoputri, daughter of the former Indonesian president, was given a tumultuous welcome at her first appearance at a pro-reform protest. The diminutive opposition figure, Amien Rais, leader of a Muslim organisation claiming twenty-eight million members, made a speech saying the army had two choices: to support President Suharto or to support the people. There were sporadic disturbances in different parts of the city that afternoon.

Thursday morning, the day of anarchy, started quietly enough. I took a taxi for the thirty-minute journey from the Hilton Hotel to the University of Indonesia medical campus at Salemba, a complex of elegant Dutch colonial buildings where another anti-Suharto demonstration was planned. Everything appeared normal on the streets, but the driver refused to wait, and drove off at speed. The students held their demonstration under the palm trees on a grassy fringe between the university buildings and a busy main road. As they did so, large crowds of mainly poor local residents wearing sandals and T-shirts gathered silently outside the railings. At midday, as the demonstration ended, these people started casually pulling down lampposts, railings and road dividers. Young men climbed the traffic lights at a junction and punched out the green and orange, leaving the red permanently on. More crowds spilled out of side streets and filled the carriageway in both directions. A detachment of helmeted riot police at the campus gates just watched. They either had instructions not to intervene or were afraid. It was the first sign that events were slipping beyond the control of the security forces, perhaps deliberately so.

An anarchic situation developed quickly all around the university. A truck was overturned and burned. Cars were pulled from a dealership connected with "Tommy" Suharto, the son of President Suharto, and set alight across the highway. Approving crowds gathered on pedestrian overpasses and on rooftops to watch. Word reached us that the disturbances were spreading right across the city of eight million people. A popular uprising was under way against Suharto's corrupt and repressive administration. Just as in Beijing in June 1989, an Asian city was slipping out of the control of an authoritarian government.

Then an extraordinary thing happened. Fifty soldiers in two lines came strolling along the highway past the university, waving their fists in the air in solidarity with the rioters. The crowd went wild with delight. "They are marines, they are on our side, they are not soldiers or police, who shoot us," said an excited bystander, waving at the men in neat camouflage uniforms and purple berets, with automatic rifles slung behind their backs and swagger sticks in their hands. The marines gave "high fives" to street urchins, who a few minutes before had been smashing the panes of the glass-walled Mayapada Bank. They walked past burning cars to the cheers of massed onlookers. I watched from the café of a little hotel beside the burning car showroom, where I managed to get a coffee and cheese sandwich. The son of the manager joined me, shaking his head sadly. "They will destroy everything," he said. "Indonesia is finished."

Since all traffic had stopped, I set off to walk to the Jakarta Hilton where I was staying, a distance of several kilometres, accompanied by a German correspondent who, like me, found himself stranded in the middle of the chaos. As we made our way through the crowds, we were easy prey for street thugs and we gave lots of high-fives ourselves. Most people grinned and waved, but one aggressive young man stopped us and said, "Hello, mister, what you think?" "It's a revolution," I replied. "Yes, yes, a revolution," he cried, as his companions cheered. At one point a train slowly passed over a bridge and dozens of passengers leaned out from the carriage windows to yell encouragement to the mob below. Arsonists by then were hard at work. Shopping malls, restaurants, food stores and electronic goods outlets were being looted and set on fire. Some kids were gorging themselves on the contents of a Dunkin' Donuts café.

In the middle of all this, a lone jeep came by and the driver, an engineer working for Digital, called to us to get in, saying, "It's too dangerous that way, sir, people are going crazy." We drove back along a deserted main highway, usually jammed with traffic, and reached the business district, where he had to do a U-turn. "Look, people are running amok," he said, using an English word adopted from the Malay language, *amuk*, meaning "mad with rage".

In an elegant boulevard in the city centre, soldiers in riot gear lounged around four troop carriers and fraternised with the throng, but they had erected barbed wire to protect the American embassy and the glitzy mall by the Hyatt Hotel that was popular with the wealthy. A convoy of British-made Scorpion armoured cars with long guns drove slowly by, the troops giving the thumbs-up to cheering youths. The engineer dropped us off and we walked the last kilometre to the hotel. Some shops had the word *Pribumi*, meaning native Indonesian – i.e. not Chinese – painted on their doors to keep the arsonists at bay, sometimes to no avail. As always when running amok, thugs attacked the better-off Chinese minority. Motorcycle taxi drivers still plying their trade were warning non-Chinese customers not to pull down their helmet visors or rioters might think they were Chinese trying to escape detection.

We eventually reached the Hilton Hotel (since renamed the Sultan), set in extensive gardens near the parliament building. As we ducked through the gates, I heard a "poc, poc, poc" sound. A colleague, who wrote for a Sunday newspaper, was playing tennis with the hotel tennis coach. Inside the vast marble-floored foyer there was pandemonium. Dozens of panicking middle-class Chinese families had come to seek refuge in the 1,350-room complex until the storm outside had exhausted itself. They mingled with American, Australian, British, German and Japanese expatriates who were afraid to stay in their houses. Men shouted into mobile telephones and Malay nannies soothed crying Chinese infants, as the sound of gunfire came from the adjacent expressway where soldiers were at last dispersing the crowds. As armoured cars and troop carriers roared by on the other side of a thick hedge, children cavorted in the swimming pool and sweating foreigners sipped iced pineapple juice in wicker armchairs. A notice was put up by the lifts: "Please be informed that we will not be able to change the linen in your room due to the emergency situation." From my window I had a panoramic view of the sprawling city. As far as the eye could see and in every direction, large plumes of black smoke rose into the air. On the horizon the smoke merged into a dark grey wall, shutting out the sun as it set on Jakarta's darkest day.

Officials from the international institutions whose harsh fiscal prescriptions had helped ignite the fury of the mob now had only one thought in mind: to get out. Many fled to the airport where a chartered plane flew them to Singapore. Children at the British International School were kept in the assembly hall that night and then ferried in a convoy of cars to the airport in the morning, crashing through the yellow-striped wooden barriers of the abandoned expressway toll gates. Some shaken and exhausted foreigners heading for the airport had to run a gauntlet of rioting teenagers from roadside slums, who jumped on the cars, wielding long sticks and demanding money.

On Friday morning the shocked citizens milled around, awe-struck at the extent of the damage. Streets and shopping centres were reduced to smoking ruins. I made my way to Ciledug, a long commercial strip thirty-five kilometres south of Jakarta. All along the way there were burned-out shops, wrecked mini-malls, looted banks and the skeletal remains of cars and mini-vans. Blackened squares of concrete marked the homes of ethnic Chinese families. At a new shopping mall, the charred corpses of 122 trapped looters were being taken from the fourth floor. The stench was overpowering. Heads and other body parts were placed by the mall entrance for examination by relatives.

Over 1,000 people lost their lives in the city's meltdown and, it would emerge, there were mass rapes of women, particularly Chinese. A government minister would later itemise the damage: 2,479 shop-houses, 1,026 ordinary houses, 1,604 shops, 383 private offices, sixty-five bank offices, forty-five workshops, forty shopping malls, thirteen markets and twelve hotels.

Jakarta buzzed with rumours that General Prabowo, Suharto's son-in-law and head of the feared Special Forces Unit, Korpassus, had engineered the chaos, to weaken the forces of democracy, justify a crackdown, and gain the upper hand in a political power struggle with General Wiranto, head of the Indonesian armed forces. Unleashing the mob to destroy the city and indulge in acts of racial violence against the Chinese minority – shopkeepers and white-collar workers whose ancestors came as traders centuries before and who were used by Dutch colonists as middlemen and revenue collectors – served to discredit the peaceful student movement for reform.

The following Monday morning, Suharto's survival became impossible when General Wiranto allowed students to occupy the Indonesian parliament building to demand that the President resign. They set out at 9.30 from the medical campus of the University of Indonesia, in a convoy of battered green coaches led by a 1954 black Mercedes with running boards, which once belonged to Suharto and now carried the university dean. Horns blaring, they passed through diplomatic suburbs, where Marine PT 76 light tanks guarded the crossroads, and raced through the centre of town as people waved from the pavements. At one point two Scorpion tanks made by the British firm Alvis accelerated alongside the convoy, dripping water from their tail pipes, their drivers giving the thumbs-up sign. At the gates of the parliament a line of heavily armed soldiers grudgingly allowed the 2,500 students through the gates in small groups. These soldiers were the notorious green berets from a regiment loyal to General Prabowo. A student handed one soldier a red rose as a sign of peace but he took it disdainfully, glanced at his stony-faced comrades, then tossed it behind him.

The power struggle in the military clearly had not been resolved. A line of four tanks and three trucks suddenly rumbled through the ornamental gardens behind the parliament building. Two hundred soldiers in bullet-proof vests leaped down and jogged into position between the students, who were staging a sit-down, and the main parliament building. They carried rifles, tear-gas canisters and bamboo sticks. The students, in blazers of blue, orange and other colours to denote their universities, greeted them with a barrage of taunts, at one point chorusing in

English "Fuck Suharto!" The soldiers grew edgy. They cocked their rifles in a menacing fashion. An American radio journalist, Mary Kay Magistad, who had seen someone shot dead near her in similar circumstances in Bangkok in 1992, pulled me gently away from the line of fire.

But the moment passed. At three o'clock, a convoy of thirty coaches, led by eight army buses, arrived to take the demonstrators back to their universities. After they had gone, in a scene reminiscent of Boris Yeltsin mounting a tank during the abortive Soviet coup, retired General Ibrahim Sali came hurrying from the parliament building, climbed up on a tank guarding the entrance and informed startled passers-by and street traders that the speaker of parliament, Harmoko, the third most important politician in the land, had called for Suharto to step down.

Events moved quickly after that. On Wednesday, 20 May, General Wiranto called on Suharto at his bungalow in Jalan Cendana, a leafy Jakarta avenue, to tell him he no longer had the support of the army. The seventy-six-year-old President announced his resignation at ten o'clock the next morning and handed over to his vice-president, B.J. Habibie. The students, who had reoccupied the parliament building, danced on the roof and leapt into the ornamental fountain outside in a paroxysm of delight. Some wept, others prayed, couples hugged each other, incredulous that just nine days after troops had killed four of their number at Trisakti campus in Jakarta, they had managed to bring down the leader they held accountable.

Their outpouring of joy contrasted with the fate of the students who had demonstrated for reform in Beijing a decade earlier and had been crushed in a brutal military crackdown. In Jakarta, as in China, the catalyst for revolt was a protest by students, the conscience of society, against corruption and in favour of democratic reform, and in Jakarta, as in China, the army had decided the issue. But in Beijing, the authoritarianism of the ruling Communist Party was being challenged, while in Jakarta it was the future of one ageing corrupt ruler that was at stake and the army turned its back on him.

Wiranto won the power struggle in the Indonesian military. Late on the evening after Suharto resigned, Prabowo arrived at the presidential palace, demanding that he be made chief of the armed forces, but Habibie avoided seeing him by leaving through a back door. Next day General Wiranto sacked Prabowo as head of Kostrad, the Strategic Reserve Command, though he remained a general.

The joy of the students gradually evaporated as they realised that little had really changed. They saw Habibie as a puppet of Suharto and protector of the power structure, and they changed their "Down with Suharto" placards to read "Down with Habibie". They were outraged that no general or senior official was to be held accountable for the May events. Their protests continued during the summer. On Friday, 20 November, during a demonstration in Jakarta calling for the arrest of Suharto on corruption charges and for the end of the army's role in politics, Wiranto unleashed his soldiers against them. In two hours of firing they killed eight students and wounded scores of others.

But the pro-reform forces prevailed. On 7 June 1999 Indonesia had its first free elections in nearly half a century and the parliament selected Abdurrahman Wahid as the new President of Indonesia. He was succeeded by Megawati Sukarnoputri in 2001, who in turn was succeeded in 2004 by current Indonesian President Yudhoyono, a retired general. Wiranto entered politics and in 2004 ran unsuccessfully for president. No charges were ever laid against him for army excesses. General Prabowo fled the country, amid accusations of his participation in killings and torture, but he eventually returned; he also avoided criminal charges and became involved in politics. Attempts to try Suharto failed because of his ailing health and he lived in seclusion until his death in January 2008.

Tempo magazine, banned under Suharto, resumed publication and is now a respected and influential journal. Its editor, Goenawan Mohamad, who so accurately predicted to us on the day of the Trisakti shootings that the country was about to explode, was one of four winners of the Committee to Protect Journalists Press Freedom Awards in 1998, and in 1999 he was named International Editor of the Year by *World Press Review* magazine.

30

Liberating the Turismo

Every conflict zone has a hotel favoured by journalists. In East Timor it was the one-star Turismo Beach Hotel, in the sleepy little capital, Dili. More of a two-storey motel, it faced the silky waters of the Timor Sea on Marechal Carmona Avenue, where goats foraged on the grass verge and fishermen laid out their catch. During the Indonesian occupation, the hotel was favoured by aid workers, doctors, peace campaigners, nuns and the odd tourist who ventured to Indonesian-occupied East Timor on the cockroach-infested Fokker 100 of Merpati Airlines which flew in from Bali three times a week. News and gossip was shared under the sandalwood trees of the overgrown garden, which was inhabited by two scrawny orange cats, or in the dim light of the dining-room, where the menu was always chicken or fish. Pro-independence figures flitted in and out, giving revolutionary handshakes, wary of the government spies in Hawaiian shirts who lounged on plastic chairs by the hotel entrance.

Most places of importance were within walking distance of the Turismo. The residence of Bishop Carlos Belo, the spiritual leader of the largely Catholic people, who shared the 1996 Nobel Peace Prize with exiled resistance spokesman José Ramos-Horta, was just along the seafront. A few minutes' walk farther west was the old Portuguese governor's mansion, occupied by Governor Abilio Soares, a hardline opponent of independence, and beyond that the disused parliament building and several private seaside bungalows with lush gardens of oleander and acacia, commandeered by Indonesian officials after the occupation of the former Portuguese colony in 1975. From their verandas, they could see two of the landing craft used in their invasion, rusting in shallow water. A half-hour walk away on the far side of Dili was the Santa Cruz cemetery where, on 12 November 1991, Indonesian troops massacred over 200 people protesting peacefully against the occupation.

My initial sojourn at the Turismo Hotel, in November 1998, coincided with the first big anti-Indonesian demonstration in East Timor since the day of that massacre. Emboldened by the spirit of *reformasi* sweeping through Indonesia, which had brought down President Suharto six months earlier, hundreds of Dili University students occupied the parliament building and demanded the release of resistance leader Xanana Gusmão, who was serving a twenty-year jail term for rebellion in the Indonesian capital, Jakarta.

East Timor's military commander, Colonel Tono Suratman, agreed to meet a student delegation in the governor's mansion. There he assured them he would begin a dialogue on human rights. Before they left, some students attempted to pull down the red-and-white Indonesian flag on the lawn, but were prevented by their own stewards. Ironically, three Indonesian soldiers appeared a few minutes later and lowered the flag ceremonially for the night.

Inside the mansion that day, I came across East Timor's police chief Hulman Gulton, lounging on a carved high-back chair in a blue-carpeted corridor. Emphasising his point with a silver-handled cane, he told me, "*Reformasi* is going on all over, so people are getting a chance to express their opinions." He added, "I love these people like my own family." That evening a young man wearing a Virgin Mary medallion came to the Turismo, to whisper that eight months earlier, four of his friends had been killed by soldiers in Dili and that repression was continuing in the mountains. It emerged later that twenty-eight East Timorese had been killed by soldiers since the start of the year.

Two months later President Suharto's successor, B.J. Habibie – bowing to the pressures of *reformasi* and international opinion – announced in Jakarta that East Timor could have a referendum to decide on autonomy or independence, and he transferred Xanana Gusmão from prison to house arrest in a Jakarta bungalow.

The news came as a shock to the suave Indonesian Foreign Minister, Ali Alatas, who had made a career out of justifying the occupation. Four years earlier at United Nations headquarters in New York he had complained to me about an article that the Minister for Foreign Affairs, Dick Spring, had written in *The Irish Times*, condemning Indonesia's brutal annexation of East Timor. This amounted almost to a "declaration of war", Alatas had said furiously. Spring was reflecting popular Irish sympathy for a small Catholic country abused by a large aggressive neighbour. Irish foreign policy had been influenced by the East Timor Ireland Solidarity Campaign, founded by Dublin bus driver Tom Hyland after he saw a harrowing television documentary on the Santa Cruz massacre made by camera-journalist Max Stahl.

Colonel Suratman did not keep his promise of a dialogue. After the referendum announcement, his soldiers began recruiting disaffected young East Timorese into paramilitary groups, with names like Aitarak (Thorn) and Besi Merah Putih (Red and White Iron), to intimidate East Timorese into voting against independence. Thuggish militia groups began assaulting supporters of independence. On 6 April 1999 members of Besi Merah Putih, high on a cocktail of alcohol, animal blood and drugs, and led by Indonesian officers in plain clothes, attacked a church in Liquiçá, west of Dili, shooting and hacking to death up to 200 people who were taking shelter inside.

Shortly afterwards the Aitarak group announced ominously that on Saturday, 17 April, they would "invade Dili" to commemorate the 1975 Indonesian occupation. That, coincidentally, was the day that Irish Minister for Foreign Affairs David Andrews planned to visit East Timor – the first European Union minister to do so – to draw world attention to what was going on.

On 14 April Andrews arrived in Jakarta from Dublin en route to East Timor with a small official delegation, including Tom Hyland. He got permission to visit Xanana Gusmão in the suburban Jakarta bungalow where he was being held under house arrest, and invited me to join them. The slightly built, grey-bearded guerrilla leader, dressed in neat blue shirt and tie, received us in a small, tiled room with a crucifix on the wall. It was an emotional moment for Hyland, whom Gusmão embraced warmly for his solidarity. Gusmão warned us gravely of the dangers we faced going to Dili.

In the circumstances David Andrews made a courageous decision not to cancel his trip to East Timor on the grounds of security, which he could easily have done. We flew into Dili on a private aircraft early on Saturday morning. As a military jeep escorted our car to the governor's mansion, we saw scores of Aitarak militiamen brandishing knives and home-made guns being driven around in trucks adorned with red-and-white Indonesian flags. The militia ranks had been inspected approvingly that morning by Governor Abilio Soares in whose presence the Aitarak leader, a petty gangster called Eurico Guterres, had told his men to "capture and kill" all those who betrayed integration with Indonesia. Now Governor Soares sat calmly in his reception room, offering tea to his Irish visitors. As Andrews made the case for an end to repression, the governor yawned, looked at his watch, examined his brown batik shirt and at one point formed his lips into a silent "Oh!" on hearing Xanana Gusmão described as a man of peace. "He is tricky enough," he said. He added, "If they want all of East Timor, it means war."

We next visited the air-conditioned bungalow of Colonel Tono Suratman, who dismissed what was going on in the streets as a matter for the East Timorese. "Xanana Gusmão does not want to follow the peaceful way," said the immaculately attired officer, sipping sweet black tea, as trucks packed with screaming militia roared past the windows. Police chief Hulman Gulton, who had told me how he loved the East Timorese like his own family, sat smiling politely. "What can we do?" he said. "It's their affair." Outside, there was a brief commotion when a young woman arrived in tears to plead for something, but an Indonesian police officer sent her packing.

After lunch in the Turismo, we went to Bishop Belo's residence. We sat in a semi-circle of chairs in a cool, curtained parlour, beneath Belo's gold-framed Nobel Peace Prize citation. "There is no plan for free elections here," the bishop said, matter-of-factly. "The paramilitaries are going every place, obliging people to show Indonesian flags. The message of the Indonesian police and military is, 'You like to be independent? You will have nothing!'"

Suddenly the door burst open. A gaunt, grey-bearded man appeared in the door frame. He spoke rapidly in Portuguese, the language of Dili's educated elite. Belo answered. The man turned and left. The Bishop translated for us. "He said, 'They are killing my son.'" There was a shocked silence. "You mean a man is being murdered?" asked Andrews. The bishop explained that the militias had come to the man's house nearby to assassinate him and now they were killing his son instead. "What can we do?" he said quietly. "Their aim is to destroy and kill, and keep us feeling afraid."

The man was Manuel Carrascalão, an intellectual leader of the independence movement. His house had become a place of refuge for dozens of terrified villagers fleeing intimidation and murder in the countryside. It had been attacked by a gang under Eurico Guterres. It emerged later that Carrascalão's seventeen-year-old son, also called Manuel, had been shot in the leg and finished off with a machete and that eleven other people were killed inside the building during our meeting with Bishop Belo nearby. It was Carrascalão's daughter who had appeared outside Colonel Suratman's bungalow to plead, in vain, for help. Carrascalão later told me that he, too, had appealed to the military commander for protection but had got the reply, "It's your problem."

Badly shaken, Andrews and his team left that evening to inform the world what they had witnessed. Next day I tried to approach the Carrascalão house. The street was closed by barbed wire, with police and militiamen lounging together on plastic chairs at the barricade. I went by taxi to the university and found a student activist, Antero Da Silva, whom I had befriended on my previous visits and was hiding there. He feared for his life and asked me to drive him to a safe house across town. On the way there he lay on the floor of the car. He told me that he never slept twice at the same address.

Eurico Guterres looked more like a minor pop star than a militia leader, with his good looks and shoulder-length brown hair cascading down under a white baseball cap. I met him some days later when he invited a group of correspondents to a Dili warehouse used for pro-Indonesia militia gatherings. He was flanked by three Indonesian policemen in neatly pressed grey uniforms. He addressed us from behind a black plastic stretcher, on which lay the almost naked corpse of one of his followers, a diminutive dark-skinned man, who had been found that morning on the beach. The dead man had ten knife wounds, in two neat rows, across his chest, and his face was battered beyond recognition. But now, speaking to us over the body of his subordinate, Guterres said that he had urged his militia not to react. Indonesian police officer, Lieutenant-General J.J. Sitompul, put a friendly hand on his shoulder and repeated,

"From the statement Mister Eurico made, there will be no retribution." It was evidently a show for our benefit. Guterres had been cynically co-opted by the authorities and was paying lip service to law and order for the foreign media. Dili police chief Colonel Timbul Silaen had just that week appointed him head of civilian security in the capital.

Meanwhile, Governor Soares organised pro-integration rallies across the territory. At Aileu, in the dense eucalyptus forests of the mountains, a dozen East Timorese and Indonesian officials lined up on a wooden stage to have their fingers pricked, so that drops of their blood fell into glasses of whisky. The contents were poured into a bowl and each drank a spoonful in a ceremony of blood-bonding. A teacher in the crowd whispered to me that all local headmen had been ordered to attend and to bring at least twenty villagers each.

A United Nations mission of 1,000 unarmed personnel arrived in East Timor to prepare for the referendum, scheduled for 30 August, and made their headquarters in a teacher-training college in a Dili suburb. A panel of three poll commissioners, including Northern Ireland's chief electoral officer Pat Bradley, flew in to monitor the process and authenticate the result. Suddenly everything seemed hopeful. There were prominent acts of reconciliation and promises from the militias to ensure a peaceful polling day. On 28 August David Andrews returned to East Timor, this time on a chartered Boeing 737 as one of a large team of EU observers. He visited polling stations in mountain villages and gave revolutionary hand clasps to voters waiting in long lines. UN officials recorded an astonishing ninety-eight per cent turnout on a largely incident-free day. They said the result would be announced within a week.

Immediately following the vote however, anticipating a defeat for integration, militiamen with automatic weapons, machetes, swords, knives and clubs began to attack houses in some parts of Dili. Smoke rose from the sprawling suburb of Bacora to the east.

Families began fleeing to convents and churches, afraid to stay in their homes. In the seaside town of Hera, south of Dili, four students were pulled out of a Toyota Kijang by armed men and killed. Next day a group of us negotiated a roadblock at Hera manned by guards dressed in fatigues and carrying automatic weapons, who claimed to be militia but were almost certainly Indonesian soldiers. High above the village we encountered about a hundred young supporters of independence with arrows, knives and swords. Their leader, a middle-aged man named Marcus Manek, showed us his homemade gun – it had no trigger and was fired by lighting a match to the barrel.

Two days after the referendum, I walked across town to the UN headquarters to interview some refugees who had sought shelter there. I was standing with other journalists and UN officials at the gate of the compound when dozens of youths came running past. Then gun shots rang out. We took cover behind parked UN vehicles. Armed militiamen appeared outside and we retreated into the college building. BBC journalist Jonathan Head, stranded outside, was beaten up and sustained a fractured arm when he fell.

Some 300 local people, mostly women and children, fled into the compound. They sat on the tiled floor of the assembly hall, holding children round-eyed with terror, as the gunfire intensified. A woman led them in the rosary and UN officials distributed water, among them Pat Bradley, his eyes glistening with tears of sympathy. It took an hour for two truckloads of Indonesian police to arrive in response to UN appeals for help, though the main Dili barracks was nearby. They fired in the air in a theatrical show of authority. Later the police officers, exultant at our discomfort, took us back to the Turismo in open trucks.

As I worked in my room in the Turismo the following morning, I heard shouting and crossed the garden to the hotel dining-room. Four women staff cowering in the corner cried out,

"Go back to your room, mister. Lock the door. Aitarak is here."
Five gang members had pulled up in a truck and raided the hotel.
Spotting a Canadian observer from Parliamentarians for East
Timor, they had given her a vicious kicking, then left, shouting,
"We'll be back tonight." The raid seemed part of a deliberate
campaign to intimidate the media into leaving, so the militias
could complete a coup out of the world's view. The next day
BBC and ITN crews, and about fifty other members of the
international media, left in a chartered aircraft.

The result of the referendum was announced by UN officials
in the Mahkota Hotel in the centre of Dili next day, 3 September
1999, at 9.10 a.m. The people had voted by 78.5 per cent for
independence over autonomy. Almost immediately, furious
opponents of independence, dressed in militia gear and carrying
M16 assault rifles and grenades, took over the streets. One of
them fired at journalists watching from the flat roof of the three-
storey hotel. We saw them giving instructions to the Indonesian
police, some of whom responded with thumbs-up gestures of
support.

That afternoon another one hundred international
journalists, including CNN, left for the airport in police trucks.
Pat Bradley and his two fellow-commissioners came under fire
and had to sleep that night in a vehicle in the UN compound,
before being flown out next day. I moved to the "safety" of the
UN compound, since the Turismo was now too dangerous. UN
headquarters in New York prepared an order for evacuation. I
heard that Korean journalists had chartered a plane to Jakarta
and decided to join them. It was time for me, too, to leave.

In the end the United Nations was saved from humiliation by
the heroic decision of the UN officials in Dili, prominent among
them deputy chief of information Brian Kelly – son of the
legendary *Irish Times* columnist Seamus Kelly – to refuse to obey
instructions from New York to abandon the UN compound and
the refugees there. They stayed, cooped up in the compound,

along with a few brave colleagues, as the Indonesian Army and the militias went on a rampage of destruction. General Wiranto, head of the Indonesian Armed Forces, announced that he was sending in three extra battalions "to bring under control the two parties which are fighting there following the referendum". There was, however, but one party to the conflict and it was murdering with impunity. The pro-independence fighters remained in the hills, resisting the trap of rushing to the people's defence.

By coincidence, world leaders were gathering in Auckland, New Zealand, at a summit of the Asia-Pacific Economic Cooperation group. Indonesia found itself facing a diplomatic and economic abyss. Outraged at reports of the forced movement of population, the massacres of refugees, the killing of priests and nuns, and the humiliation of the UN mission in East Timor, they forced the Indonesia government to agree to the entry of a UN peace-keeping force, without delay, to supervise the withdrawal of the Indonesian armed forces. Australia began assembling a military force in Darwin, across the Timor Sea, supplemented by a British destroyer, a Gurkha battalion, two battalions from Portugal and extra troops from New Zealand.

Hundreds of foreign correspondents, most of whom had never been to East Timor, gathered in Darwin for the "invasion", set for 20 September. We were told that two planes, one Australian and one British, would make room for reporters seeking to cover the first day of the deployment but would take only their own nationals. Concerned at being left behind, I called David Andrews's spokesman, Declan Kelly, to ask if the Minister could use his influence to get me, along with reporter Aoife Kavanagh and cameraman Paddy Higgins from RTÉ, onto the British plane. Declan had been in East Timor with Andrews, and he knew how closely the story was being followed in Ireland. Andrews asked the Irish Ambassador in London to request the British Ministry of Defence to accommodate us. Shortly afterwards a British officer, clearly somewhat put out, called me on my mobile phone to say he had been instructed to assign us seats, but he warned that if the plane was overweight, "you will be the first to be bumped". By then I had unexpectedly been offered a lift on a UN Hercules going in at dawn, along with Canadian journalist Patrick Graham and Doug Struck of the *Washington Post*. I couldn't risk getting bumped. I took the UN flight and arrived in Dili along with the first contingent of troops. RTÉ's crew made it on the British plane.

At Dili airport, the Australian and British forces kept their reporters corralled at the terminal, while soldiers in battle gear secured the buildings. With no one stopping us, Patrick, Doug and I simply left the Hercules and started walking along the deserted road into town. We flagged down a mini-van that came by, driven by Sister Marlene Bautista, an extraordinarily beautiful and cheerful Salesian nun from the Philippines, who had been sheltering scores of women and children in her convent in Bacora and was looking for food supplies. "I came out today because I heard the peace-keepers were coming and also to do some looting," she said. Her companions, two other nuns and four women, giggled loudly. We crushed in beside them and headed into town.

All across Dili, almost every important building had been burned or was still on fire, including the Mahkota Hotel. Indonesian soldiers still occupied several barracks, but of the militias there was no sign. Bishop Belo's house was a smoking ruin. Only a life-sized statue of the Blessed Virgin was left standing, its face smashed. Sister Margareta, old and stooped, emerged to say, "Thank you for coming. It is the grace of the Lord."

At the Turismo the reception area had survived but some rooms were stinking of excrement and a few were burned out. There was no electricity or water. We requisitioned three small rooms where we could spread our bedrolls and joked how, like Max Hastings who had famously "liberated" the Upland Goose pub in Stanleyville at the end of the Falklands War, we had "liberated" the Turismo. Only the old caretaker, Jon, was still there. He greeted me with tears in the trashed back office. "I saw them on December 7th, 1975, destroying everything," he said, recalling the invasion by Indonesia. "They came again on September 7th, 1999, and did this." Just then, a contingent of Australian soldiers, kitted out for war, roared up in a truck to secure the hotel for their own media. The caretaker's little granddaughter went rigid with fright when she saw the soldiers. "It's okay. They are our friends," he said.

Early next morning the three of us set off walking along the deserted three-kilometre avenue, lined with bougainvillea and frangipani, that ran through the suburb of Bacora. High in the hills beyond Bacora we came across hundreds of men, women and children, sheltering in little valleys and in groves of banana trees, afraid to come down. With different deadlines we split up and returned individually. As I strolled back through Bacora, I glimpsed among the bushes and foliage dozens of tin-roofed houses that had been burned. There were no people to be seen, other than half a dozen Indonesian soldiers sitting on plastic chairs outside a small military base, listening to pop music on a radio. They stared at me without smiling as I walked by.

At the Turismo more journalists had just arrived on a flight from Indonesia. I renewed acquaintance with Sanders Thoenes of the *Financial Times*, whom I once had to dinner in my apartment in Moscow. He gave me his email address. It was the last entry in my notebook that day. Shortly afterwards Sanders hired a motorbike and driver and set off on the same road through Bacora. Some hours later, his driver, Florinda Da Conceiro Araujo, turned up at the Turismo. He had cuts and bruises and was trembling. He told us that six members of the 745 Battalion (mainly East

Timorese) of the Indonesian Army had blocked the road and started shooting at them, and he had crashed. Sanders had been knocked unconscious, but Araujo had escaped on foot. As night fell and Sanders did not return, we got very alarmed for his safety. It was too dangerous to go looking for him.

Aoife Kavanagh had also rented a motorbike and, with Paddy Higgins on the pillion with his TV camera, had set off along the same road around the same time as Thoenes. She saw six soldiers wearing militia-style bandanas and pointing guns at them and quickly turned back. Doug returned soon after me, and Patrick much later after darkness, but both were safe. Jon Swain of the *Sunday Times* and American photographer Chip Hires had also gone missing on the same road. It emerged later that they were ambushed by the soldiers at the same spot, and fled into the bushes. They were rescued by helicopter early next day after making a mobile phone call from their hiding place to the *Sunday Times* in London, which then appealed to the Australian forces for help.

For Sanders, there was no happy outcome. The body of the thirty-year-old *Financial Times* journalist was found the next day. He had been shot in the back and his left ear was hacked off and his face mutilated.

The death of Sanders Thoenes was a shock. Patrick realised he had walked right past his body without seeing it. We had thought Dili was relatively safe and that the militias had melted away. We hadn't bargained for rogue Indonesian soldiers. In fact it would be many days before the city was secured. During that time Indonesian officers, knowing they would soon be evacuated, instructed their soldiers to set fire to the remaining buildings they were occupying in the city. Not willing to provoke a fight, the Australian forces did little to stop them,

A bespectacled Australian captain, who wore leather gloves despite the heat, lectured us daily in the Turismo lobby on security and on our behaviour – no walking in bare feet, no cooking food in the rooms, no stroking the hotel cats, as "they carry diseases". That risk was soon eliminated as an Australian soldier kicked one of the skinny orange cats to death in the garden and the other fled. Food and water ran desperately short. In an act of pettiness, the Australian officer told his pool of reporters not to give army-issue drinking water to the non-Australian reporters like ourselves. We got spider bites from sleeping on the concrete floors of burned-out rooms. When I mentioned to Doug a few days after we'd arrived that it was my birthday, he produced a quarter bottle of whisky which we shared on empty stomachs, and had the effect of making me feel rather ill.

The situation gradually improved, as the Australian-led peace-keepers spread out across East Timor, joined by a thirty-member platoon of Irish Army Rangers, which patrolled a section of the border with Indonesian West Timor. Brigadier David Richards, commander of the British contingent, told us he saw East Timor as a "tropical Northern Ireland". He said he advised the Australians they should keep helicopters in the air, as he had done over Belfast, because "they think you are better than you are". After that, three Australian Black Hawk helicopters roared low over Dili every day, as remnants of the militias were flushed out.

On 30 October 1999, after an occupation lasting a quarter of a century, and having overseen the vengeful destruction of seventy per cent of the country's infrastructure, Indonesian troops finally left East Timor for good, the last contingent slipping away at dead of night from the port of Dili in an old troop ship, naval vessel No. 513.

East Timor came under the control of an enlarged UN mission, headed by Sergio de Mello (who would later be assassinated in Baghdad). There was considerable Irish involvement. A Dublin lawyer, John Ryan from Rathgar, was appointed UN administrator of Dili and began the process of reconstruction. The Irish government pledged IR£1 million for humanitarian assistance and opened an aid office in Dili. In Aileu, where the militias had made their blood oath, Irish volunteers from the aid agency GOAL began rebuilding homes. Another Irish aid agency, Concern, set up an office in Dili to help with the democratisation process. Tom Hyland took up residence in Dili as a teacher.

In February 2000 Indonesian President Abdurrahman Wahid visited Dili, laid flowers at Santa Cruz cemetery and apologised for human rights abuses committed against the population. On 27 September 2002 the former Portuguese colony was recognised at the United Nations as the independent country of Timor-Leste, with Xanana Gusmão as its first elected President and a population of just over one million. Gusmão was succeeded in 2007 by José Ramos-Horta, and became Prime Minister instead. In February 2008 both men survived assassination attempts by disaffected soldiers from the Timor-Leste armed forces.

In 2006 President Xanana Gusmão submitted the 2,500-page report of the Timor-Leste Commission for Reception, Truth and Reconciliation to the UN Secretary-General. It blamed Jakarta for more than 100,000 deaths from killings, starvation and disease during the twenty-four-year occupation, but in the interest of good relations, he said they would not seek punitive action against Indonesia.

Former East Timor governor, Abilio Soares, was indicted for crimes against humanity before a human rights court in Indonesia and sentenced to three years in prison. He was never jailed. Hulman Gulton was charged with failing to prevent the killing of seventeen-year-old Manuel Carrascalão and eleven others on 17 April 1999 and sentenced to three years, which he also never served. Eurico Guterres left East Timor and formed a new militia named the Red and White Warriors in Indonesia's restive Papua province, where Brigadier General Timbul Silaen was made police chief, raising fears of another bloody campaign against separatists. However, in 2006 Guterres was brought to Jakarta and placed in Cipinang Prison to begin a ten-year sentence for his part in the killings. He was released in April 2008 after serving less than two years. His mentor, Colonel Tono Suratman, was acquitted of human rights abuses and received a promotion to brigadier general.

A Dutch police investigator concluded that Sanders Thoenes was shot dead by Lieutenant Camilo dos Santos, an East Timorese officer serving in Battalion 745 of the Indonesian Army. Now serving in Indonesia, dos Santos was promoted to the role of general's adjutant.

The Irish government made Timor-Leste a development aid priority. Between 2003 and 2007 it contributed over €20 million in aid. In March 2008, as part of its effort to help the former East Timor find a path from conflict to sustainable peace and development, the government appointed Nuala O'Loan, who had been the first police ombudsman for Northern Ireland, as Roving Ambassador for the Conflict Resolution Initiative with the role of Special Envoy to Timor-Leste.

31

A Long Wait for a Train

A large sign stating, "Welcome to the World's Most Dangerous Golf Course" greets visitors to the "clubhouse" at Panmunjom. Another notice warns me that if I drive my ball into the rough from the first tee, I shouldn't go looking for it. That's because the rough is part of the world's biggest minefield, which straddles the 248-kilometre Demilitarised Zone (DMZ) between North and South Korea. In fact Panmunjom Golf Course consists of just one 192-yard, par-three hole, with a peeling Astroturf green. It is a tourist gimmick; nothing to die for.

I arrived at the most heavily armed border in the world in early June 2000, just after the announcement of the first-ever summit between North and South Korea, which was stirring hopes of eventual reunification. To get to Panmunjom, the site of the armistice which ended the 1950–53 Korean War, I had to take a special bus along a tarmacadam road through the minefield lined with red warning triangles hanging from strands of wire. It ended at the "Reunification Observatory" where tourists sit on plastic seats arrayed in terraces and peer through powerful coin-operated binoculars into no-man's land.

South Koreans are obsessively curious about the North, which has been separated from the South since the Korean War, and news of the summit had brought a big increase in the number of visitors arriving in smoked-glass buses from Seoul, an hour's drive to the south. They could see terrain that would be familiar to viewers of the American television series *M.A.S.H.*, with camouflaged bunkers and missile silos, and rusting military helmets with weeds growing through the holes. In the distance lay Gijeong-dong, or "Peace Village". This was a fake hamlet, where no one lived except for caretakers who switched on the lights at night and who maintained loudspeakers that broadcast North Korean propaganda across the DMZ – which was countered with South Korean pop music.

"I wonder what kind of lives people live over there," mused a teenager, peering through her binoculars as the morning mist began to evaporate in the warm sunshine. "I think they live like South Koreans did in the 1960s," said her friend, before they both set off to descend seventy-three metres through a damp, sloping shaft and walk along part of the "Third Tunnel", the biggest of several tunnels dug through bedrock by the North Koreans during the 1970s, in a foiled attempt to mount a surprise attack.

The DMZ holds one million mines, most of them planted to deter the one million-strong North Korean army from invading the South. The arithmetic is neat: one mine per communist soldier. But almost half a century after the end of the Korean War, the mines along the southern section of Korea's 38th Parallel were still killing and maiming soldiers and peasants at the rate of fifteen a year. The previous October, Private First Class Ban Yoon-soo of the South Korean army was blown up while digging a bunker, and two other privates were killed when a mine exploded in March. Farmers were sometimes torn apart when they stepped on mines that had been swept by landslides and floods outside the officially mapped minefields. According to the International Campaign to Ban Landmines, the United States military here also had stocks of hundreds of thousands of smart mines, as small as jam-jar lids, which could be scattered by air, artillery and vehicles in the event of an invasion.

The inhabitants of the village of Sung Dong live just a few hundred metres from this killing zone. They were fed up with the non-stop propaganda from the giant loudspeakers on both sides. "It gets on my nerves, sometimes it goes on all night," said a white-haired grandmother, as a martial song echoed across the rice paddies. "I'm not worried about North Korea attacking us any more, but I am worried about the South being taken advantage of by the North," said an old woman crossly as she sorted baby onions outside her house. "All the food aid we sent them did not make them change." Sitting cross-legged in his farmhouse, sixty-four-year-old Kim Jungchul said that the soldiers had stopped making them wear ID cards, though he put his on proudly to pose for a photograph with his wife Ju Young Ok. "I'd like to see North Korea one day," he said, "but there is no chance of that."

Most South Koreans accepted the necessity of the militarised zone and did not want their American protectors to leave. But many Koreans were critical of the US military. The Itaewon red-light district of Seoul, called "Hookers Hill", where bars are typically called Tight Tavern or Texas Club, enabled off-duty American soldiers to engage in behaviour that was illegal for South Koreans. It was almost deserted when I went there one afternoon. A teenage girl, her face caked with make-up, beckoned to passers-by from the doorway of the Rocky Top Bar and an old woman emerged from an alleyway to ask, "Want a nice lady?" One of the smallest bars, the Amazon, was locked and deserted: it had been shunned since a thirty-two-year-old hostess called Kim Sung-hi was beaten and strangled in a back room some weeks earlier by twenty-two-year-old Corporal Christopher McCarthy of the 2nd US Infantry Division, who would later be sentenced to just six years in a Korean jail. This incident had aroused popular anger, already stirred up by new research

313

detailing American atrocities committed against civilians in the Korean War and alleged US connivance at the May 1980 massacre by Korean special forces of some 2,000 pro-democracy demonstrators in Kwangju in South Korea.

The environmental impact of US military bases was also stirring up strong feelings. In the village of Maehyang, eighty kilometres south of Seoul, violent anti-American protests had become almost a daily occurrence since 8 May 2000, when a US A-10 jet, on a practice run at the nearby Koon-ni range, inadvertently dropped six live bombs so close that houses shook as if in an earthquake. A fisherman, Kim Jun Pong, showed me cracks in his plaster and the wall clock lying where it fell on the floor. "The aircraft come in so low that we can see the pilots' faces," said another villager, Park Jangsun, as we walked past part of the razor-wire fence torn down by protesters the previous week. "I understand the need for having the US planes, but the suffering of the villagers has been going on too long." It had become unbearable for Mr Kim, owner of a little village store, who claimed his house was within permitted practice range. Jabbing his finger at a large sketch which he spread out on the floor, he said: "If they hit this part, they get seven points; if this part, five points; and if they accidentally hit the village, they get three points." An unarmed ten-kilogramme bomb had dropped through his bedroom ceiling two years before, while he was in the shop, he said. "It scared the living daylights out of me. They came and collected it and said, 'Sorry.' I had to patch up the roof myself." But when asked if they wanted the Americans to leave, the village elders gave an emphatic "no". They emphasised how grateful they were to the United States for its protection against the communist North, as the two Koreas were still technically at war.

For many North Koreans, like Kim Gun-il, who had defected two years earlier and whom I met in Seoul, the DMZ is not a tourist attraction, but a barrier to freedom. Wearing a plaid shirt and with a tiny silver mobile phone hung round his neck, he could have been any South Korean twenty-one-year-old. But he was rather undersized, weighing just fifty-three kilos, and still hadn't quite mastered the attitude and the walk. "The problem is the posture," he explained. "We North Koreans have no self-respect, no self-confidence and our eyes dart around everywhere when we move around. But I've almost got over that." He recalled the culture shock of finding himself in the prosperous capital of South Korea. "I was always told South Korea was full of poor people," he said. "I saw some kids who had cut their jeans and I thought they were beggars. Also, there is so much sex here. You can sleep with anyone. When I first saw South Korean girls walking down the street exposing half their breasts, I thought they'd had plastic surgery."

What Kim Gun-il found hard to take was the indifference of many young South Koreans to their fate. "In the North everyone wants reunification but here people don't care, they don't want it; I think it is because they are rich," he said. "When I first saw so many wealthy people, I hated them. Many people laughed at me because I didn't understand some of the English words they use." He had won a scholarship to study theology and had found God, but sometimes was overcome with homesickness. "I often feel alone here," he said. "I don't even have a picture of my father, who starved to death."

When Lee Min Bok fled across the Tumen River from North Korea into China, he thought he was in "paradise" because the shops were full of food. The forty-three-year-old agriculture researcher from Pyongyang was stunned when he reached Seoul, with its traffic jams and high buildings topped with giant TV screens. "The gap between the two Koreas is so huge, it's indescribable," he told me. "But what I couldn't get over were small things, such as individually wrapped candies, and this sort of thing" – he picked up a toothpick encased in paper from the restaurant table where we were having tea. "Only high officials in North Korea had toothpicks." In North Korea Lee worked on solving food shortages and developing related technologies. "The problem was the collective system. As an experiment, I tried Chinese methods and got an increase in output of 300–500 per cent. I wrote a letter to then North Korean leader Kim Il Sung. Top officials of the Communist Party came and said, 'You are right but don't do it any more or you will get hurt.'" He failed in his first attempt to flee and was put in the political prison. "I was made to sit up all night and not allowed to go to the toilet. They did not give me any food. My finger and toenails stopped growing because of malnutrition." He was eventually released and succeeded in his second attempt to escape through China.

Before and during the Korean War, millions of North Koreans fled to the South to avoid coming under communist rule and found themselves stranded when the armistice came in 1953. The partition was absolute. Even postal communication between separated relatives was forbidden by the North. The only way to make contact with lost parents, brothers and sisters and children was by paying ethnic Koreans from China, who had special access to North Korea, to bring letters to relatives. The first generation of separated families had now started to die out, and any easing of tensions would come too late for most of them, said seventy-seven-year-old Dong Young Cho, who ran the "Korean Assembly for the Reunion of Ten Million Separated Families". In his Seoul office lined with thousands of files, Dong told me in a faltering voice how he was separated from his parents and two brothers and sisters by the Korean War; and then in December 1998 he received a letter from a woman in North Korea. "She wrote, 'I think I am your sister', and told me she had raised two children. You can't imagine what it felt like. It was like a dream."

Hong Kun-sik, also then seventy-seven, the youngest of seven brothers and sisters who remained in the North, despaired of any of them remaining alive. "In the South, among the second generation, there are two types of children, A and B. The A type says, 'I was born in the South so I don't really care about the North.' The B type says, 'I was born in the South and my parents cried all the time about the North, so I am interested.' I have two boys and two girls and they are all of the B type, I am happy to say." Hong, who was president of the Association of Lost Home Towns, dreamed of the collapse of communism in the North. "I have been waiting for fifty years. I am tired of waiting. I think reunification should happen right away."

The historic summit got under way on 13 June 2000 in the North Korean capital, Pyongyang, between South Korean President Kim Dae-jong and the North Korean "Dear Leader", Kim Jong-il. It was the first top meeting between the two sides since the Korean War. They agreed on a "road map" for national reconciliation, starting with a token act of harmony: a brief visit by one hundred family members from each side. A total of 76,000 South Koreans applied to go to North Korea, desperate to find lost relatives.

On 19 August, two months after the summit, the visits took place. A North Korean aircraft took one hundred people south to Seoul to meet their relatives, assembled in a convention centre under the glare of television lights, and the same day the aircraft took one hundred South Koreans to Pyongyang. The North Koreans were carefully selected, and were led by Yoo Mi-young, the elderly widow of a former South Korean foreign minister who defected in 1986. But there was nothing contrived about the emotions we witnessed. What does one say to a mother or a brother after a separation of half a century? Words failed many Koreans at their tear-drenched reunions. They hugged in fierce embraces. Ninety-five-year-old Chung Sun-hwa from South Korea collapsed and required medical attention on meeting her son for the first time in half a century. "I thought all of you were dead," said a man when he met his two elderly sisters. Many frail and ailing relatives did not recognise each other.

Slowly, and with several stops and starts, the thaw got under way. More ministerial meetings took place. The propaganda broadcasts across the DMZ ceased. South Korean businesses and individuals were able to initiate contacts with the North, under President Kim Dae-jong's "Sunshine Policy". South Korean investment began to flow into North Korea along a newly opened road link to the Kumgang Mountain tourism resort and Kaesong industrial park, where thousands of North Koreans were employed in South Korean factories. The defence ministers on each side agreed to reconstruct the railway line through the DMZ. It took five years for enough mines and tank traps to be removed and for the tracks to be reconnected to form the start of what President Kim hoped would be an "Iron Silk Road". It was a long wait for a train. But after a second summit on 2–4 October 2007, the first goods train headed northwards to restart a regular service in both directions. The soldiers of the opposing armies continue to stare at each other at Panmunjom, however, and there are no plans, as yet, to build the remaining seventeen holes of the Panmunjom golf course.

32

All is Not Forgiven

In April 2000, hundreds of American visitors came to Ho Chi Minh City, formerly Saigon, to mark the twenty-fifth anniversary of the end of what they call the Vietnam War and what Vietnamese call the American War. Dozens of veteran US correspondents also arrived, and staged a noisy reunion on the roof garden of the Rex Hotel, where US military briefers used to hold the "Five o'clock Follies", the often fictional accounts of progress in the war. Many celebrated chroniclers of the war were there, including Stanley Karnow, Pulitzer Prize-winning author of *Vietnam: A History*. In his old haunt, the Givral Café, he reminisced over Vietnamese coffee about how *Time* correspondent Pham Xuan An used to pass on gossip at the tables. When the communist tanks arrived, Pham revealed himself to be an undercover colonel in the North Vietnamese army. "Times have changed; our two daughters now hang out together," said Karnow. Outside, prostitutes on motor scooters circled around looking for clients and urchins hawked crude copies of Karnow's book and other Vietnam-related classics, like Graham Greene's *The Quiet American*.

Among the American visitors was Senator John McCain, a former prisoner of war, who gave several interviews from the Rex

Hotel to American TV and cable networks. His message was, "The wrong guys won." It was not a view shared by many Vietnamese. However, the Americans found themselves greeted with a surprising degree of friendliness. Many of their reports and broadcasts spoke of an attitude of "forgive and forget". Most Vietnamese seemed to make a distinction between the American government, which waged the war, and the American people, many of whom, the Vietnamese knew, opposed it.

Everywhere there are memorials of the war. In a forest of eucalyptus trees near Cu Chi, sixty kilometres north-west of Ho Chi Minh City, I was able to enter a Viet Cong tunnel and take tea and *khoai-mi*, the white cassava roots (quite tasty when dipped in salt) that formed the staple diet of Vietnamese fighters, with a veteran Viet Cong guerrilla called Le Van Tung. US military veterans occasionally turned up and "sometimes they cry," said Tung, and "they say that they hate war". If they felt like reliving the fighting, however, they could, for a dollar a bullet, fire M16s and AK47s on an open range behind the tunnels. The tunnels were a reconstruction, made wide to accommodate overweight western tourists. The real network of tunnels, which had provided munitions dumps, hospitals, dormitories and kitchens for the Viet Cong, remained mostly inaccessible to the public.

Some of the most protracted fighting of the war occurred in the Mekong Delta where military patrol craft – including the Swift Boat of John Kerry, later Senator of Massachusetts – tore along the wide river and canals, their guns raking the palm fronds. Now boatloads of tourists aimed only cameras at the flaming red summer trees and green coconut palms on the peaceful banks. They were taken to villages like Ankhan, once designated a strategic hamlet by the American forces. The residents echoed the government line. "Maybe we had hatred in the past but now we are friends," said bee-keeper Tam Khuynh, over a thimble of honey wine in his hardwood and woven rattan home. By his account, there was much to forgive. US troops forced everyone to come into one village, "and if they didn't comply, the soldiers destroyed the houses," he said. Now seventy-seven, he still mourned two brothers he lost in the fighting.

With a Canadian colleague, Miro Cernetig, I ventured deeper into the Mekong Delta, along rivers and roads not approved for tourists. We took a rusting, Danish-built car ferry across the Co Chien River, and reached Vinh Long, 150 kilometres from Ho Chi Minh City, where the streets were filled with men on motorcycles and women in diaphanous pyjamas. An elderly woman stopped to practise her French. "I much preferred the French to the Americans," she said, echoing a sentiment I heard many times from Vietnamese who credited the French for at least giving them a sense of style when they ran the country as a colony from 1859 to 1954.

Here we came across a former Viet Cong nurse, called Dung, who managed a little provision shop. She was watching a black-and-white documentary called *The Wide Field*, the official account of the victory over the Americans, on a little Daewoo television set in the back room. She offered us tea among boxes of soap and electric fans and a parked Honda motorcycle. The sound of B52 bombers and anti-aircraft fire from the television formed a background to our conversation. Dung felt very proud to be celebrating the anniversary of liberation that weekend, but her round face became heavy with sadness as she recalled her days in action.

"I think often, especially at this time, of the people who died in the war," she said. "My older brother's seven children were killed, all but one. My mother was beaten by American soldiers who broke her ribs. She passed away just last year." She paused, blinking back tears. "I saw Agent Orange being sprayed from a plane," she said. "The Viet Cong soldiers had masks but the people did not. The leaves fell off the trees and the baby bananas suddenly grew big and nobody would eat them. People got cancer afterwards." What did she feel about Americans twenty-five years later? "I have a lot of hatred for Americans," she said. "I will hate them till I die. I cannot forget the sight of people dying and being raped by American soldiers." She lapsed into silence and stared up at the television screen, where a US helicopter pilot was falling to the ground in a staged scene, brought down by a heroic Viet Cong gunner.

Outside Vinh Long, we left the car and paid local youths to take us on the back of their motorcycles a further fifteen kilometres to the little town of Huu Thanh. We crossed several canals bridged only by planks and made treacherous by torrential rain. Outside the town, a hoarding warned residents not to allow "cock-fights, gambling, sex videos, prostitution or begging".

A bloody battle of the Vietnam War was fought around Huu Thanh in October 1972, when Viet Cong guerrillas attacked a South Vietnam Army base. Only twenty-three of the 320 South Vietnamese soldiers stationed there survived the fighting, among them an army sergeant called Son who was airlifted to hospital at the height of the battle after being wounded in fourteen places. He now lived in a little concrete house and raised pigs. He could never forget the war, he said, not least because a fragment of an M79 bullet was still lodged painfully in his left chest.

"When the Americans left, I felt despair; I felt like dying," he said, as he cut slices of fresh star-fruit for his visitors. "When the war ended, I just waited around to be arrested. The local Viet Cong were pretty obnoxious at first. I was sent for re-education to a camp and told to forget what I had learned in the past and learn about the new government. After my release I had to report regularly as an American collaborator. Now I am left alone. When I meet local Viet Cong we never discuss the past. After so many years, we have to co-operate with each other." He felt nothing but resentment, however, for his former protectors. "The Americans abandoned us," he said bitterly. "After the war we got no help from them."

The war was also more than a memory to people living around Khe Sanh, the remote battlefield on a barren plateau just south of the demilitarised zone that once separated North and South Vietnam. We flew north to the city of Hue and drove through Dong Ha and across the Ho Chi Minh trail, now a tar-macadam track, to reach Khe Sanh, where American marines held out for seventy-five days in 1968. All around the former base, the land is barren, the legacy of the tons of phosphorous shells, Agent Orange and napalm dropped by American forces in one of the heaviest bombardments in the history of modern warfare. There was so much unexploded ordnance still lying around that villagers planting coffee were regularly maimed, said Le Suc, a thirty-two-year-old peasant who made a living by selling old bullets and US army dog tags to the trickle of visitors. "One of my friends was killed last year when he was searching for scrap metal with a detector and he disturbed an old grenade." In the twenty-five years since the fighting stopped, more than 5,400 people had been killed or injured by landmines and unexploded ordnance around Khe Sanh, out of a total of over 100,000 in all Vietnam.

"It wasn't worth one dollar or one American life," a US tourist had scribbled in a well-thumbed visitors' book in a one-room Khe Sanh museum erected on an abandoned runway. "Who won? Who lost? Who knows?" wrote another. A veteran artillery sergeant from Oklahoma confessed, "Am truly sorry for what we have done. Have learned much here." Other visitors struck a more defiant note. "Ultimately the American way is winning," wrote Gary from California. "That's true, there's nothing like a Big Mac," responded the next visitor. "We love you America."

Five hundred Americans, 10,000 North Vietnamese and countless civilians died at Khe Sanh in a battle which achieved no strategic gain for either side, but helped to break the will of the Americans to stay in Vietnam. The words of "Born in the USA", sung by Bruce Springsteen, ran through my head as I looked around at the desolate landscape: "Had a brother at Khe Sanh, fighting off the Viet Cong. They're still there. He's all gone."

In Hanoi, the Vietnamese capital, there is little evidence today of the devastation wrought by Operation Rolling Thunder, the American air bombardment of North Vietnam, which US pilots boasted "made the rubble bounce". A quarter of a century after the war ended, the capital of Vietnam still awakens to the sound of communist slogans from loudspeakers and there are portraits everywhere of the revered war-time Communist Party leader, Ho Chi Minh. But the French colonial buildings in the centre have been restored to their original elegance and several new hotels built. Young people on Suzukis and Hondas jostle in the streets with pedicabs and peddlers in conical hats. In the old quarter, traders in rows of fantastically narrow shops sell everything from silk pyjamas to engraved headstones. The day we arrived, the National Symphony Orchestra was playing at the Opera House and there was classic piano in the Luna d'Autunno Theatre. American popular culture had intruded in the shape of several bowling alleys and a concert movie by Metallica called *Cunning Stunts Live in Texas* at the Fansland Cinema. There was even a golf course outside town, where former American pilots could play nine holes, and reflect on how much the world had changed. We played a round there just so we could say we did.

As a US Air Force pilot, John McCain was shot down and imprisoned in Hoa Lo Prison, known to the French as Maison Centrale, and to the Americans as the Hanoi Hilton. The prison had been part demolished to make way for a twenty-storey luxury condominium and only the front had been retained as a museum honouring Vietnamese patriots of the French era, displaying leg irons, a guillotine and a bucket for severed heads. One small room recalled the American POWs, with photographs of McCain and other prominent inmates. It had an inscription saying, "Despite their terrible crimes against the Vietnamese people, American pilots were well treated and given food, clothing and shelter." One of the prisoners was the pilot of a B52 Stratofortress bomber brought down by a SAM missile in 1972.

The wreckage still protrudes from an oily pond called Jade Lake, located at the end of a narrow lane that runs past an ochre-coloured temple and a garden with tangerine trees. A young man angling for snake fish told me that the pilot of the B52 came to see it one day after his release.

The memories of past wars are also kept alive in the Hanoi Military Museum, where schoolchildren in red neck scarves and peasants with blackened teeth sit in rows to watch re-enactments of epic battles, such as that against the French in Dien Bien Phu in 1954, and the liberation of Saigon in 1975.

In the corridor of a clinic of Bach Mai hospital, the consequences of the war were still being felt. Bewildered children waited to be fitted with thermo-plastic braces from a prosthetics workshop or to have their deformed limbs gently stretched and massaged by therapists. All the children had mental and physical defects. Between 1962 and 1971, US Air Force C123s sprayed seventy-six million litres of defoliants, including Agent Orange, over fourteen per cent of the land surface of Vietnam. An estimated 300,000 children, born long after the war, suffered from a range of afflictions: mental retardation, spina bifida, cerebral palsy, immune deficiencies, liver damage, nervous system disorders, tumours and other cancers. Vietnam lacked the resources to prove the connection with Agent Orange, but for the hospital doctors the circumstantial evidence was overwhelming. "I know of a woman from the Mekong Delta who had a normal healthy child in 1968, then had three children after exposure to Agent Orange who were all severely disabled and mentally retarded, and two were blind," said Dr Tran Thi Thu Ha, who headed the clinic. The United States had spent more than $200 million on research into the effects of Agent Orange on US veterans, but accepted no responsibility for the consequences on the ground where its dioxin ingredient – the most toxic man-made organic chemical – entered the food chain through soil, fish and ducks. It was left to individuals like Chuck Searcy, a Vietnam veteran from Georgia, to make amends for America's chemical warfare. He represented the Vietnam Veterans of America Foundation, which had established two children's clinics. "I'm not seeking redemption, but I do feel responsible for the destruction and tragedy of the war, and America's role in it," he said as we walked around the Bach Mai clinic. Now he found joy in seeing "a kid beaming with new self-esteem as it walks for the first time".

We arrived back in Ho Chi Minh City in time for the official ceremonies to mark the anniversary of the fall of Saigon. The occasion stirred patriotic emotions for Ngo Si Nguyen, one of four North Vietnamese soldiers on tank No. 843, which smashed down the wrought-iron gates of the palace on 30 April 1975, and who had returned to Saigon for the first time. "Exactly twenty-five years ago history gave us the honour of being here on behalf of the millions of soldiers who died in the war to liberate the South and reunite the country," he said, as soldiers carrying rifles goose-stepped past a huge picture of Ho Chi Minh at Reunification Palace, followed by a women's rifle contingent in black pyjamas.

Among the onlookers, author Le Ly Hayslip told me, with tears in her eyes: "I'm here to celebrate twenty-five years of peace." She has good reason to despise war. Born into a peasant family near Danang, Le Ly was recruited as a child by the Viet Cong, tortured by the South Vietnamese army and forced to flee her home. She survived a spell as a prostitute to marry an American and emigrate to the United States, where her story was told by Oliver Stone in his 1993 film *Heaven and Earth* and where she founded the East Meets West Foundation in California to care for children in Vietnam. (This had more profound implications than she could have realised. When researching a biography of the Irish-American philanthropist Chuck Feeney several years later, I found that a 1997 article in the *San Francisco Examiner* about Le Ly Hayslip's struggling foundation had inspired him to get involved in funding education and health care in Vietnam, which by 2006 totalled $220 million.) There was something missing, said

Hayslip – that was, any expression of regret from the US. "Such a move would mean much to Vietnamese people."

"The US media are always concentrating on how the Americans feel, but we have many scars here," she said, pointing to her heart. She would even love to see a visit by President Clinton, who normalised relations in 1995. "He wouldn't have to apologise if he came," said Chuck Searcy, standing nearby. "He could simply acknowledge America's role in the suffering caused by the war."

Bill Clinton did come to Vietnam, six months later, arriving in Hanoi on 16 November 2000 as traders put up Christmas trees and models of Santa Claus and reindeers. He didn't apologise for the American War but, in a televised speech at the National University, he said there was "another side" to the Vietnam Memorial Wall in Washington, famous for its inscriptions of the names of the 58,183 Americans who died. This was the "staggering sacrifice of the Vietnamese people on both sides of that conflict, more than three million brave soldiers and civilians". Then he went off around the city to a tumultuous welcome.

I went for a meal at the KOTO restaurant in a narrow Hanoi street. "It's a bit chaotic," said manager Jimmy Pham, as he apologised for the slow service in the downstairs dining-room. "Table twelve upstairs is keeping us busy." The customers weren't complaining, however. In fact, they were beaming. For at table twelve on the upper floor, tucking into grilled vegetables served with hummus and pitta bread, was the President of the United States.

33

You Read It Here First

On 17 January 2004, more than eight months before the 2004 US presidential election, the following headline appeared above my name in *The Irish Times*: "George looking good: All the signs point to President Bush's re-election". I had returned to the United States in 2001 and was once again plunged into a presidential election. My forecast was largely based on a poll showing George W. Bush's approval rating at over fifty per cent. I pointed out that Americans didn't like to change presidents in wartime or when the economy was doing well. Moreover, the core constituency of the Republican Party, the Christian right, which deserted George H.W. Bush in 1992, was solidly behind his son. They liked his frequent references to God, his appointment of conservative judges, his opposition to abortion and his promotion of conventional marriage. And he had kept his promise to cut taxes. By contrast, the Democrats were split on several issues, such as the Iraq war, free trade and gay marriage. The polls also showed that voters, by three to one, expected Bush to win re-election in November. I concluded, "At this stage, these are probably about the right odds."

That was then. Five weeks later, on 21 February 2004, I reversed my prediction and wrote: "You read it here first: Bush will be beaten". A lot had happened in a short time to make me (unfortunately) change my forecast. Bush's credibility had taken a tumble. His Iraq weapons inspector David Kay had resigned. The Carnegie Endowment for International Peace in Washington had found that Bush "systematically misrepresented" the danger of Iraq's weapons of mass destruction. (A study by the non-profit Center for Public Integrity in Washington would later find that Bush made a total of 259 false statements to justify attacking Iraq, 231 about weapons of mass destruction in Iraq and twenty-eight about Iraq's links to al Qaeda.) Meanwhile Senator John Kerry of Massachusetts, a decorated Vietnam veteran, had emerged as the Democratic front-runner and his party had united behind him.

As time went on, Bush was increasingly portrayed as a duplicitous president who had deceived the nation into a war. During the musical *Frogs* at Manhattan's Lincoln Center, when the actor Nathan Lane, playing an ancient Greek, proclaimed, "We are still at war, a war we may not be able to win, a war we shouldn't even be in," the audience around us broke into applause. Michael Moore's *Fahrenheit 9/11*, which portrayed Bush as a simpleton whose gang stole the 2000 election, opened in June 2004 to packed houses across the US. At the Loews cinema in New York's East Village, the audience applauded loud and long at the end of the documentary. In Dayton, Ohio, a local newspaperman told me that delighted local Democrats were coming out of the cinema "levitating".

Kerry looked like an ideal candidate for the Democrats. Just before the Iowa Caucus I accompanied him to a rally in Des Moines, where a retired police officer called Jim Rassman turned up unexpectedly and told an enraptured crowd how, under fire in the Mekong Delta, Kerry had turned his Swift Boat around and pulled him out of the water, saving his life. If anyone could beat George Bush, who had avoided service in Vietnam, it was a genuine war hero. At subsequent Kerry rallies in New Hampshire, the crowds grew bigger and more enthusiastic. A Gallup poll on 19 February showed Kerry trouncing the President in an election by fifty-five to forty-three per cent. I was convinced. A decade earlier I had used the expression "You read it here first" to predict, against the odds but correctly, that Bill Clinton would be returned to the White House. I thought I could throw the dice and be proved right again.

At that point the election was Kerry's to lose and he set about doing just that. Confident of nomination, he went off skiing at his $4.5 million vacation home in Sun Valley, Idaho. George Bush meanwhile went on the offensive. He seized on a comment made by Kerry about a bill in Congress to fund the war in Iraq. "I actually did vote for the $87 billion, before I voted against it." Bush accused Kerry of flip-flopping and the Republican strategist, Karl Rove, arranged for supporters to turn up at rallies with pairs of flip-flops to slap together mockingly. By 1 April, a Gallup poll showed that the Massuchusetts senator had lost his lead and trailed Bush fifty-one to forty-seven per cent among likely voters.

The strategy of the Bush campaign was to turn Kerry's best qualities against him, and make the election a referendum on Kerry rather than on George Bush. Kerry was fluent in French, Italian, Portuguese, German and Spanish and he had maternal relatives in Europe, where former French Environment Minister Brice Lalonde was his first cousin. Here was a candidate who could reach out to the world, compared to Bush, who could speak only a little Spanish – or Mexican as he once called it. When visiting Paris, Bush had famously mocked NBC's David Gregory for asking President Jacques Chirac a question in French, saying, "The guy memorises four words and he plays like he's intercontinental."

Republicans set about making Kerry's talents a handicap. Commerce Secretary Don Evans called Kerry a "fellow of a different political stripe who looks French". House Majority Leader Tom DeLay started a lunchtime speech with: "Good afternoon, or, as John Kerry might say, *bonjour*." Kerry, typically, ran for cover.

Though he privately chatted with French journalists in their own language, he refused to do television or radio interviews in French or even to reply in that language to a question if American reporters were around.

European opposition to the war in Iraq had produced widespread anti-French nativism among many Americans. A Parisian I knew told people in New York she was from Quebec to avoid trouble. In downtown Manhattan one day, a woman with a heavy accent asked me directions. "Are you French?" I asked. "Yes," she replied, cautiously. "Vive la France," I said. "I get the message," she responded, with a relieved smile.

John Kerry gave another hostage to fortune by revealing that some unnamed world leaders had told him, "You've got to win this, you've got to beat this guy and get rid of George Bush." Time and again, I heard the President at campaign rallies draw great cheers with the punchline, "Whoever these mystery men are, they're not going to be deciding the election. The American people will be deciding this election."

The Republican campaign was extremely well organised. In midsummer I received an envelope in the post containing a photograph of the President and First Lady, personally signed by each, with the message: "To Conor O'Clery, thank you for your early commitment and dedication as a Charter Member of the campaign in New York. Grassroots leaders like you are the key to building a winning team." There was an accompanying letter from Marc Racicot, chairman of Bush-Cheney '04, that started "Dear Friend", except the word "Friend" was crossed out, and "Conor" written by hand. He said he would be "thrilled to tell the President you are with us" if I would join the team as a charter member for a contribution of $1,000, $500, $250 . . . or whatever I could afford. The signatures, of course, were rubber-stamped and there were two misspellings in my name. The same letter had probably gone to everyone who ever turned up at a Republican event, as I had done in the course of my work.

All political campaign donations were recorded on a website called www.fundrace.org. I was able to establish that most tenants in my apartment block were Republicans, not surprising given that most of them worked in the financial district, and had given sums up to $1,000 to Bush-Cheney '04. The most lucrative address for Republicans was 865 South Figueroa in Los Angeles. The signatures on the photographs of the President and First Lady that hung in that building were probably genuine. The most profitable building for the Democrats was the San Remo at 146 Central Park West in New York, which housed celebrities such as Steven Spielberg.

Kerry pulled in so much money from voters who hoped he could beat George Bush that he started travelling in a chartered 757 jet with bar, first-class seats and bedroom. He laid on luxury overflow coaches for the "boys on the bus", most of whom were silently cheering him on. One CNN reporter wrote a cheque for $500 for his campaign. A survey conducted four years later established that of 143 journalists who made political contributions from 2004 to the start of the 2008 campaign, 125 had given to Democrats and liberal causes.

In an echo of the Vietnam War era, the Democratic convention, held in Boston in late July, was picketed by anti-Iraq War activists protesting against the vote in Congress by leading Democrats like John Kerry and New York Senator Hillary Rodham Clinton to authorise President Bush to take military action against Saddam Hussein. In Oliver Stone's 1989 film *Born on the Fourth of July*, wheelchair-bound Vietnam veteran Ron Kovic, played by Tom Cruise, forced his way into the 1972 Republican convention on Miami Beach, and hoisted a sign for the TV cameras that read "Stop the bombing". At this Democratic National Convention, however, many of the same Vietnam vets were inside. When Kerry took the podium to accept the nomination as Democratic presidential candidate for 2004, he was introduced by the most famous crippled war veteran in politics, former Georgia Senator, Max Cleland, who lost two legs and an arm in Vietnam.

Kerry presented himself as a commander-in-chief by bouncing on stage to salute the convention and announcing that he was "reporting for duty". Several of my press colleagues visibly cringed as they watched. Kerry had initially supported the Iraq war and knew that in post-9/11 America many voters worried about security and believed that leaving Iraq could increase the danger to the US of a new terrorist attack, but during the primaries he had attracted considerable Democratic support for his harsh criticisms of the war. Now Kerry was offering himself as Bush-lite. In a line borrowed from his opponent's patriotism textbook, he declared: "I will never give any nation or international institution a veto over our national security." He had concluded that only by stealing Republican clothes did he have a chance to win.

The Democratic convention was electrified, not by Kerry, but by a US Senate candidate from Chicago, son of a black student from Kenya and a white woman from Kansas, whose brilliant performance stilled the chatter at the back of the hall and brought people tip-toeing in from the corridors. Barack Obama gave one of the most compelling convention speeches any of us had ever heard. He castigated the "spin masters and negative ad peddlers" who would divide America. "I say to them tonight, there's not a liberal America and a conservative America, there's the United States of America. There's not a black America and white America and Latino America and Asian America, there's the United States of America." He criticised the war in Iraq, telling how he met a young Iraq-bound soldier called Seamus who had enlisted in the military from a sense of patriotism and duty. "But then I asked myself, are we serving Seamus as well as he was serving us?" The headline to my report read "Awed hush for new kid on the block". He had not been elected to the Senate at that point, however, and few imagined he would be running for president as the Democratic nominee four years later.

Bush proved to be a tireless campaigner and as consummate a performer as Ronald Reagan, delivering the same lines at rally after rally to great effect. At a typical event in Saginaw, Michigan, he was greeted like a rock star as he walked into a basketball stadium, wearing a casual shirt as if he had just been cutting brush. The crowd, bussed in from all over Michigan and waving American flags handed out at the door, had already been whipped into a patriotic fervour by the Gatlin Brothers, Larry, Steve and Rudy from Texas, introduced as "musicians who have their thinking straight". Bush had to wait several minutes, smiling and shrugging, before the noise abated. "My opponents believe you can find the heart and soul of America in Hollywood," he said. "I think you can find it right here in Saginaw." (Earlier in the day, it was in Columbus, Ohio.) As always, the President linked the war on Saddam to 9/11. "Do I forget the lessons of September the 11th and trust a madman?" he cried. "No!" shouted the fans. "See, you can't talk sense to the terrorists." "No!" "You cannot negotiate with the terrorists." "No!" "We must engage the enemies around the world so we do not have to face them here at home." "Yes! USA! USA!"

As the Bush supporters streamed out of the arena, they encountered about a hundred pro-Kerry protesters with placards, shouting, "Bush lies, soldiers die!" A man came over to tell them brusquely, "I'm a Democrat, but I have to vote Bush. I don't think John Kerry can protect this country."

Kerry then made another serious blunder. At a photo-opportunity beside the Grand Canyon, he was asked if he had known there were no weapons of mass destruction in Iraq, would he still have voted to authorise the war. He replied that he would have. Kerry was the anti-war Vietnam veteran, who had famously challenged senators in 1971 with the question, "How do you ask a man to be the last man to die for a mistake?" Now he was conceding that all the White House deceptions did not matter and Bush was right to take the country to war.

In late August Kerry failed to respond in good time to a series of mendacious television advertisements from "Swift Boat

Veterans for Truth", which vilified him as someone who had lied to get his combat medals. Most of the funding for the group came from Bob Perry, a long-time associate of Karl Rove. Kerry was also slow to respond to an attack on his record at the Republican Convention in New York in September, when a turncoat Democrat, Senator Zell Miller from Georgia, sent delegates into paroxysms of delight with his declaration that, "Kerry would let Paris decide when America needs defending; I want Bush to decide." Speaking as softly as a CEO in a boardroom, Vice-President Dick Cheney told delegates that the country could not trust John Kerry to act in defence of the US, since he would deploy American troops "only at the directive of the United Nations". At rallies Cheney would later say that electing Kerry would invite another al Qaeda attack.

Anti-war protesters tried unsuccessfully to disrupt Bush-Cheney events. When Laura Bush was addressing voters at a fire station in Hamilton, New Jersey, Sue Niederer from nearby Hopewell took off a T-shirt to reveal another underneath with the words "President Bush, You Killed My Son", and a picture of her son, Army First Lieutenant Seth Dvorin. She was dragged to the door as people chorused, "Four More Years!" Outside Niederer began telling me how her twenty-four-year-old son was killed in Iraq while trying to disarm a bomb, but she was handcuffed and driven off in a police van when she refused a police order to move away.

Sometimes it doesn't pay to be an insider. During election day, 2 November 2004, a contact in the *New York Times* called me a number of times with confidential updates on exit polls his newspaper had commissioned, which could not be published until after voting ended. The first batch of polls showed Kerry leading in the must-win states of Florida and Ohio. The data leaked and word of a probable Kerry victory flashed around the political world. At 6.17 p.m. the story burst into the mainstream media when Reuters reported a strong Kerry lead. US newspapers began to prepare spreads on how Kerry had pulled it off. In Boston, as John Kerry tucked into a meal of neck clams, sole and mashed potatoes in the Union Oyster House, his staff began making preparations for the transition. As the evening wore on and the actual counts came in, the euphoria in the Kerry camp evaporated. By midnight it had turned to despair. Bush took Florida and Ohio, and the election, and the inquests began as to how the exit polls had got it wrong.

I was correct to write in February that the Democrats were energised and united in their anger against Bush and that this would benefit Kerry. Five million more Americans voted for the ineffectual Democrat than had voted for Bush in 2000. But Republicans too were energised and turned out in even greater numbers than before and Bush still won the popular vote. But I was not alone in my prediction. Jimmy Breslin declared in his *Newsday* column in May that Kerry would sweep home. That was three months after my forecast. At least I got it wrong first.

34

The New Front Line

On 27 April 2005, when the temperature in Fairbanks, Alaska, rose to a record twenty-two degrees Celsius, the rotting ice of the Tenana River shifted beneath a tripod of black and white rods, tipping it into open water. As it floated away, it pulled a string which automatically stopped a clock on the bank. Observers noted the time – 12.01 p.m. – and relayed the news to the Fairbanks media. Contestants in a state lottery known as the Ice Classic then learned from the radio whether or not they had guessed the correct date and time of the ice break-up. Professor John Walsh of the University of Alaska in Fairbanks got the day right, but not the time, so he didn't get a share of the $285,000 jackpot. However, as a leading expert on global climate change who had been observing the warming of Alaska for many years, he did have a better idea than most that it would happen earlier than ever. In thirty years the date on which the clock stopped had advanced by nine days, a sure sign that in Alaska the winters were getting shorter and the spring was coming earlier.

Climate change is happening faster in Alaska than anywhere else and with possibly catastrophic consequences. In Fairbanks University geophysics department, Professor Walsh showed me computer projections that Alaskan temperatures could rise by another seven degrees before the end of the century. "Every month of this year was warmer than average," he said, "and March was warmer by eight to nine degrees, and that got the snow melt starting earlier." He pointed out that in the entire hemisphere, eight of the previous ten years had been among the ten warmest years on record.

A few days after the ice break-up on the Tenana River, I went for a long drive out of Fairbanks, along roads through stunted coniferous forests where old snowdrifts lurked in the shade, and blue and yellow pasque flowers and yellow-brown birch catkins were already in bloom. The birch and aspen trees in the *taiga* were bursting into leaf, in the abrupt way winter changes to spring in this latitude, and the air was heavy with birch pollen. The transformation of the landscape from brown to green was happening ten days earlier than usual. The warm winter in Fairbanks – it rained on Christmas Eve – followed the hottest summer on record. Summer lightning storms always set off a few forest fires, but the conditions were so hot and dry the previous year and there were so many fires that a toxic haze of airborne particles had enveloped the city for ten weeks. Fires had again started much earlier than usual, according to the *Fairbanks Daily News-Miner*. It was early May but there were already patches of scorched earth and wisps of smoke rising where black spruce had burned. In one hotspot near Dot Lake, south-east of Fairbanks, the Billy Creek fire that raged all the previous summer had flared up again, after smouldering all winter under snow-covered layers of dry needles and spruce cones.

Like canaries in a mine, birds are a harbinger of climate change, so I headed to Creamer's Field Migratory Waterfowl Refuge, just north of Fairbanks. This is a vast expanse of marshy tundra, where tens of thousands of migrating birds arrive with the spring. A notice-board informs birdwatchers when the different species can be expected to turn up. Canada geese normally arrived on 15 April. This year they had come early, on 6 April, and the previous year even earlier, on 3 April. A lesser yellowlegs was spotted on 25 April, though it was not usually sighted until May. The first red-necked grebes had been seen on 1 May, five days earlier than normal, and the common redpolls had already hatched their chicks and left several weeks early. The observatory's senior biologist, Susan Sharbaugh, told me the flycatchers from South America were also there already, seven days too soon. She hesitated to speculate whether or not the early arrivals were due to global warming, as there was so much year-to-year variation, but she did say, "Last week, the temperature broke records two or three days in a row, so I think something's going on." Don Johnson, a white-bearded park volunteer on the refuge, thought so too. He had seen a golden plover arrive early close to his home near Chena Hot Springs. But he questioned my motives for asking about early birds. Like many Alaskans, he regarded climate change as natural and not unduly influenced by human activity. "Take it from this old Alaskan: global climate change is an industry – and you are part of that industry," he scolded me.

However reluctant old-timers like Johnson were to accept that global warming was man-made, there was plenty of evidence that destructive forces were at work which could make parts of Alaska where he lived uninhabitable. Professor Vladimir Romanovsky, Associate Professor of Geophysics at the University of Alaska, and an expert on the permafrost that covered sixty per cent of the land around Fairbanks, told me that the frozen ground beneath the *taiga* and tundra was melting and in twenty or thirty years the permafrost thaw could become widespread. This could cause serious damage to the state's infrastructure of roads and pipes and to the ecosystem. Permafrost held water, explained Romanovsky, a graduate of Moscow University who came to Alaska in 1992, and if it died, drainage of rain and snow melt would be faster. With only 300 millimetres of precipitation a year, the land surface would become drier and the fires even worse. "I'm not an alarmist like some extreme environmentalists, but I can, at this time, see what is happening."

Romanovsky took me on a permafrost tour around town to make his point. We hadn't far to go. Some suburban roads were cracked and had deep dips where permafrost had melted. A tarmacadam cycle path running alongside a raised commuter highway was buckled and misshapen. He showed me a grove of spruce trees leaning drunkenly against each other, and a row of abandoned bungalows with walls tilted at an angle. This was the result of the melting of thermokarsts, giant ice wedges that had been frozen since the last Ice Age.

Permafrost is defined as land where the temperature beneath the surface stays below zero for two consecutive years and it can be hundreds of metres deep. Measurements taken by the institute had produced ominous signs of widespread permafrost retreat. In some places, the active layer, the surface area that melted in summer and could support plant life, had not frozen that winter and it was growing deeper. Following the hot summer of 2004, and heavier snow than usual in the winter which protected the ground from the hardest frosts, Romanovsky expected the permafrost to warm more than usual again. Typically minus two degrees Celsius near the surface, the permafrost around Fairbanks was alarmingly close to zero. Many Alaskans were happy with the warmer weather. In the long term, the effects of warming could be beneficial, with a longer growing season and less harsh winters. The problem was they did not realise that the transition period of about one hundred years would be "very hard", said Romanovsky.

There was another worry, he explained. Deep permafrost contained organic matter such as grass and stems – some still green after thousands of years – which, if broken down, would release billions of tons of stored methane. The effects of such a large body of greenhouse gases in the atmosphere were incalculable. "We are already at much higher levels than in several hundred thousand years and we are now in an area we have never been before."

I asked the Russian scientist what he would say to President George W. Bush, if he ever got the chance, about his refusal to impose curbs on carbon monoxide emissions. "Why say anything?" he replied. "He doesn't listen."

Next day I took an hour-long flight from Fairbanks to the North Bank, the polar wilderness along the Arctic Ocean, from which the sea ice has been disappearing in recent years. The Alaskan Airways plane flew over boreal forest, granite ridges and vast snow fields. It landed at Barrow, 550 kilometres above the Arctic Circle, the most northerly town on the American continent. Barrow, population 5,000, consists of a few streets of single-storey homes, seven churches, four hotels and a supermarket, and has cable television, flush toilets and a single traffic light that is always green until someone wants to cross the road. Its homes are heated by gas, piped in from a nearby field. It boasts a Mexican restaurant named Pepe's with a Filipina waitress, a Japanese restaurant run by Koreans, and a restaurant called Northern Lights serving Chinese and Italian food. There could have been an Irish bar, too, if the largely Inupiat town wasn't officially "dry".

The wilderness that stretches for hundreds of roadless kilometres around is inhabited by polar bears, Arctic foxes and half a million caribou of the Central Arctic and Teshekpuk herds. It is home to many different species of birds, including snowy owls, Arctic terns and geese. Just outside town I saw glaucous gulls and snow buntings and a little group of willow ptarmigans that took off from a snow bank as my guide, Bunna Edwardson, walked towards them. Here too, bird life betrayed the shifts in the climate. The robin started nesting on the Arctic coast some years ago. Never having seen one before, the Inupiat people had no word for it.

It was well below freezing, but Edwardson, a burly native with black, shoulder-length hair, trod the snow in open-toed sandals. He liked to show visitors how acclimatised he was to the cold, though he admitted that after he jumped into the sea once in a show of bravado, he "wasn't a man for ten minutes". He related proudly how the old ways were still followed in Barrow, called Ukpeagvik in Inupiat, meaning "place where snowy owls are hunted" (today they are protected). He loved the solitude and the pristine remoteness of the Arctic, he said, as we drove around trying (in vain) to find the first snowy owl of the spring that he had spotted on a telegraph pole the day before. But he also enjoyed the amenities that allowed him to indulge his craze for cribbage by challenging competitors in London on the Internet.

Many Barrow residents still hunt and fish for much of their food. The first bowhead whale of the season had been harpooned at the end of April by whalers in sealskin boats who took advantage of a windbreak in the sea ice. That day the fourth bowhead was hauled in across the pack ice by a few hundred volunteers, who converged in pickups and snowmobiles, and stayed around to help themselves as the eight-metre mammal was butchered on the shore.

Here winter was still hanging on. It was minus ten degrees at noon and the ocean pack ice, or *sarri*, was jammed up against the shore, forming a jagged green-white landscape as far as one could see. The *sarri* would disintergrate and blow away in late May, leaving open water for up to six months. That was two months longer than a generation ago, said Edwardson. In the 1970s, summer pack ice sometimes prevented supply ships finding a passage around the Arctic coast to the oil-drilling installations at Prudoe Bay. Now the sea surface was clear in summer. In the previous three years, people in Barrow had even spotted tourist cruise ships on the horizon. The loss of the late-year ice made the town vulnerable to sea erosion, as the autumn storms, more ferocious than before, whipped up huge waves on what should be a frozen ocean. A gravel berm had been pushed up by diggers to protect the coast road. "There used to be icebergs as big as houses that would block the waves," said Edwardson. "Now there is no ice and we have big waves that eat up all the beach."

There were other strange happenings, he said. "My grandfather saw lightning only about three times in his life. It comes once a year now. Last year it was awesome. The storm came on the night of 3 July and went on for seven hours, with purple and violet lightning. And last year the temperature went up to twenty-five degrees one summer day and the kids were swimming in the sea. When I was a kid we never swam in the sea."

On a community bulletin board in Barrow High School, a paper had been pinned up by Bowhead Transportation, an Inupiat corporation that runs supply barges from Seattle to Barrow every season. It said that "because of the general shift in weather patterns", sailings would start on 17 June, two weeks earlier than before. In this building five years previously, officials from the US, Canada, Denmark, Finland, Iceland, Norway, Russia and Sweden had met to consider global warming, and a summary of their Arctic Impact Climate Assessment, released in Iceland the previous November, had caused a sensation: it concluded that the Arctic was heating twice as fast as the rest of the globe and that human activity was the dominant factor. "Over the next one hundred years," it warned, "climate change is expected to accelerate, contributing to major physical, ecological, social and economic changes, many of which have already begun." The authors estimated that by 2050 there would be very little summer ice off the Arctic coast and after 2070 some years would have no summer ice. The loss of sea ice meant a loss of the world's reflective surface which reinforced the process.

Before leaving Alaska, I had one more observation I wanted to make. Scientists from the University of Alaska had measured the thickness of more than seventy glaciers across Alaska and had found they had all been thinning since the 1950s. The rate had doubled in the previous decade, contributing to global sea rise. I flew south to Anchorage and drove about seventy-five kilometres along the Seward Highway to see the famous Portage Glacier, the state's most frequently visited sight-seeing destination. Arriving at the tourist centre, I found that I could barely see the glacier's "tongue" behind a distant mountain slope. It had retreated by between seven and ten kilometres in the previous fifty years. From the official viewing point, the once-majestic glacier had been reduced to a vast expanse of melted ice.

I left Alaska convinced that for the coming generation of correspondents, global warming is the "next big thing". Journalism will increasingly play a key role in informing the world's population about the causes and consequences of global warming: analysing the reports of scientists, including the alarmists and sceptics among them; investigating the influence of oil and coal industries on government policies; exploring the measures needed to save future generations from the looming disasters of extreme weather and world food shortages; and above all, as in any war, going to the "conflict zones" to carry out one of the basic tasks of journalism – reporting the impact of great events, in this case climate change, on ordinary people's lives. It will mean chronicling a gigantic struggle with nature, and a force that threatens to destabilise societies across the world in decades to come.

35

That the Wrong May Cease

I did not start out with a burning desire to change the world when I became a journalist. I just wanted to write stories. But journalism challenges those in power by chronicling the consequences of their actions. It can never be completely objective. The way a correspondent sees and reports an event is determined by a combination of things, from personal bias, nationality and family background to the culture of the newspaper and one's perception of its readers' preferences. Impartiality is well-nigh impossible, even if one sets it as a goal. The very choice of words – "terrorist" or "freedom fighter," "country" or "province" – betrays one's sympathies and makes us all advocacy journalists to a great or lesser degree, whether we like it or not. As the French writer Marguerite Duras once put it, journalism without a moral position is impossible.

As far as I was concerned, the stories I found myself reporting with the greatest enthusiasm were those that detailed and exposed wrongs and hardships being inflicted on people, especially by authority. Conveniently this was in tune with the articles of the *Irish Times* Trust, drawn up in 1974, which requires its reporters to promote "understanding of other nations and peoples with a sympathetic concern for well-being". Under the

glass top of his editor's desk, Douglas Gageby kept a note of the words of the Chicago editor Finley Peter Dunne, that a newspaper *"comforts th' afflicted, afflicts th' comfortable"*. (He also had the famous epigram of Humbert Wolfe: *"You cannot hope to bribe or twist/ thank God! The British journalist./ But, seeing what the man will do/ unbribed, there's no occasion to"*.) I reckon my upbringing in Northern Ireland programmed me to be sympathetic to the underdog and I found myself naturally siding with the afflicted on a personal level. I quietly cheered on the pro-democracy students in Tiananmen Square, the nationalists in the Baltics, the Democrats in communist Russia, the pro-independence Tibetans, the anti-apartheid activists in South Africa and the students in Indonesia. The line, "that the wrong may cease and the right prevail", from the ballad about the 1798 rebellion, "The Man From God Knows Where", resonated with me as I witnessed the liberation of East Timor, where the right did prevail and the wrong ceased when the Indonesian army was evicted.

Nevertheless, I also learned to appreciate that the righting of wrongs is not always the end of the matter. Newly won freedoms often lead to bloody civil conflicts, as in East Timor and the Caucasus republics. We hoped for the defeat of the Russians in Afghanistan, only to see the conditions created for al Qaeda. I found myself wondering, as China became prosperous and stable, if the crushing of the Tiananmen Square demonstrations might actually have averted something worse, such as civil war. If Tibet was left to its own devices, would there still be sex slaves in the Potala Palace? The "afflicted" too can sometimes become the "comfortable" in remarkably quick time, the victims can turn into oppressors and the heroes of freedom – the name Boris Yeltsin comes to mind – can evolve into corrupt rulers in short order. A correspondent sometimes has to combat cynicism to maintain "a sympathetic concern for well-being".

Nor was I ever a gung-ho war correspondent. War is exciting. It gets the adrenalin going, and I have seen colleagues become

addicted to it, but ultimately it is about death, and journalists are not immune. Some I knew were desperately unlucky, like David Blundy of the *Sunday Times*, shot dead in El Salvador, and Sanders Thoenes of the *Financial Times*, killed in East Timor. Writing "the first rough draft of history" has become much more dangerous in modern times. The Committee to Protect Journalists recorded sixty-five journalists killed in direct connection with their work in 2007, and a total of 676 in the period 1992 to 2008, a third of whom were "pencils", print reporters like me. During the Cold War, journalism seemed to be a much less hazardous occupation.

The life of a foreign correspondent has more highs and lows than most professions. One can be breakfasting by the pool in a tropical location one day, and bedding down in a mosquito-infested hovel the next. But mostly it is exhilarating. It can bring one into contact with iconic figures like Graham Greene, Yoko Ono or Bill Clinton, to name(drop) some of the people I have interviewed. If lucky, we get to witness and record great historical events.

My good fortune was to work for *The Irish Times* when it was in the process of shedding a provincial mentality inherited from pre-independence days and looking beyond its old horizons. Despite its interest in foreign news, *The Irish Times* rarely had anyone corresponding from abroad before modern times. There were some notable exceptions. John Edward Healy, editor from 1904-34, reported from the western front during the First World War and R.M. (Bertie) Smyllie covered the Versailles Peace Conference at the end of that war. After Smyllie became editor in 1934, he sent Lionel Fleming to cover the Spanish Civil War, though Fleming's even-handed despatches from the Republican side angered prominent Catholic advertisers so much that it is said he was withdrawn to prevent a boycott of the paper. John Horgan, now the press ombudsman, spent much time in Rome from 1962 to 1965 to report on the Second Vatican Council.

It wasn't until 1971 that the first foreign bureau (outside of London) was opened, by Fergus Pyle in Paris. Two years later when Ireland joined the European Economic Community, now the European Union, *The Irish Times*, along with the other main Irish newspapers and RTÉ, opened a staff bureau in Brussels. As Ireland subsequently adjusted to its expanded role in Europe, it became apparent that *The Irish Times* needed more of its own foreign correspondents to provide news and analysis. It was no longer sufficient to take British news agencies or syndicated reports from sometimes jingoistic London dailies, which gave Irish newspapers the same outlook on foreign news as that of newspapers in large British cities. The opening of the Moscow bureau in 1987 launched a new era in the *Irish Times*'s foreign coverage. Since then, the paper has been serviced by resident correspondents in Beijing, Berlin, Brussels, Johannesburg, London, New York, Paris, Rome and Washington. With the ease of foreign travel in modern times, writers from all sections of the newspaper now think little of crossing the globe to report, not just "hard" news, but on issues such as property and fashion. Staff posts in key cities abroad are still essential, however, because the correspondent can bring continuity and a distinctly Irish perspective to bear on political and business news, and is a lot freer than a stringer to service the newspaper uniquely through informed knowledge of the country and of the needs and priorities of the different editorial sections of the newspaper, while having the authority and financial backing to act on his or her own initiative. This is more important than ever at a time when journalism is under siege from low-cost proprietors and dumbed-down cable news channels.

My career as a foreign correspondent resembled the cycles of the Soviet economy, which were predicated on the "five-year plan". I was never required to remain longer than five years in any of my postings: London, Moscow, Washington, Beijing and New York. I did not consider staying permanently in any of the overseas cities I lived in, much as my life was enriched by contact with different customs and languages, and new and lasting friendships. I never really left Ireland. There was never a year that I did not return for several weeks. Whenever I was abroad, I communicated every day with the foreign desk, finding out what was going on back home, always conscious that I was writing for a particular readership which I sensed I knew. Dublin now is one of the most cosmopolitan cities in the world and – I say this on good authority – Ireland is the most desirable place to live on the planet, recent economic turmoil notwithstanding. To borrow a favourite line from American R&B singer-songwriter Donell Jones, this is "Where I Wanna Be". It is a paradox that I had to spend so many years abroad to find that out for sure.

INDEX

352